TABLE OF

HISTORY A.

TRAVELING IN ISRAEL

Explore the World

NELLES GUIDE

ISRAEL

WEST BANK · EXCURSIONS TO JORDAN

Authors:
Hans-Günter Semsek, Carmella Pfaffenbach

*An Up-to-date travel guide
with 167 color photos
and 19 maps*

Dear Reader: Being up-to-date is the main goal of the Nelles series. Our correspondents help keep us abreast of the latest developments in the travel scene, while our cartographers see to it that maps are also kept completely current. However, as the travel world is constantly changing, we cannot guarantee that all the information contained in our books is always valid. Should you come across a discrepancy, please contact us at: Nelles Verlag, Schleissheimer Str. 371 b, 80935 Munich, Germany, tel. (089) 3571940, fax. (089) 35719430, e-mail: Nelles.Verlag@T-Online.de

Note: Distances and measurements, including temperatures, used in this guide are metric. For conversion information, please see the *Guidelines* section of this book.

LEGEND

▨ Public or Significant Building	Lahav Place Mentioned in Text	▬▬▬ Expressway	
■ Hotel	◪ International Airport	▬▬▬ Throughway	
▦ ○ Shopping Center, Market	⊞ National Airport	▬▬▬ Principal Highway	
✝ ✡ Church, Synagogue	12 Route number	▬▬▬ Main Road	
☾ Mosque	\25/ Distance in Kilometers	▬▬▬ Other Road Paved	
★ Place of Interest	Mt. Nebo 802 Mountain Summit (Height in Meters)	▬▬▬ Other Road Unpaved	
∴ Ancient site			
♠ Nature Reserve	▬▬▬ National Border	---- Track	
● Water Source	▬ ▬ ▬ Armistice line	▬▬▬ Railway	

ISRAEL – West Bank,
        Excursions to Jordan
© Nelles Verlag GmbH, D-80935 München
  All rights reserved

Second Revised Edition 2001
ISBN 3-88618-223-1
Printed in Slovenia

Publisher:	Günter Nelles	**Translations:**	Ross Greville,
Editor-in-Chief:	Berthold Schwarz		Jacqueline Guigui
Project Editor:	Hans-Günter Semsek	**Cartography:**	Nelles Verlag GmbH
Editor:	Susanne Braun	**Color Separation:**	Priegnitz, München
Photo Editor:	K. Bärmann-Thümmel		
English Editor:	Anne Midgette	**Printed by:**	Gorenjski Tisk

                                                             - T04 -

GUIDELINES

MAP LIST

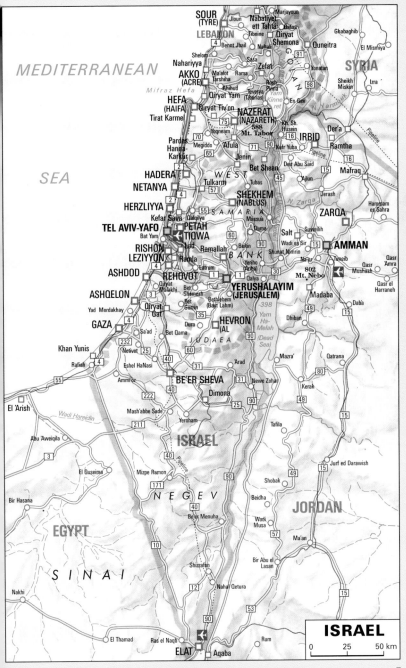

ISRAEL

0   25   50 km

H. PISAN

HISTORY
AND CULTURE

Palestine

Palestine is one of the cradles of Western civilization. More than 12,000 years ago the world's first fortified city stood on the soil of the Holy Land: Jericho. It was Palestine that saw the unfolding of the history of the Jewish people. Originally a minor and indigent group of tribes, the Israelites were always surrounded and occasionally overrun by the powerful empires of the Egyptians, Babylonians, Assyrians, Persians, Greeks and Romans, all of which left their own marks on the land. Even back in those days, hundreds of thousands of people were victimized by oppression.

In Israel today, you can still visit the places where Christ lived and taught; places well known from the Scriptures to millions of Christians worldwide. Names of cities such as Capernaum, Tiberias, Nazareth, Jerusalem, or of places such as the Mount of Olives, Golgotha, the Sea of Galilee (Lake Genezareth) and the Garden of Gethsemane, are all an essential part of the Christian heritage. The history of the region, from earliest settlements up until the crucifixion of Christ, is recounted in the most frequently printed book in the world, the Bible.

But all of these important reminders of ancient history should not entirely distract us from the current situation in the Near East. Almost 50 years after the foundation of the modern state of Israel, there are still serious problems that have yet to be solved, with the Palestinians

Preceding pages: Timna Valley in the Negev Desert. Spectators at a bar mitzvah celebration in Jerusalem. Left: Moses with the Ten Commandments (woodcut by Gustave Doré, 1865).

quite justifiably demanding their own sovereign state. However, the partial autonomy of the Gaza Strip and of the Jericho region has paved the first steps along the road to peace.

The Second Millenium B.C.
Political Structures in the Near East

Israel's history commenced 5,000 years ago, on a patch of land around 130 kilometers across and 240 kilometers long, or "from Dan to Beersheba" in the biblical phrase (2 Samuel 17:11). As part of the fertile crescent running in an arc between the Mediterranean Sea and the Persian Gulf and wedged in between the mighty empires of Babylonia in the east and Egypt in the southwest, this small but important piece of land attracted the covetous attentions of other nations right from the start.

It was through Palestine (the name Herodotus gave to the region), this bridge of land between Africa and Asia, that the caravan routes passed, and control of these routes brought economic advantages. The fertile farming land promised rich tributary payments to anyone able to get the area under their control. In addition, you could catch and check enemy invasions here, long before they had reached your own front gates.

The first political and territorial structures appeared in Palestine as early as the end of the third millenium B.C. The pre-Israelitic Canaanites had established a number of independent city-states throughout the region, of which the most famous (to us today) were Megiddo, Jericho, Gezer, Lachish and Jerusalem. The economies of these communities were founded on already well-developed agriculture, such as fruit-growing, viticulture, the production of olive oil and livestock farming.

During this time, Palestine's neighbor Egypt (whose history would remain closely connected with that of Palestine

13

for thousands of years to come) was enjoying a period of political stability. Around 1700 B.C., Semitic invaders known as the Hyksos overran Egypt using a hitherto unknown method of warfare: horses and war chariots. These "foreign rulers", as the Egyptians used to call them, brushed the armies of the Middle Kingdom (2040-1785 B.C.) aside with one fell swoop and remained in power until 1550 B.C.

After the expulsion of the Hyksos, the pharaohs of the 18th dynasty (1551-1306 B.C.) succeeded in becoming a major power in the Near East. Within a very short time Palestine fell under the supreme rule of the Egyptians, who controlled the entire region through the Canaanite cities. The kings of these cities, who already belonged to the ruling class elite, were appointed by the pharaohs and

Above: The power of the Egyptians; 19th-century color lithograph. Right: The Israelites depart Egypt (wall mural, tomb of Chnumhotep, 19th century B.C.).

saw to it that the local aristocracy kept tribute payments flowing to Egypt. The initially relaxed Egyptian rule in Palestine became much stricter following a number of city-state rebellions. Now, Egyptian officials exerted their control over the trade routes and, with military support from Nubian soldiers, enforced collection of tolls and duty. At the same time, the city kings used their charioteers to collect taxes required for the upkeep of their royal households. Therefore, the population was being doubly exploited.

At the beginning of the 13th century B.C., the pharaohs' power in Palestine diminished as a result of invasion by the so-called seafaring peoples, in particular the infamous Philistines. Although the Egyptians succeeded in repelling the invaders, this effort and expense had so weakened the country that Egyptian rule in Palestine soon came to an end.

The Philistines became the political heirs and ruled Palestine by means of the pentapolis – the five cities of the Philistine confederacy (Gaza, Ascalon, Ash-

dod, Ekron and Gath). Their supremacy was solidly supported by a well-trained army, whose cutting edge was the heavily-armed, single-combat warrior. One example of this kind of soldier is the biblical character Goliath, although he is somewhat caricatured.

It was during the rule of the Philistines in Palestine that the Hebrews began acquiring land.

The Territorial Expansion of the Hebrews

The Hebrews were semi-nomads who tended small herds of sheep and goats, using the donkey as their beast of burden (the camel, which made full nomadism possible, was not domesticated until the 12th century B.C.).

During the rainy season, the steppe supplied the herds with nourishment, but when the dry summer came the tribes moved to the fringes of the fertile regions, where they had long-standing arrangements with the farmers. Once the wheat had been harvested, the nomads' already easy-going herds found ample foraging to satisfy them. At the beginning of the rainy season, when the farmers went out to plow, the nomads left for the steppe once again. This harsh living required social structures dominated by collective rather than individual interests.

But even solid group cohesion was of little use when the regular succession of rainy and dry periods was disrupted. If a year saw too little or no rain at all and if such drought persisted for a number of years in succession, the nomads would find themselves in danger of starvation.

In such times of famine and hardship, Egypt provided the only hope. Here agriculture did not depend on rainfall but on the reliable seasonal flooding of the Nile. At the well-guarded borders of the pharaoh's empire, the emaciated herdsmen, hoping to survive, were registered and then drafted as unpaid laborers on the construction of military projects and temples. In the 12th century B.C. one civil servant reported the following to the

15

pharaoh: "We have finished the task of allowing the Shasu tribe of Edom to pass through the Merneptah fortress in Tkw and travel as far as the ponds of Pithom of the Merneptah in Tkw so that they and their herds can preserve their lives on the great estates of the pharaoh, the good sun of every land."

And so it also went for the Israelite tribes: even Abraham sought shelter in Egypt, and after him the twelve sons of Jacob – Joseph and his brothers – who were saved from death by emigrating to the land of the Nile. However, getting into Egypt was one thing, getting out was quite another. The pharaoh's reluctance to let people leave is clearly illustrated by his dramatic altercations with Moses. Only the direct intervention of God, according to the Bible, enabled the Hebrews to succeed in fleeing the country.

Above: "The Egyptians drown in the Red Sea," woodcut by Schnorr of Carolsfeld, 1860. Right: Israelite clay pots (7th century B.C.): early sign of a settled lifestyle.

The myth of the Hebrews and the rise of their god, Yahweh, begins with the success of the Exodus. Particularly significant was the defeat of the pharaoh's chariot phalanx, since the Egyptians were not only faster than the fleeing nomads but also far better armed. According to the Bible, it was thanks to divine intervention that the Egyptians' attempt to prevent the escape of their unpaid drudges ended in disaster for them. The Bible celebrates it with the words: "Sing ye to the Lord, for he hath triumphed gloriously; the horse and his rider hath he thrown into the sea" (Exodus 15:22).

The Hebrews did not by any means take the shortest route to the "Promised Land." According to the Bible, God himself worked out an alternative itinerary so that his people would not be demoralized right at the start of their flight by any clashes with other tribes and thus be inclined to return back to Egypt. The fastest way would have been down the Sinai coast, but this route was, at that time, an international trade route which Pharaoh

Seti I (1303-1290 B.C.) had secured with a network of fortresses; the nomads would hardly have been able to pass these unscathed. For this reason the tribed traveled southeast, traversing the interior of the Sinai peninsula and parts of Transjordan before finally crossing the river Jordan into Canaan.

Upon their arrival in Canaan, the Hebrews were faced with a political power vacuum. The invasion of the seafaring peoples, particularly the Philistines, and the resulting decline of Egypt's power, ultimately led to extensive migration of the population, including not only the Hebrews but also other Aramaic peoples such as the Edomites, Moabites and Ammonites. Until then, only the pharaohs had ever been able to establish any kind of central administration; once this was gone, a power struggle ensued between the various tribes, from which the Hebrews ultimately emerged victorious. During this period, the acquisition of land was not, as the Bible implies, a well-planned project. In those early days the

Israelite tribes simply didn't have the strong political or military leadership to direct and coordinate such a task.

The immigrants, still the semi-nomads they had always been, passed through Palestine in small clan groups. Just as in the old days, the herdsmen reached understandings with the farmers about letting their herds forage in the fields. Gradually, the first permanent settlements began to spring up, centered around paddocks for small livestock. In the mountain regions, woodland was cleared, land reclaimed and tilled.

This initial occupation of land was peaceful: the Hebrews kept out of the way of the native population as much as possible. Furthermore, the land they were settling was generally uninhabited and unclaimed by anyone else, and the nomads were very well acquainted with this sort of countryside. They knew how to adapt to natural conditions, and could thus proceed to settle down in peace, at their own pace. Two important innovations facilitated this change: first, the He-

17

brews were now able to construct cisterns sealed with waterproof lime plaster to catch and store rainwater, and second, they were learning how to manufacture tools and implements out of iron, which were much more efficient than the conventional copper and bronze tools used for work such as clearing woodland.

The Hebrews did not begin to descend down into the valleys, where the Canaanites had their towns, until their tribes had gained a foothold in the hills and were ready to continue their quest for land. This second phase of farmland acquisition was not at all peaceful, as by now, the Hebrews had strategic aims as well. For the more established they became in the mountains, the more the Canaanite settlements at the edges of their tribal territories came to represent potential threats. It was, therefore, necessary to curtail the power of these cities.

Above: Israelite warrior under King David (19th-c. lithograph). Right: "David's Coronation," Byzantine illumination (10th c.).

This gave rise to the question of how a former nomadic people, who had only just begun to settle down permanently, would be able to defeat these well-fortified Canaanite towns. One major factor contributing to the Hebrews' military success was the impoverishment of the country caused by the Egyptian occupation; another was the constant bickering and squabbling of the Canaanite cities amongst themselves. At that time, the Canaanites were strangers to the sort of unifying national consciousness the Hebrews enjoyed. Another point working in favor of the Israelite tribes was their efficient secret service: not only military but also economic and population-specific intelligence was gathered and analyzed and spies, saboteurs and traitors were recruited by the tribes.

The Hebrews even had the logistic problems, which are often a weak point in large-scale expansion plans, under control. They either prepared large stockpiles of food and supplies in advance or scheduled their attacks for just before the harvest, so that their troops could sustain themselves from the enemy's crops while at the same time reducing enemy reserves by rustling livestock.

Hebrew military operations, therefore, were based on a functioning organization, yet wars were ultimately decided on the battlefield. Here, the Hebrews were faced with two problems: first, the strong defenses of the Canaanite towns, and second, their disciplined professional soldiers, whose very effective chariot units could wipe out troops of foot soldiers with extreme rapidity. The Israelite tribes were without siege machines or other technology to attack the fortifications, and had only foot soldiers to set against the chariots. They countered these deficiencies with what strategists term as an indirect approach: stratagems and ruses, feints, refusal to participate in fixed battles, ambushes, sabotage – in short guerilla tactics. Bethel and Jerusalem were conquered by strategy rather than might: the stronghold of Bethel fell by treachery (Judges 1:21-25), while Jerusalem was taken by troops creeping into the city along the conduit which brought drinking water in from the Gihon spring outside the walls. This, at least, is one interpretation of the rather obscure Bible passage that runs: "Whosoever getteth up to the gutter, and smiteth the Jebusites, he shall be chief and captain" (2 Samuel 5:8). In the conquest of Ai, the Hebrew troops besieging the city simulated flight, enticing the city's garrison in pursuing them. Left thus defenseless, the town was then easy prey for the major part of the Israelite forces which were standing by.

Other city conquests were decided in open battle with the Canaanites, but for these, too, the Israelites had prepared very well, winning them not so much by the superiority of their troops as by the element of surprise. At the battle of Gibeon, the Israelite army advanced at a fast march under cover of darkness and overran enemy troops just before dawn – something no one had anticipated. Similar night marches followed by surprise attacks in the early hours of the morning were features of the battle with the Medianites, the attack on Shechem, and Saul's battles with the Ammonites and Philistines.

By means of tactical tricks of this sort the Hebrews were even able to neutralize the feared chariots of the enemy. In the battle which Deborah and Barak conducted against the oppressor Sisera, they were able to make maximum use of the geographical and climatic conditions of the region. First of all Sisera's chariots were forced to form up in a narrow valley where they could make absolutely no use of their superior speed nor even deploy properly. Secondly, the Hebrews delayed the battle itself until the rainy season, when the enemy and its chariots bogged down in the mud. Sisera himself was forced to flee, humiliatingly, on foot.

As the Hebrews consolidated their new role as a settled people and continued to expand their territories, the need arose for new social and political organizations in which one institution, as centralized as possible, defined the nation's political and military goals. At first this function was exercised by the "judges," whose responsibility during the military conflicts resulting from Hebrew territorial expansion was to ensure that the people pulled together and kept up morale even in adversity, and that in victory their fighting spirit was not allowed to dissipate uselessly but was channeled in a beneficial way. For this kind of government, exercised purely sporadically and in which day-to-day affairs continued to be controlled by family heads and patriarchs, what was required was not rational legitimization, but rather charisma.

However, as the population grew and the Hebrew territories expanded, it was clear that a new form of government would have to be found. Only a central power would be able to introduce new

19

laws and have the organizational muscle to protect national territory. The time was ripe for the founding of a royal house.

Excursus: Life Before the State

The extended family was at the center of the Israelite communities. Described in the specialist terms of ethnography, it was endogamous, patrilocal, patriarchal, patrilinear and polygynous.

Endogamous means that an individual must marry within his group; in other words, marriage of blood relatives. The advantage of this practice was that property remained within the family. This in turn strengthened the relationships between kin, increased the inner cohesion of the family unit and resolved tensions and conflicts almost as they occurred when a family head married his

Above: "Cain slaying Abel," from the Verdun Altar, 1181. Right: The father's blessing kept the family together ("Jacob's Blessing," Rembrandt, 1656).

male relations to his daughters. This practice didn't cease when the nomads became a settled people. The Hebrews made sure they kept as much as possible to themselves and out of the way of the native population.

The stability of the extended family was also bolstered by patrilocality, which means that even after marriage, the sons and their wives continued to reside under their father's roof, and raised their own children there. The more sons there were, the more productive was the family unit, and the better able it was to defend itself.

These family groups were ruled by one man who wielded absolute authority; in other words, it was patriarchal. What was required was not individuality, but rather the collective: each family member was important only as a cog in the family machine, with the patriarch standing at the controls and assigning everyone his task.

Anyone who was forced to leave the solidarity of such a group would have no chance whatsoever of surviving. Cain the fratricide, expelled by God from his community, cried out in despair: "I shall be a fugitive and a vagabond in the earth; and it shall come to pass, that every one that findeth me shall slay me" (Genesis 4:14).

Patrilinear means that bloodlines – and, in the concrete individual case, much more importantly matters of inheritance – are defined on the basis of the relationship to the father. Male descendants were therefore a boon and cause for rejoicing; while lamentation was raised if the first-born was a daughter. Sons, on the other hand, led to power and wealth, as they could in turn beget more sons of their wives. This is the origin of the custom of the dowry. Since a daughter went to live with her husband, bore him children and contributed to work in the new household, her own family only regard her as an economic loss, for which the dowry was intended to compensate.

Polygynous indicates that a man may take more than one wife. In practice, this

was reserved for a few rich males, since a dowry had to be paid for each wife. If a fairly poor member of the community did happen to have two wives, this was frequently a result of the obligation of the levirate: the requirement, formulated in Leviticus, that if a man's brother dies he must marry his childless widow and take her into his household. Since the widow inherited the property of her deceased husband, this legacy could be brought back under the male control of the dead man's family if his brother acquired this property by marriage. However the requirement that the widow be childless admits of another interpretation: the levirate was also a way of ensuring the dead man had descendants, albeit fictive, by his closest relative.

These family structures did not change after the Hebrews ceased to be nomads. At the beginning of the process of land acquisition, everyone worked together to clear the woods, after which the cleared land was surveyed and then distributed by lot. Hebrew law placed these parcels of land under special protection. Land could only be sold to kinsmen, ensuring that it would remain in the extended family. Within each and every clan, the ethos was strongly oriented toward preserving property and possession. If a family made new land arable, nothing stood in the way of their becoming its owners. As large family groups had more people who could work, they were able to keep increasing their lands, thus becoming richer than other families and showing this off through material possessions, such as jewelry. Wealthy patriarchs established bonds of loyalty through patron-client relationships: in times of need they gave material support to the poorer members of the community, and expected honor, respect and services (free of charge) in return. After the Hebrews had taken up the settled agricultural life, men of this type assumed positions of authority in local communities. But even these patriarchs could not exercise real power. Since there was no central political authority, there was no guarantee of

21

property either; this meant that only the strength of the family group could back up an individual's claims to property. Anyone who annoyed the clan, or was expelled and thus had no protection, soon found that he could hardly keep the shirt on his back. And a marked degree of egalitarian awareness prevented too much power becoming concentrated in one hand. Family chiefs tended to react allergically if any one of them showed interest in social climbing; their joint efforts and authorities very soon brought the ambitious one back down to earth.

The Kingdoms of Judea and Israel under David and Solomon

The external stimulus that led to the foundation of a kingdom came at the end of the 11th century in the form of the military expansion of the Philistines. Fur-

Above: David and Goliath, 13th-c. illumination. Right: Depiction of the Arc of the Covenant, Capernaum, 2nd-3rd centuries A.D.

thermore, the Hebrews were already acquainted with the centralized political authority of the Edomites, Ammonites and Moabites, and they clearly registered the organizational advantages of this form of government.

Around 1050 B.C., the prophet Samuel, a judge, ruled the country. In 1012 B.C., as the Bible reports, Samuel appointed Saul to be the first king in accordance with the wishes of the people: "Now make us a king to judge us like all the nations" (1 Samuel 8:5). The Bible goes on to report how Samuel gradually withdrew his support from Saul in favor of David.

Saul had gained a reputation as a general when he defended the town of Jabesh-Gilead and defeated the Ammonites who were beseiging it. After this he was involved in fighting for the entire duration of his reign (1012-1004 B.C.), primarily against the Philistines, but also against the Moabites, Amalekites and Edomites. Samuel withdrew the royal mandate from Saul after the battle against the Amalekites – Saul had failed to "slay both man and woman, infant and suckling, ox and sheep, camel and ass," as the Lord bade, sparing the king and the best animals! (1 Samuel 15). He was still, however, able to unite the Israelite tribes. His era saw the end of the patriarchal system, as well as other important social changes. For example, the king rewarded his trusty supporters, and also the greater part of his family, with lands he had conquered. In order to support the court, tithes were levied on agricultural products, although loyal (or toadying) courtiers were freed from such obligations. There was a surge of fierce and widespread resistance to these practices, utterly alien as they were to a nomadic people who had only recently become settled. All the same, before the king entered office, Samuel had, as the Bible reports, expressly and insistently warned his people and given them a long list of

the services they would have to render him, finally predicting that "ye shall cry out in that day because of your king which ye shall have chosen you" (1 Samuel 8:10-18). The final years of Saul's rule were marked by violent conflicts between the king and the traditional elite. In the long run, it was David who benefitted the most from this; he had always enjoyed the high regard of the people, and Saul suspected him of harboring treasonous plans in his heart. David had no choice but to flee.

With a band of 400 to 600 fighters – social outsiders like himself, men with nothing to lose – he roamed, marauding, through the land of the Amalekites and even made a loose alliance with the arch-enemies of the Jews, the Philistines. After these hated adversaries of the Chosen People had inflicted a crushing victory on Saul at Mount Gilboa, when Saul's sons were killed and the king himself fell on his sword in despair, David was the only person with enough leadership qualities to protect the people. Accordingly, the

elders of the southern tribes anointed him king, and in 1004 B.C. the northern tribes of Israel quickly followed suit. A unification of Judea and Israel in this manner was something that the Philistines did not welcome. They invaded, but suffered such high losses that they never again amounted to a significant influence in the region.

Then David turned to Jerusalem, a city which its inhabitants considered impregnable; they were, furthermore, utterly scornful of the new king's abilities: "Except thou take away the blind and the lame, thou shalt not come in hither" (2 Samuel 5:6). But Jerusalem advanced to become the capital of the united kingdom, as well as its religious center, once the Ark of the Covenant had been installed there.

Victorious in a string of battles, David secured the boundaries of his realm. As far as domestic policies were concerned, he continued with the changes which Saul had set under way, creating offices for royal ministers, developing an effec-

building program. Among the many new buildings erected in Jerusalem was the magnificent First Temple. The reign of Solomon was a time of peace and security for his countrymen, as David's era had been. Solomon swiftly and severely quashed the only uprising against his rule, instigated by Jeroboam, the administrator of the king's estates. Jeroboam fled and sought refuge in Egypt. Solomon died in 930 B.C.

Solomon's eldest son Rehoboam (930-913 B.C.) ascended the throne after his father's death, but the northern tribes were only willing to acknowledge his sovereignty under certain conditions, notably a reduction in taxes – they wanted the expensive administration which devoured them to be abolished or at least considerably cut back. They told Rehoboam "Thy father made our yoke grievous: now therefore make thou the grievous service of thy father, and his heavy yoke which he put upon us, lighter, and we will serve thee" (1 Kings 12:4). Rehoboam wished to demonstrate royal strength and leadership qualities and replied, rather undiplomatically, "My father made your yoke heavy, and I will add to your yoke: my father also chastised you with whips, but I will chastise you with scorpions." (1 Kings 12:14). The northern tribes could not swallow such an insult, and with the cry "To your tents, O Israel!" (1 Kings 12:16) they went to their homes, calling Jeroboam (c. 930-908 B.C.) to return to Egypt, and appointing him ruler of the northern state. The days of peace in both kingdoms was past, and to all intents and purposes they were in a state of war.

tive administration, and curtailing the rights of the elders. Rumblings of discontent were once again heard among the people, and David's son Absalom put himself at the head of the protests, which were so successful that David actually had to flee Jerusalem. He gathered an army and defeated his son's troops. As Absalom fled the field, his hair caught in a tree, and David's nephew Joab murdered the crown prince, in direct disobedience of the king's orders.

David suppressed a second revolt, appointed his son Solomon as his successor, and died soon afterwards in the year 965 B.C. Solomon's first official act upon taking office was to eliminate all those who disputed his right to the succession, after which he reigned for the most part in a peaceful fashion, held the kingdom together and initiated a major

The Northern Kingdom of Israel

The most significant event on the international stage during Jeroboam's rule was the invasion of the Egyptians under their pharaoh Sheshonq, who had very probably come to hear of the riches of

Above: King Solomon, 17th-century Russian icon. Right: "The Destruction of Jerusalem and the Israelites' Flight to Babel," woodcut by Schnorr of Carolsfeld, 1860.

Solomon. Otherwise, Jeroboam steered his country fairly competently through the troubled waters of his reign. He was succeeded on the throne by his son Nadab, who not long afterwards was murdered, together with his entire family, by a certain Baasha (908-883 B.C.) of the tribe of Issachar.

The two rulers who followed suffered similar unhappy fates; it took the military leader Omri (881-871 B.C.) to restore peace and order to the land. He put a stop to the border squabbles with the southern kingdom of Judea and had a new capital city built, called Samaria; the northern kingdom was thenceforth called the kingdom of Samaria. Omri was succeeded by his son Ahab (871-852 B.C.), who immediately recognized that the kingdom was threatened by Assyrian expansionism and acted swiftly. He had the cities' fortifications improved, supplies and provisions stockpiled, the water supply systems extended and chariots built. Also in response to external pressures, he concluded a peace treaty with Judea.

15 years later, in 853 B.C., the Assyrian king Shalmanezer III really did launch an invasion of both Israel and Judea. The two kingdoms merged their armies in response, and the Assyrians were virtually annihilated. Ahab alone furnished the greater part of the troops: 10,000 foot soldiers and 2,000 chariots. This is an indication of how well he had prepared his kingdom for the Assyrian threat. In 841 B.C., after the fourth invasion attempt by Shalmanezer, the Assyrian king finally managed to incorporate Israel into his empire and Jehu paid tribute. A good hundred years later Hoshea (731-724 B.C.; not to be confused with the prophet Hosea) ceased making these payments. Shalmanezer V struck back and in 721 B.C. his successor Sargon II, as recorded in his annals, led 27,280 Israelites – the entire upper class and most of the population – into slavery. Sargon flooded the depopulated country with foreign settlers, and the remnants of the Israelites were eventually simply absorbed. Israel had ceased to exist.

The Southern Kingdom of Judea

It was Solomon's son Rehoboam who became ruler of Judea. In 926 B.C. he stopped the invasion of the Egyptian pharaoh Sheshonq by simply handing over to him a large portion of the temple and palace treasures. The centuries which followed were marked by border disputes with the more powerful kingdom of Israel, but a peace treaty ws finally signed in 868 B.C.

The Arameans conducted the next attack of a foreign power during the reign of Josach (839-801 B.C.); but these forces, too, were able to be bought off with the payment of tribute and withdrew their armies. The reign of Uzziah (786-736 B.C.) brought the Judeans half a century of peace, and their prosperity increased accordingly.

Above: Nebuchadnezzar before Jerusalem, lithograph by R. Weibezahl, 1832. Right: Antiochus IV plunders Jerusalem, manuscript illumination, 15th century.

In 734 B.C., the region was overrun by the forces of Tiglath-Pileser III. Judea acknowledged the sovereignty of the Assyrians and paid regular tribute. After the death of Sargon II, when many of the Assyrian vassal states revolted, Hezekiah (725-697 B.C.) also refused to pay taxes, but soon recognized that the Assyrians were too powerful to withstand and recommenced payment. His son Manasseh (696-642 B.C.) presided over another 50 years of stability and prosperity. In 609 B.C., the pharaoh Necho advanced into Palestine in order to prevent the Babylonians from taking over the region. King Josiah (639-609 B.C.) sided with Babylon and was killed at the battle of Megiddo as he tried to stop the Egyptian advance. Once again, Judea had become a vassal state, paying tribute first to the Egyptians and, once they had been defeated by the Babylonian King Nebuchadnezzar at the battle of Charchemish, to the Babylonians. When Zedekiah (597-587 B.C.), whom the Babylonians had set up as a puppet ruler, called for Judea's independence, Nebuchadnezzar sent his troops in, and in 587 B.C. conquered and plundered Jerusalem. His men destroyed the Temple of Solomon and the Ark of the Covenant, and led the inhabitants off into slavery.

Persians and Hellenes

After the death of Nebuchadnezzar II in 562 B.C., only weak kings ruled in Babylonia and so it was an easy matter for the Persian king Cyrus to snatch the Babylonian empire in 539 B.C. The Jews had not assimilated during the captivity, and returned to Judea which was, after all, another Persian possession. In Jerusalem, they rebuilt the Temple on its old site, reconsecrating it in 515 B.C.

When persecution of the Jews commenced in Persia in 452 B.C., more Jews returned to Jerusalem, this time largely people who had amassed some wealth.

Under Nehemiah, the autonomous governor of the province of Judea, a new city wall was built around Jerusalem.

After the death of Alexander the Great in 323 B.C., his Macedonian generals, the Diadochi, divided up his massive empire between them. Egypt went to Ptolemy, who went on to capture Palestine after a surprise attack in 320 B.C. A century later, the Seleucids, who ruled over Syria and Mesopotamia, desired fertile Palestine for themselves. In 217 B.C., Antiochus III of Syria marched in for the first time, but was repelled. He had to wait another 17 years before he finally managed to defeat Ptolemy V at the battle of Baiyas. The Jews were now subjects of the Seleucid Empire; and this occurrence sped up the Hellenization of the country.

The Age of the Hasmoneans

The Hellenes quickly made themselves unpopular with the Jewish people. In 167 B.C., the Seleucid king Antiochus IV prohibited the Jewish religion and forced the Jews to participate in heathen rituals, fully intending to completely wipe out Judaism.

In the village of Modin, located on the Lydda plain northwest of Jerusalem, a Jewish citizen who was about to celebrate the Hellenic rites was murdered by the high priest Mattathias. The aged priest fled with his family into the desert after the deed was done, and many supporters rallied around him ready to fight. They called themselves Hasmoneans, after Hasmon, an ancestor of Mattathias. When the high priest died, his sons Judas, Jonathan and Simeon assumed leadership of the rebellion. Judas, in particular, proved to be a military genius, and was nicknamed Maccabaeus, meaning "the hammer." Since the Hellenes did not take the matter very seriously, they did not send in their best troops to put the rebellion down. Judas Maccabaeus and his band defeated the Seleucids twice and in 164 B.C. he actually took Jerusalem, sweeping the Hellenes away and reopening the Temple to Jewish rites.

Lysias, the Seleucid governor and regent for the underage Antiochus V, now assembled a large army and reconquered one town after the other until he was standing before the gates of Jerusalem. But at that point news reached him that his main rival was heading back toward Antioch with the intention of seizing power. Although on the verge of victory, Lysias had no choice but to abandon further military action and return home. He offered the Hasmoneans a peace settlement and the freedom to exercise their religion. But Judas Maccabaeus wanted more, dreaming of political independence. He fought on and was finally killed in battle in 160 B.C. Hastily the Hasmoneans retreated into the safe but inhospitable desert. Under the command of Judas' brother Jonathan, they followed a policy of inflicting military pinpricks.

In the ensuing conflicts, Jonathan had achieved a string of political successes, only to fall victim to an intrigue, resulting in his murder in 143 B.C. The reins of power were then picked up by Simeon, the last of the three sons of Mattathias. Simeon came to an agreement with the Seleucid Demetrius II and was appointed to the office of high priest. Now he could call himself the leader of the Jewish people, and was able to act with a fair amount of political autonomy. In 140 B.C. the great assembly confirmed the hereditary nature of his offices. Thus the Hasmonean dynasty was established and the country was given the name of Israel. In 134 B.C. Simeon was visiting Jericho in the company of his two sons Judas and Mattathias when they were murdered by his power-hungry son-in-law Ptolemy. But the Hasmoneans were firmly in the saddle and happened to be popular as well. Simeon's sole surviving son, John Hyrcanus I, ascended the throne of his father with the enthusiastic backing of the people and put down his brother-in-law's rebellion with brusque severity. Hardly had he sorted out his domestic adversaries when he was confronted with the army of the Seleucid Antiochus VII Sedetes. The war lasted some two years, a war that neither side could win. After the death of Antiochus, John Hyrcanus was able to further expand Jewish territories by means of a series of successful military campaigns.

When John died in 104 B.C., the question of his succession did not turn out to be an easy one. For a year, his widow acted as ruler; but then John's son Aristobulus had himself appointed king, arrested his mother and allowed her to starve in a dungeon. He also took three of his brothers prisoner, and had a fourth murdered. When Aristobulus died he was succeeded by his brother Alexander Janaeus (102-76 B.C.). The new king married his sister-in-law Salome Alexandra, and, just to be on the safe side, had another brother murdered. After the conquest of the coastal cities, Galilee and Transjordan, Israel's borders had reached their greatest extent. Upon the death of Alexander Jannaeus, there were once again struggles over the succession. Into this power vacuum stepped the Romans, who had become the dominant power in the region after the breakup of the Seleucid Empire. The new rulers quickly merged Syria and Palestine into the Roman province of Syria.

The Roman Yoke

In 47 B.C., at the height of his power, Julius Caesar visited Syria and confirmed Hyrcanus, the son of Alexander Jannaeus, as the hereditary high priest. Antipater, an old fox from the top levels of government in the former Edomite territory of Idumea and a loyal follower and supporter of Hyrcanus, was granted Roman citizenship by Caesar himself and appointed the procurator of Judea. Anti-

Right: "The Massacre of the Innocents," fresco by Giotto di Bondone from around 1315.

28

pater bestowed influential positions upon his two sons, Phaseal and Herod, before dying, poisoned, in 43 B.C. Caesar was assassinated a year later, and the ensuing power struggles of Antony, Octavian and Lepidus dragged the region into civil war. As if this was not enough, the Parthians attacked the Roman provinces in the east, and everyone of any rank of importance went over to them. Herod, meanwhile, installed his family in the safety of the mountain fortress of Masada and only got to Rome by the skin of his teeth. Mark Antony and Octavian received him with great honors, as he was their only ally in Judea. So necessary was he to Rome that he was even allowed the title of King of Palestine. With the help of Roman troops, Herod conquered his kingdom, and in 37 B.C. Jerusalem fell into his hands.

He had the high-ranking defenders of the city executed; the same fate befell the greater part of the Sanhedrin, or high council. The king filled every important position with his chosen henchmen and stayed true to Rome. He was the country's greatest builder since Solomon, and his rule was characterized by a long period of peace – in foreign affairs. On the home front he exerted a brutal reign of terror. The splendor of his reign was stained and besmirched again and again by suspicions, denunciations, intrigues and executions. As a vassal of Rome and a supporter of the cult of Caesar, the king earned the hatred of the Jewish people; furthermore, he counted as a foreign occupier, coming as he did from Idumea (formerly Edom, where the population had actually been converted to Judaism by force), and with a Nabataean mother. As the years went by, Herod ruled more and more ferociously, not sparing even his closest family. He had Aristobulus, the brother of his favorite Jewish wife Mariamme, who had been appointed high priest by Antony and who was highly respected by the people, drowned in Jericho, disguising the murder as an accident. He also had Mariamme herself, whom he doubtless loved, executed,

29

together with one of his friends, on suspicion of adultery; her mother, Alexandra, also had to die on charges of being involved in a rebellion. Two sons of Mariamme as well as Antipater, his son by another wife, fell victim to the paranoid delusions of their father; so did more than 5,000 Pharisees who refused to take the oath of allegiance to the king. The hatred of his people knew no bounds, but as long as Herod still lived public life was, for the most part, at a virtual standstill. Into this foreboding atmosphere stumbled the Three Wise Men from the East, asking the dangerous question: "Where is he that is born King of the Jews?" The Evangelist's commentary on this is succinct and very characteristic of the situation at the time: "When Herod the king had heard these things, he was troubled, and all Jerusalem with him." (Matthew 2:3). In the year 4 B.C., the king died at

Above: Flavius Josephus, marble head, 1st century A.D. Right: Emperor Hadrian, portrait head from Ephesus.

the age of 69 and an audible sigh of relief went up from the people.

All of Jewish writing is permeated with hatred of Herod. In the Talmud we read: "A slave of the Hasmonean state who treacherously raised himself up over his masters," and in another place: "He will destroy their leaders with the sword and bury their bodies in unknown places; he will kill both old and young and show no mercy. Great fear of him will come over them in their land." And the striking judgement of one contemporary was: "Herod stole the throne like a fox, ruled like a tiger and died like a dog!"

Herod left his kingdom to his three surviving sons, and the Romans did not change a line of his testament. But the sons were incapable of agreeing on the succession, and by 44 A.D. the country was ruled by Roman procurators, men whose main aim was to line their own pockets. Soon, nothing worked in Palestine any more, and the roads were plagued by marauding bands who robbed travelers and attacked entire villages. Anarchy ruled in Jerusalem, the public administration was totally corrupt and run down, and the last procurator, a man named Gessius Florus, was personally guilty of robbery, murder and blatant embezzlement.

Revolt broke out in May of 66. One leader of the rebellion was Eleazar ben Hananjah, son of an influential family of priests. Jerusalem quickly fell into Jewish hands, and in many other cities the Jews were able to drive out the hated Roman occupiers. Not until autumn did Cestius Gallus appear outside Jerusalem with his troops; they managed to take the town, but could not capture the Temple Mount. When the Romans withdrew to wait for reinforcements, they ran into an ambush and the legion was almost completely annihilated. The Jews went wild with excitement and already regarded themselves as a liberated nation. Those who had hesitated now joined the uprising.

In the summer of 67, Nero's general Vespasian marched down from the north, while his son Titus approached Palestine from the south; the combined forces numbered some 60,000 soldiers. Their first goal was to take the strongly-fortified Galilean fortress of Jotapata which was commanded by a certain Joseph ben Matthias (this is the Jewish name of the most important chronicler we have from this period, Flavius Josephus). The disciplined Roman legions captured the fortress in less than two months. As was customary in those days, the men were executed and the women and children sold as slaves. Josephus managed to hide, but surrendered to the Romans when they promised they would not put him to death. Josephus, clearly pretty familiar with the power situation in the Roman Empire, behaved cleverly: he prophesied that Vespasian would soon become emperor. The latter took Josephus into his entourage, almost as a kind of luck mascot, and over the next two years conquered the rest of the country. Just as he was moving to take Jerusalem, a message reached Vespasian with the news of Nero's fall and death.

Flavius Vespasian was proclaimed emperor, fulfilling Josephus' prophecy. Vespasian freed him from custody, granted him Roman citizenship and provided him with a pension for life. The fortunate man assumed Vespasian's family name, calling himself Flavius Josephus from then on. He emigrated to Rome, where from 75 to 79 he penned *The Jewish War*, our most important source for the history of the period and the state of Judeo-Roman relations. His next work was the massive Jewish Antiquities, which in twenty books covers the entire history of his people from Adam to the eve of the rebellion of 66. Josephus died in Rome about 100 A.D.

In the spring of 70, Vespasian's son Titus commenced preparations for the siege of Jerusalem. By autumn his legionaries had captured the city. In the street fighting, the Temple, the religious and political center of Judaism, went up in flames. The Jews thereby lost the concrete symbol of their national consciousness; a new Diaspora, or dispersal among the nations, had begun.

Nothing much happened over the next fifty years; in 130 the emperor Hadrian visited Palestine and gave orders that Jerusalem should be rebuilt. With particular malice, he had a temple to Capitoline Jupiter erected on the site of the Temple. For the Jews, this action was yet another last straw which broke the camel's back. In the year 132 they rebelled a second time against the Roman oppressors; historians refer to this as the revolt of Bar Kochba after the name of its leader, Simeon ben Kochba ("son of the star"). Rapidly the Jews gained control of the entire country, and, skilfully applying the tactics of guerilla warfare, they wore down the VI Legion and the X Legion, which was traditionally stationed in Palestine. Bar Kochba had his own coins

31

minted and set up administrative centers in the areas he had conquered.

Publius Marcellus, governor of Syria, now marched on Palestine with his standing army, reinforced with units and auxiliaries stationed in Egypt, only to have his nose bloodied. The Egyptian XII Legion was practically wiped out. Hadrian now placed the entire affair in the hands of Julius Severus, whom he summoned from Britain. Severus adopted the guerilla tactics of the Jews, as the toll in Roman lives had so far been uncommonly high. A decisive battle was fought in the summer of 135, and this time the Romans emerged victorious. Almost 600,000 Jews lost their lives in the revolt, as did countless thousands of Romans – so many that in his address to the Senate, Hadrian abstained from the conventional introductory formula: "I trust that you and your children are in good health; my soldiers and I are in good health."

Excursus: Judaism, Torah and Talmud

The Torah, commonly known as the Law, is one of the sources of Judaism; the word means teaching or instruction. The Old Testament used the term to refer to individual regulations and explanations, as well as for the five books of Moses.

In post-Biblical or so-called rabbinic Judaism, the term Torah was used in the sense of wisdom, truth and divine revelation. The Torah governs a Jew's entire life; not only does it set forth guidelines for his religious and devotional life, but it also decisively influences all his worldly actions. For this reason it would be incorrect to see the Torah simply and solely as "law": this would be a reduction of the word's meaning and not do it justice.

In the Bible, the image of a marriage is a metaphor for the relationship between

Right: Reading from the Torah rolls is a central part of the Jewish tradition.

God and his people. The rabbis have modified this idea by representing the Torah as the bride and Israel as the bridegroom. The *simhat torah*, or festival of joy in the Torah, in which the Jews respond with effusive joy to its "teaching and instruction," contradicts the Christian stereotype that the Jewish "Law" is a form of ritualized constraint which binds its people like a straitjacket.

Rabbinic Judaism distinguishes between the written Torah – originally only the five books of Moses, but later expanded to encompass all of the books of the Old Testament, all divine revelation – and the Torah which was orally transmitted. According to Jewish tradition, both were delivered to Moses in Sinai.

When the Romans destroyed the second Temple in Jerusalem in the year 70, which meant that the Jews no longer had a concrete religious center, it led to a fresh religious reconsideration and reevaluation of the Torah.

Up until then, the written Torah had been supplemented by the oral Torah: the latter, as *mishnah*, was committed to the memory by constant repetition and recitation (the word derives from a Hebrew root meaning "to repeat").

This oral tradition included not only explanations and interpretations of the written Torah but also directives and legal teachings which were not to be found in the recorded version (the so-called *halachah*). The contents of the *halachah* are either derived from the written version or arose in the course of rational reflection and logical inference. After the destruction of the Temple, the rabbis sorted and ordered the contents of the constantly increasing body of orally transmitted knowledge, and then recorded them in writing.

However, even the Mishnah, once it had been fixed in written form, was the subject of unceasing theological debate over the following centuries, which created a whole new body of explanatory

material and commentary. This was collected under the term *Gemara* (literally "completion"). The Mishnah and the Gemara together make up the Talmud (from a Hebrew root meaning "to study") in which the Mishnah consists of the individual Halachah, while the Gemara comments in detail on each Halachah. In addition, the interpretations, homilies, moral reflections, anecdotes and aphorisms of famous rabbis are frequently quoted, and these are grouped within the Gemara under the name of *Haggadah* (literally "narration").

Both Judaism and Christianity have in common their hope for a better future for mankind. Both Jews and Christians also believe in life after death, and in a transformation of the world triggered by God sending the Messiah. Christians, however, believe that the Saviour has already come for the first time in the person of Jesus, while the Jews are still waiting for their Messiah, and are therefore in a constant state of unbroken hope for the future. In contrast to Christians and Mus-

lims, who pray on a much more individual basis, Jews place more emphasis on community prayers, underlining the social nature of prayer in their religion.

In synagogue services, no priests mediate between God and man; rather, both parties communicate directly through the medium of prayer (as is also the case in Islamic services). "The priest, whose functions are described in such detail in the Bible, disappears from religious life; his place is taken by the rabbi, who is neither a mediator of salvation nor an administrator of the sacraments but rather someone who has knowledge of the teachings, knows how to interpret them, and is able to explain them to the enquirer. He indicates the direction that Jews should take in shaping their lives in accordance with tradition. The priest-layman division no longer exists; instead, there's a division between the learned and the unlearned, the uneducated."

The oldest and most important Jewish liturgical formulation is the *Shema* (literally "Hear!") prayer, which takes its

33

the coming of the Messiah, and closes with a prayer for peace.

When visiting sacred sites, such as the Wailing Wall, men and married women wear some form of head covering (small caps of cardboard are always provided for foreign visitors). This rite of covering symbolizes the belief that profane man should not step before his creator without preparation.

At morning prayers, men wear the talith, a white prayer shawl with black or blue stripes along its edges. In addition to this, orthodox Jews also don tefillin or "phylacteries," fastened to the upper left arm (in other words, near to the heart) and the brow. Within a kind of small box or locket are verses from the Bible written on parchment: Deuteronomy 6:4-9; 11:13-21; Exodus 13:1-10 and 11-16. According to Jewish tradition, these are a reminder to the faithful of the revelation of God and the escape from Egypt.

name from its first word: "Hear, O Israel! The Lord our God is one Lord: and thou shalt love the Lord thy God with all thine heart, and with all thy soul, and with all thy might" (Deuteronomy 6:4). The prayer is a composite of these parts of the Pentateuch: Deuteronomy 6:4-9; 11:13-21; Numbers 15:37-41. It swears to the unity of God and thus implies monotheism, includes the love of God and the Torah, expresses the concepts of reward and punishment, and recounts the flight from Egypt. This prayer is uttered daily.

The principal part of the three daily prayers is the prayer of the nineteen (formerly eighteen) benedictions which is also known as the *tefillah* (liturgical prayer), or the *amidah* (literally "standing") since it is recited while standing. The Amidah starts with the declaration of belief in God; this is followed by pleas for the rebuilding of Jerusalem and for

This community religious service is held in the synagogue. This Greek word comes from the Septuagint (the Greek translation of the Bible) and means "house of assembly," as originally a synagogue was a council or court building in which the citizens gathered for public meetings. Like a mosque, the synagogue is not exclusively a place of worship nor in any way sacred in and of itself: it only becomes a sacred place when the faithful, the members of the community, gather there to practice their holy rites.

Rabbi Lionel Blue penned a good characterization of the atmosphere in his book *How Does a Jew Get to Heaven?* "When you enter the synagogue, you're greeted with a roar of prayer and talking. A conversation between two neighbors mingles with the murmurs of a man at prayer. The rabbi reads silently to himself on the riser, while two representatives of the congregation discuss details of the service. People are constantly coming and going. You hear muffled laughter, or a Jewish joke. The spirit of the outside

Above: Men wear the tallit, or prayer shawl, when at prayer. Right: Your head must be covered when visiting holy sites.

world flows into the holy place, and it doesn't seem to be a holy place at all. A synagogue, therefore, isn't the highest or most holy place, but it's certainly the busiest place, the center of religious life, and one infers that no kind of life exists that is not religious life. The synagogue is not the temple of Jewish life, but rather its religious town hall."

The Byzantine Period

In 324, Constantine became absolute ruler of the Roman Empire. He and his mother Helena immediately had churches built at the most important places where Jesus had ministered. The emperor Justinian (527-565) later emulated their example. Gradually pilgrims began to journey to the Holy Land, bringing prosperity to the inhabitants of the region. But, in 529 the Samaritans instigated an uprising and destroyed many churches; then in 614 the Persians raged through Palestine, plundering and killing. The Persian king Chosram II handed Jerusa-lem over to the Jews, who, once back in possession of their national religious center, destroyed all the impious sacred edifices the Christians had built.

The Arab Period

Caliph Omar I (634-644) conquered the entire Middle East for Islam in a very short time. Yet there were no great outbursts of lamentation in Palestine, since the Muslims were known to be tolerant and accepted Jew and Christian alike as "people of a Book;" the Muslims also guaranteed laws of property. However the did demand the djiza, a poll tax levied on all those who did not convert to Islam. In 660 Muawiyya founded the Umayyad dynasty and send his armies off on further campaigns of conquest. But within 90 years his family's power was exhausted, and the Abbasids ruled thenceforth from their headquarters in Baghdad for the next 500 years.

Jerusalem became the most important religious city of the Muslims after

35

Mecca, since the Koran stated that it was from a rock in Jerusalem that the prophet Mohammed mounted his horse Buraq and started on his ride to heaven. In the 7th century the Dome of the Rock was erected on this spot; it remains one of the most beautiful Islamic buildings and an important place of worship.

In 905, the Shiite Fatimids conquered Egypt and threatened the supremacy of the Abbasids. The Byzantines also went back on the offensive, capturing parts of Syria and Antioch. The Fatimid sultan Hakim was the first in Palestine to turn against the Christians, ordering churches and cloisters to be burned down; but he was assassinated in 1021. The fifty years or so following his death were another period when peace prevailed and groups of pilgrims streamed back into the Holy Land. This era of tolerance came to an end with the Turks who were the new

Above: Koran suras ornament the Dome of the Rock. Right: Washing of feet and hands is a ritual purification before prayer.

masters in Palestine and who put an abrupt stop to the pilgrimages.

Excursus: Islam

Three basic principles rule the lives of Muslims: Islam, religion, faith. Islam means "submission to God," but also at the same time "established religion." This means that not only do the faithful live in accordance with the precepts of the Koran (or, in stricter orthography, the Qur'an) but also make public acknowledgement of belief (see below) to the communality of all Muslims (the 'Umma), thus ensuring the solidarity of all members in that community of faith ('Asabiyya).

Religion, in Arabic *din*, includes the injunction to obey the precepts of the Koran and to apply them in their best spirit for the benefit of the entire community of the faithful. *Din* also means faithfulness to the sources, to the Koran and to the Sunnah (see below). Finally, *din* is also the domain in which the Muslim lives: his daily affairs, in which no distinction is drawn between religious and worldly actions. This precept is illustrated in the phrase *din we dunya*, religion and the world, the two forming a single unit.

Faith (*iman*) means "entrusting oneself to God," and thus also means regularly making open acknowledgement of one's faith.

Alongside these three central principles stand the five pillars of Islam, which are the religious acts required of each Muslim. In the first place comes the declaration of faith (*al-shahadah*) as follows: "There is no god but Allah and Mohammed is his prophet" (*La illa lah wa Muhammed rasul lah*). Through ritual prayer (*al-sallah*), every Muslim turns five times each day to his God. He washes himself symbolically beforehand so that he is in the required ritual state of purity, and creates a sacred space by means of his prayer mat. When he prays, he orients himself towards the *qiblah*, that is to say, toward Mecca; in every mosque, the *qiblah* is indicated by a niche in the wall called the *mihrab*. Every Muslim should pray as often as possible with the others in the mosque (*masjid*) so as to strengthen the community of the Prophet, the *'ummat an nabi*. Anyone who prays throughout his life in the prescribed manner is assured of entry into paradise.

By giving alms (*al-zakah*) to the poor and needy, the faithful cleanse themselves of sin, thereby achieving rich blessings in the afterlife.

Then there is the duty to fast from sunrise to sunset during the month of Ramadan (*al-sawm*); only after the sun has gone down are the faithful permitted to eat, drink or smoke. Fasting during Ramadan may be waived, but generous alms are expected in compensation. Every Muslim should make the pilgrimage to Mecca (*al-hajj*) at least once in his life time; such a pilgrimage washes away

sin and strengthens the solidarity of the community of the faithful.

In addition to these five pillars, another important element in Islam is holy war (*al-jihad*) – although the English translation "holy war" is tinged with the ethnocentrism of the last century. Jihad actually signifies that "the entire community has to make an effort to spread the laws of God and of man throughout the world in accordance with the precepts of the Koran": not, therefore, war and extermination, but rather missionizing.

The Koran, Sunnah and Hadith are the sources of Islam. The word Koran (*Qur'an*) derives from the same root as *qara*, to read, and is generally translated as "recitation." According to Islamic tradition, God, in his revelations, transmitted the contents of the Koran directly, sura by sura, to Mohammed; the book sets forth both religious and legal rules for the way people should live with one another. The Koran, also referred to as simply *al-kitab*, or "the Book," is comprised of 114 of these sura, or chapters.

The Sunnah, short for the *sunnah an nabi*, the Actions of the Prophet, is the collection of all *hadith*, or traditions. A *hadith* recounts events, aphorisms, actions or sayings from the life of Mohammed and is thus, for all intents and purposes, a commentary on the Koran. A *hadith* has two parts: first, it states the name of the person who originally made the report, followed by the chain (*isnad, silsillah*) of those who handed down its contents; second comes the report (*matn*) of the event itself. All Muslims revere the Sunnah and consider themselves to be the *ahl al-sunnah al-jama'a*, the people of the Sunnah and of the community.

The Age of the Crusades

At the synod of Clermont on November 27, 1095, Pope Urban made a fateful

Above: "Godfrey de Bouillon's Conquest of Jerusalem in 1099," painting by K.T. von Piloty, around 1855. Right: Crusader (Mehrerau monastery, c. 1300).

speech in which he called for a Crusade – a military campaign to liberate the holy places of Palestine from the hands of the infidel. The Crusades were to cost millions of lives and immerse Palestine in a bloodbath for almost two centuries. The First, or "People's," Crusade – an undisciplined mob of around 20,000 men (and also women) – set out in the spring of 1096 in a state of religious hysteria, only to be completely annihilated after crossing into Turkish domains. Further columns followed, leaving a swathe of devastation in their wake, until the Byzantine emperor had to drive them back with his troops.

Finally the better-equipped armies started to arrive, under the command of Godfrey of Bouillon, his brother Baldwin, Bohemund of Otranto, his nephew Tancred, Raymond of Toulouse, and William the Conqueror's son Robert II of Normandy. Around 90,000 men went out to the Holy Land, inspired by the vision of the Crusades and the prospect of eternal life in Paradise and material riches on earth. On July 15, 1099, they stormed Jerusalem, plundering, killing and simply slaughtering anyone who got in the way of their swords: Muslims, Jews, men, women, children, the old, or the sick.

"In all of the city's streets and squares you could see mountains of heads, hands and legs. People walked over corpses and dead horses. But I have as yet only described the lesser horrors... If I were to describe what I really saw, you would not believe me..." wrote Raymond of Aguilers, an eyewitness of the fall of Jerusalem.

Godfrey of Bouillon died one year later, and his brother Baldwin had himself crowned King of Jerusalem on Christmas Day in the Church of the Nativity in Bethlehem.

The news of the glorious victory of the First Crusade reached home quickly. Suffused with heroic courage and excited by the prospect of fabulous riches, three more crusading armies departed, but these were completely wiped out in Asia Minor (present-day Turkey). With the aid of a considerable Genovese fleet, Baldwin was able to capture the coastal cities of Arsuf, Caesarea (where the entire population, except for a few children, was massacred by the Christian knights), Acre (today Akko), Sidon and Beirut. In the years which followed, Acre became the Crusaders' most important port, both strategically and economically.

Baldwin died in 1181, and his kinsman Baldwin of Le Bourg was appointed to succeed him. It was during his reign that the first military orders were founded. The Knights Hospitallers originated in a hospital which cared for poor pilgrims, while the Knights Templar were named after the Temple Mount, where, in the former Aqsa mosque, they had their headquarters. The avowed purpose of these two military orders was to protect the routes taken by the pilgrims. The Muslims intensified their struggles against the invaders, managing to take

Baldwin prisoner in 1123. He was finally released after payment of an enormous ransom, amounting to some 80,000 dinar. Baldwin II died in 1131, and his son-in-law, Fulk of Anjou, succeeded him as King of Jerusalem.

In 1141, the Saracens captured the city and county of Edessa, and Queen Melisende, the widow of Fulk (who had died the year before) and regent for the underage Baldwin III, appealed to the Pope for help. It was Bernard of Clairvaux, the founder of the Cistercian order, who called for a second Crusade in his sermons, and inspired great popular enthusiasm for the idea.

King Louis VII of France and the German king Conrad III each raised an army and set off by separate routes for the Holy Land. The German main force divided in Asia Minor. Bishop Otto of Freising led one part of the army and the pilgrims to Jerusalem, while Conrad, with the greater part of the troops, attempted a raid on the Muslim caliphate of Iconium at Dorylaeum (in the eastern part of present-day

Turkey). Conrad, however, was utterly defeated, and was forced to retreat to Constantinople, while the remainder of his forces attached themselves to the army of the French king. In the spring of 1148, Louis and Conrad met in Jerusalem. From here they conducted fruitless campaigns against Damascus and Acre.

After the failure of the Second Crusade, the Muslim states in the Near East were able to build up their forces under great leaders. In 1169, Nur al-Din gained control over Egypt and put his general Saladin (Salah al-Din) in charge of administering the country. In 1187 Saladin, who had in the meantime become Sultan of Egypt, crossed the Jordan with around 30,000 men. Guido of Lusignan, King of Jerusalem, commanded the 20,000 soldiers of the Christian army.

The further destiny of the Crusaders was decided in the hills known as the

Above: Suleiman II, the Magnificent (Kunsthistorisches Museum, Vienna). Right: Theodor Herzl, photograph of around 1900.

Horns of Hittim, west of Tiberias. Saladin utterly defeated the Christian army on its way to relieve that city. In the months which followed, Saladin conquered all the rest of the Crusaders' fortresses and cities, and entered Jerusalem victoriously on October 2, 1187.

The sheer scale of his successes revived European enthusiasm for yet another crusade: things were back exactly as they had been a hundred years before, except that the Muslim world was now united. Accordingly, Richard the Lion-Hearted of England, Philip Augustus of France, and Emperor Frederick Barbarossa set out with their armies to recapture the holy places of Christendom. July 10, 1190 was a catastrophic day for the Crusaders: Frederick, 70 years old and a veteran of the previous crusade, drowned while his troops were crossing the river Saleph in Armenia. His giant army broke up and dissipated. Richard and Philip Augustus, on the other hand, pushed on towards the Holy Land. The first city they conquered was Acre (Akko) where, after capturing the city, they followed the tradition of the First Crusade by slaughtering the 3,000 Muslim inhabitants — men, women and children alike.

Richard then continued southwards and inflicted a decisive defeat on Saladin at Arsuf. He refortified the port of Jaffa (Yafo) and planned to use this city as his base for the reconquest of Jerusalem. But things never actually got that far; Richard never lost sight of the reality of the military situation and conditions, and did not intend to risk his army unnecessarily. He actually opened negotiations with Saladin, even at one time proposing a strategic marriage of his sister to Saladin's brother.

When Saladin proposed a peace treaty and guaranteed unimpeded access to the holy places, Richard agreed in 1192 and set off for home. Saladin died a year later.

The following hundred years saw four further crusades. Emperor Frederick II was able to win back Jerusalem, Bethlehem and Nazareth once more in 1229, but by diplomacy rather than war. But the Muslims conquered the Kingdom of Jerusalem for the last time in 1244, and the last Christians quit Palestine in 1271; only Acre, the last city to fall to the Muslims, managed to hold out until 1291.

Turkish Rule

After the Crusades, Palestine was incorporated into the Mameluke Empire, ruled from Cairo, and assumed a rather peripheral role. In 1516, the Ottoman sultan Selim defeated the Egyptian army of the Mamelukes at Aleppo, occupied Jerusalem a year later, and a few months after that marched into Cairo. This was the beginning of the four hundred years of Turkish Ottoman rule in the Middle East. Selim's son, Suleiman the Magnificent, had splendid mosques, Koran schools, palaces, public fountains and much more built in his major cities. In 1799 Napoleon arrived, and attempted to invade Asia from Egypt. He was opposed at Acre by Ahmad al-Jezzar, nicknamed "the butcher," with the support of the British, and Napoleon's grandiose expansionist plans were thwarted.

In 1874, Jews from Jerusalem set up the *Palestine Exploration Fund* and four years later launched the first agricultural settlement of the country. 1882 saw the first stream of immigrants from Eastern Europe starting into Palestine; fourteen years later, Theodor Herzl published his book *Der Judenstaat* (The Jewish State), in which he called for the formation of a Jewish nation in Palestine. He was, therefore, the founder of Zionism.

In 1901, the Jewish National Fund was set up at the instigation of Chaim Weizmann to provide financial assistance in the purchasing of land. Between 1904 and the eve of World War I, a second great wave of immigration flooded into the country; many new Jewish settle-

mentrs sprang up and the first kibbutzim were founded (farm collectives organized and run on socialist principles). The Arab Palestinians slowly began to grow mistrustful, watching with disquiet as the Jews ceaselessly continued to acquire land, and particularly fearing the Zionist propaganda calling for the foundation of a Jewish state in Palestine. The year 1908 saw the first actual use of violence in Arab attacks on Jewish villages.

In World War I, many Jews fought in the British army and made a great contribution to expelling the Turks from Palestine. Parallel to the Jewish colony's military involvement in the Holy Land, leading Zionist politicians were determining the future of the region along diplomatic channels. They scored their first great success in June, 1917, when the French foreign ministry issued a communiqué to the effect that the French state would be amenable to the foundation of a state in Palestine under the protection of the Allied powers. The British, who were on the point of bringing Palestine under their control, naturally could not take a back seat here, and on November 2, 1917, the famous Balfour Declaration was issued. The British Foreign Minister, Lord Balfour, declared that his government would support the formation of a Jewish state in Palestine. This was the second great victory for the Zionists.

The British Mandate

In April, 1920, the League of Nations awarded the British the mandate over Palestine at the peace conference of San Remo, and a third wave of immigration reached the country. The Arabs were extremely dissatisfied with the situation, and the Grand Mufti of Jerusalem called for a holy war. This led to further severe unrest, in the course of which the Jews founded the military organization *Haganah* (literally "self-defense"). The British colonial secretary, Winston Churchill, who supported the idea of a Jewish state, was not able to gain acceptance for his views in the cabinet of Prime Minister Lloyd George. The British government saw the Arabs as important allies and did not wish to intimidate them by making concessions to the Jews.

The British postponed the provisions of the Balfour Declaration to a vague and distant future, denied Zionist organizations the right to have any say in the matter, restricted immigration quotas, and declared that they did not intend to make "Palestine as Jewish as England is English" – in other words, they sought the parallel development of both Zionist and Arab aspirations. This meant that the dream of an independent Jewish state again receded into the distance.

The British increasingly hindered Jewish activities with every passing year; they stopped making land available to Zionist settlement projects while trans-

Right: Israelis wait to meet arriving immigrants at the harbor in Haifa, 1949.

ferring large areas of land to the Arabs (who at this time made up more than 85% of the settled population). Despite these difficulties, the Jews did not give up, continuing to extend their self-administration in the 1920s while starting up functioning education and welfare systems. During the same period, however, Arab national consciousness was also on the rise, and the chasm separating Jew and Arab became ever wider. The Mufti of Jerusalem, Amin al Hussein, tirelessly stirred up the situation with inflammatory tracts and public speeches against the Jews; and the number of violent clashes between the country's two ethnic groups increased. An inquiry into the matter suggested that one underlying problem were Arab fears over Jewish immigration and sale of land, and recommended that immigration be more closely controlled and the Arab peasantry be afforded a greater degree of protection. The Zionists objected strongly, and to the Arab's great resentment the British government, as the mandate power, climbed down a little.

After the Nazi party came to power in Germany in 1933, more than 60,000 new immigrants flooded into Palestine within a few months, and the British army was forced to put down an Arab uprising. To prevent the unrest from getting worse, the mandate power, on the eve of World War II, decreed a halt to Jewish immigration – despite the fact that the Nazi practices of systematic racial persecution and internment in concentration camps were already known to the British.

The politically left-wing *Haganah* and the *Irgun*, the right-wing military organization of the later President Menachem Begin, were active in promoting secret immigration and were increasingly active militarily against both the mandate power and the Arabs. Illegal immigrants detected by the British were either sent back or interned on Cyprus.

The German occupation of Europe caused the death of about six million

Jews in the gas chambers of the concentration camps. Hitler's Final Solution meant the almost complete annihilation of European Jewry, the greatest concentration of Jews in the world. Only a small number escaped this terrible fate, aided by the resistance of a few individuals and national governments. Finland refused to hand over its Jewish citizens; while the Danish resistance movement managed to smuggle virtually all of the country's 50,000 Jewish citizens into neutral Sweden. In Italy, anti-Semitic legislation was passed, but both the government and the military chiefs of staff resisted German pressure to enforce these laws. The firm resolve of Bulgaria's people and government saved the lives of more than 50,000 Jews. Other Jews survived the Nazi terror due to the courage of individual Dutchmen, Frenchmen, Poles and Germans. The best-known of these, since Spielberg's film *Schindler's List*, may be German factory owner Oskar Schindler.

During the war, anti-British feeling in Palestine among the Jewish population (now around one-third of the total population) became keener and keener, and in January, 1944, the *Irgun* called for an "uprising against the British conqueror." The members of this underground organization committed acts of sabotage against British facilities, while the *Lechi*, which had splintered off from the *Irgun*, crossed the line between resistance and actual violence, murdering British policemen and soldiers. In June, 1946, the *Irgun* blew up the King David Hotel in Jerusalem which housed the mandate administration. Almost 100 British, Arabs and Jews died in the blast.

On February 14, 1947, the British declared that they were no longer in a position to reconcile the interests of the Arabs and Jews in Palestine, and referred the problem to the U.N. Nine months later, on November 29, 1947, the United Nations General Assembly approved, with 33 votes to 13, the partition of the country into an Arab and a Jewish state.

The myth survives even today that the Arab Palestinians were unanimously op-

The State of Israel

On May 14, 1948, David Ben Gurion proclaimed the state of Israel. Hours later tanks from five Arab armies – Egypt, Transjordan, Syria, Iraq and Lebanon – started advancing on the young republic, and the war of independence began. According to the official Israeli history, the Arab invasion made the war of 1948 unavoidable. In truth, however, the Arab politicians were expert in martial rhetoric, but none of the five countries was actually keen on a war. Instead, the Arabs agreed at the last minute to a plan mediated by the Americans which provided for an armistice should the Israelis prove willing to postpone their declaration of independence. But Ben Gurion was determinedly set against this plan. The Arabs, therefore, became victims of their own rhetoric, entering a war in a state of indecision, poorly equipped and miserably trained. This gave rise to the further myth that the tiny and new-born Israel, like a modern David, stood up to Goliath and ran the risk of being annihilated by a mighty war machine. Even Ben Gurion admitted that the only time this may have been the case was during the first four weeks. After that, such vast quantities of weaponry and equipment were delivered to Israel that the Israeli army, navy and air force all enjoyed clear superiority and conquered a series of territories which even today remain part of Israel.

posed to the partition plan and followed the call of the Mufti of Jerusalem in declaring total war on the Jewish state. This supposedly forced the Jews to apply military force against the Arabs. Yet after the opening of the archives in the 1980s, Israeli historians established that this was not the whole truth. The great majority of the Arabs did not obey the Mufti's call to arms, even if they were all against partition. Between the U.N. resolution in November 1947 and Israel's Declaration of Independence in May, 1948, a whole series of Arab Palestinian leaders and groups tried earnestly to talk with the Jewish politicians, in an attempt to find a way to live together. It wasn't until Ben Gurion's inflexible resistance to the creation of a Palestinian state that the Arab masses were ultimately radicalized.

Above: David Ben Gurion, first president of Israel, around 1950. Right: Armed conflict between the Arab Liberation Army and the Israeli underground organization Irgun, April 1948.

The Arab Palestinians resident in Israel fled by the thousands into neighboring countries, and the Israeli army did all it could to keep this mass exodus continuing for as long as possible. In the end, around 80% of the Arab citizens of Israel had left the country by the end of hostilities in early 1949.

In the following years, Israel's population doubled: in the course of programs such as "Magic Carpet," around 850,000 Jews were brought to the Promised Land from around the world, particularly from the Arab countries and from the Soviet Union. This mass immigration presented the little country of Israel with major social and economic problems. Furthermore, the military situation remained unsettled, and bands of marauders, or *fedajin*, were slipping into Israel from the surrounding Arab countries. Between the end of the war of independence and the Sinai campaign of 1956, around 1,300 Israelis fell victim to their terrorist attacks. Each time, the army reacted with extensive reprisals and retaliation.

In 1956, President Nasser of Egypt nationalized the Suez Canal. Britain and France pressurized Israel into war with Egypt, and themselves sent an expeditionary force into the canal zone. In response to pressure from the U.S.A., Britain and France were forced to stop their rather old-fashioned colonialist behavior; the Israelis were not permitted to annex the Sinai area which they had captured.

The situation in the region had never been so gridlocked. The Arab states now enjoyed the support of the Soviet Union, while Israel found its political friends in western Europe and the U.S.A. The Middle East gradually became the deep freezer of the Cold War. Border skirmishes and terrorist attacks were just routine dangers which the country had to endure over the coming years.

At the end of the 1950s, West Germany and Israel moved towards closer contacts. In 1960 Ben Gurion and Konrad Adenauer met in Washington, and the process of reconciliation between Germany and Israel began. From then on, the German government provided support for economic development in Israel.

In 1964, Palestinian refugees founded the PLO, or Palestine Liberation Organization, thereby starting the long process of informing world public opinion of the still-unsolved problem of the Palestinian refugees. Israel was still not prepared to allow the Palestinians to return to their old homeland, and the Arab states – with

the sole exception of Jordan – did not see themselves as capable of integrating the refugees into their social systems. The slogan which was still being mouthed by the Arab politicians – that they would drive the Israelis into the sea – fanned the flames of Jewish fears and ensured constant tension.

In the summer of 1967, Israel conducted a preemptive war against its Arab neighbors, occupying the Golan Heights, the region of Jordan west of the River Jordan, the Egyptian Sinai peninsula, the Gaza strip, and eastern Jerusalem in what became known as the Six-Day War. In the Sinai a massive tank battle took place. A considerable part of the credit for the Israelis' complete victory over the Arab countries was due to the Minister of Defense, Moshe Dayan, who was Supreme Commander of the armed forces.

In the years which followed, Palestinian guerrillas continued to operate from their bases in Lebanon and Jordan, carrying out terrorist attacks or hijacking passenger aircraft. During Israeli retalia-

tion, Egyptian territory was also bombed. The Egyptian government responded by making offers of peace negotiations which were, however, rejected by the Israelis. In consequence, October of 1973 saw the advance of Egyptian troops across the Sinai peninsula, where they inflicted heavy losses on Israeli forces. When the Egyptian army was surrounded by the Israelis and stood on the brink of another disaster, the U.S.A. and the U.S.S.R. effected an armistice three weeks after the commencement of hostilities in the Yom Kippur War. Diplomatic negotiations between the Egyptian president Anwar al-Sadat, the American mediator Henry Kissinger and the Israeli prime minister Golda Meir managed to allow the Egyptians to emerge from the war as military victors, thus saving face.

Above: Intifada – armed with stones, Palestinian youths fight for freedom. Right: Shimon Peres and Yassir Arafat shake hands on the treaty of autonomy in September, 1993.

Sadat then opened up his country to the West; and after some cautious moves toward rapprochement, Anwar al-Sadat and Menachem Begin signed a peace treaty at the beginning of 1979 (the Camp David Accords).

In 1982, Israeli troops intervened in south Lebanon in order to set up a buffer zone there, with the aim of making it nearly impossible to launch terrorist attacks from the region.

The *intifada* or Palestinian uprising against the occupying Israeli forces began in the occupied territories in 1987. Despite their brutal behavior against Palestinian civilians, the Israeli army has not been able to stamp out the fight for freedom.

The beginning of the 90s saw the start of secret meetings between Yassir Arafat and Israeli negotiators. On September 13, 1993, on the occasion of the signing of an autonomy agreement, Israeli president Yitzhak Rabin and PLO leader Yassir Arafat actually stood before the microphones and cameras with American president Bill Clinton – and together with Shimon Peres, shook hands. In May of 1994, the Israelis ended their 17-year occupation of the Gaza strip and the region around Jericho, placing the administration of these areas in Palestinian hands.

On October 26, 1994, Israel and Jordan signed a peace treaty; and on September 28, 1995, a second autonomy accord was signed in Washington, resulting in the withdrawal of Israeli troops from the Palestinian cities in the West Bank. Even Yitzhak Rabin's murder by a radical right-wing Jewish student on November 4, 1995 could not stop the momentum of the peace process. At the end of 1996, the majority of Hebron was placed under Arafat's administrative control. By the fall of 2000, however, the peace process seemed to have come to a standstill on both sides. Following fierce fighting bordering on the Palestinian autonomous regions, which claimed 100 lives, extremis-

forces in Palestine urged resumption of the intifada. Observers feared the outbreak of renewed far-reaching conflict in the Middle East.

Israel Today

Israel today has a population of five million, but only half of these residents were actually born in the country. The natives are called *sabres*, named after the cactus fruit which is spiky on the outside but is tender and sweet on the inside. The other half of the population consists of immigrants, many of whom have arrived in the "promised land" within the last few years. In the wake of the break-up of the Soviet Union, half a million Russian Jews emigrated to Israel between 1989 and 1992 alone; at the same time, 30,000 Ethiopians arrived in their new homeland. In these few years the population as a whole rose by more than 10%.

At the beginning of the last century, it was mainly the well-educated European Jews, or Ashkenazim, who emigrated to Palestine; in the kibbutzes, these emigres became the planners and instigators of the creation of a Jewish state. Today, they and their descendents are known as the *planter aristocracy*. After the state of Israel was established, the immigrants during the 1950s and 60s were almost exclusively Sephardim. These oriental Jews were settled in the almost uninhabited regions of northern Galilee and the Negev; the government saw its main task in integrating its new citizens into Israeli society as quickly as possible. But this wasn't quite so simple. Jews had streamed into Israel from almost one hundred different countries, from different regions, with different backgrounds and different cultures. Their only common link was religion.

The small country, therefore, has become a bubbling melting pot of nationalities, and despite all efforts to develop a national identity and unify society, tensions between the various social classes and ethnic groups have arisen and persisted. While the Ashkenazin, who no

47

longer constitute the majority, still occupy political, economic and military key positions and are consistently regarded as prosperous, the Sephardim live in much more modest or even poor circumstances and are not often found in leading positions. Fortunately, people in Israel are very much aware of this disparity in social classes, and are making conscious efforts to counteract it. Due to a consistent national education system, increasing mixing of ethnic groups, the universal compulsory military service, and the strong emphasis on personal achievement, ethnic differences are becoming increasingly irrelevant, and concrete steps are being taken toward social equality.

There are also tensions between secular and religious Jews. The latter, many of whom are immigrants from the United States, are acquiring more and more influence in key political and social fields. These groups are endeavoring to in-

fluence the way people think and to affect and define the national identity of the state of Israel.

The pressure of orthodox Jews on social areas of all kinds is increasing, and questions of religion and faith have never taken center stage in public discussion in the way they have come to in Israel today. Hard-line Jews, for example, are demanding the strict application of the Halachah, the Talmud's religious laws, in the country's legislation.

Since its foundation, the state of Israel has conceded three points to its religious lobby: observance of the Sabbath, observance of the ritual dietary laws, and respect for the Biblical laws of purity as they affect marriage. The orthodox are now interpreting these precepts more and more strictly. For example, a rabbi in Tel Aviv refused to marry a young couple because the celebration was held in a restaurant which also had non-kosher food on the menu. By pushing a new piece of legislation, the Ultras have accomplished a ban on the importation of non-kosher

Above: Ethiopian immigrants have found work on a construction site.

meat. One influential Jewish scholar issued the decree that no pious Jew should enter a Christian church – not even to take shelter from the rain. On the wall of a public swimming pool, other fundamentalist zealots sprayed, "We'll turn this swimming pool into a mikveh," or ritual bath.

Some time ago, the magazine *Jerusalem Report* stated that "the ultra-orthodox are slowly but inexorably increasing their grip on the capital," and the well-known liberal historian Tom Segev complained publicly that "there is a clear about-face underway in the political climate, and the country is becoming less and less Israeli and instead more and more Jewish."

The religious Schas party, which is represented in Parliament, would also like to force legislation along an ultra-orthodox course. "The courts must recognize that Israel is not just any democracy, but rather a Jewish democracy," declared one of its representatives in the Knesset.

Ever since Israel's foundation, the country has had severe economic problems, and things would be pretty bleak today were it not for the constant influx of money from the U.S.A. The government apportions two-thirds of the budget to paying off debts and defense spending, which means that only one-third can go toward social development. Israeli citizens pay one of the highest tax rates in the world, yet the government's economic policies have not, as yet, managed to get the widespread unemployment (11.2%) and the long-standing high rate of inflation (9.6%) under control. Agriculture only contributes 2.4% to the gross domestic product, industry around 32%; high, on the other hand, is the contibution of the service sector, at 56.8%. Special emphasis is laid on high-technology manufacturing, and for years the government has been investing a great deal of money in research in this area. Israeli engineers and technicians have made advances in medical electronics; in military engineering, of course; in telecommunications, and in solar energy. Tourism is a great source of foreign income; around 1.6 million visitors come each year from all over the world, bringing in around two billion U.S. dollars.

During the war of independence in 1948, the army drove many Arabs out of their villages and towns; many also fled from the fighting or went voluntarily into exile in neighboring countries. However, around 150,000 Arabs remained in their country and became citizens of the new state of Israel. Today, around 1 million Arab Israelis live in Israel, of whom 80% are Muslim, the remainder Christians and Druses. They enjoy the same rights as Jewish citizens, although they are not obligated to serve in the military – so that no Arab citizen will be forced to shoot on fellow Muslims in a war. Arabs can, however, enlist in the army of their own free will. Enlistment in the Israeli army helps form the identity of soldiers and citizens alike, and the army helps generate a strong awareness of national consciousness; young Arabs who do not enlist are therefore in a sense left out of measures central to the development of the national community. In practical terms, this means that they have problems finding jobs, since anyone who has performed his or her national services receives preferential treatment, and not just from the government agencies.

Naturally, Arab Israelis hold Israeli passports and identity cards, but the fact that the state specifies their religion in their identification papers effectively makes them, as Muslims, second-class citizens. Accordingly, the Arabs live apart from the Jews in their own settlements: the cities of Yafo (Jaffa), Haifa, Akko (Acre), Nazareth, Jerusalem and Ramla have a high proportion of Arab citizens. However, religious confession or ethnic membership are not registered at Israeli universities, which means that around 5,000 Arab students do study there. But it was not until 1989 that the first Arab Israeli was appointed as a lecturer at an Israeli university.

Israel has six universities: the Hebrew University in Jerusalem, the universities of Tel Aviv and Haifa, the national-religious College of Bar-Ilan in Tel Aviv, the Ben Gurion University of Be'er Sheva, and the Israeli Institute for Technology (Technikon) in Haifa. You could also include the Weizmann Institute, where graduate scientists study, teach and research. According to a survey, it's the Ben Gurion University of Be'er Sheva which is most highly regarded throughout the country.

But all of the universities enjoy a generally high popular regard. Only the armed forces, in fact, can record a higher degree of acceptance. As might be expected, a disproportionate number of academics are founders of citizen and peace pressure groups, and the higher the level of education, the more ready are the Israelis to let go of territory and conduct peace discussions with the Palestinians.

A familiar sight throughout Israel is that of young people doing their military service; at crossroads and bus stops, you often see groups of young soldiers waiting for the bus or trying to hitch a ride. In cafés, restaurants, department stores, pedestrian zones, by the main tourist sights, everywhere you see young male and female soldiers in uniform – all of them carrying their weapons with them, complete with extra magazines of live ammunition. It takes a little getting used to the image of an attractive young woman soldier in her green uniform skirt hurrying across the street, her handbag suspended from one shoulder and her submachine gun from the other.

Military service lasts three years for men and two years for women. The navy and the air force each add one more year

Right: Soldiers – both men and women – are a normal feature of daily life in Israel.

to this. Even after completing this period, men have to don their uniforms again for up to 35 days a year, for reserve forces exercises, until the age of 50; women, however, are not under this obligation.

Despite the length of service, Israelis seem to like serving in the armed forces; in fact, applications for pilot training or for the élite units are so high that not everyone can find a place. The sheer numbers of uniforms on the streets would lead you to believe that Israelis are a martial or militaristic people, but this impression is not quite correct: many families lost members during the four wars of the last decades.

Israeli Literature

When Eliezer Beh Yehuda came to Palestine with his family in 1881, they decided to speak nothing but Hebrew in the new land. We therefore have Eliezer to thank for the fact that one of the most ancient languages in the world has developed into a modern, living idiom with new expressions and words, now wholly adapted to today's high-tech environment. Ben Yehuda was supported from 1889 on by the Council for the Hebrew Language, which helped to bring about the fact that today, Hebrew is the national language of Israel.

Accounted the fathers of modern Hebrew literature are Chaim Nachman Bialik (1873-1934) and the Nobel prize-winner for literature, Samuel Joseph Agnon (1888-1970). Both came from eastern Europe and emigrated as grown men to Palestine in 1924; their books deal with the long years of the diaspora, Eastern European Yiddish culture, and the desire for a country of their own. Other members of this generation of writers include Chaim Chasas (1898-1973) and the third President of Israel, Salaman Schneur (1887-1959).

The next generation of writers was also born in Eastern Europe but grew up in

Palestine. The works of Abraham Schlonsky (1900-1973), Nathan Alterman (1910-1970) and the right-wing Zionist Uri Zwi Grinberg (1896-1981) no longer deal with the old homeland and the diaspora, but rather with Zionist ideals and the development of a strong Jewish society.

Writers who were born before or after the foundation of the state of Israel – the so-called '48 generation – cover the great political changes in the land in their books. Take, for example, Jishar Smilansky, born in 1916, who published under the nom de plume of S. Yizhar. His book of short stories *Khirbet Khiseh* (1949) deals with the war of independence, the expulsion of Arab neighbors and the guilty conscience of the Israeli soldiers. Even then, Smilansky already saw that the Jews were pushing the Arabs into the role of the victim, indeed, that they were making the Muslims into what they had only just themselves left behind: a people deprived of its rights without being a nation. In his great epoch *Days of the Zyklag (Jemei Zyklag)*, published in 1958, he again describes the war of 1948 and its effects.

Smilansky's younger colleagues – the internationally-known Amos Oz (born 1939), Abraham B. Yehoshua (born 1936), Joram Kaniuk (born 1930) and David Grossman (born 1954) – also take a critical, even accusing stance in their books, questioning the cost of the successes of Zionism and urging the Israeli public to move toward peace. The Arab Israeli Anton Shammas writes wonderful prose in both Arabic and Hebrew: best-known abroad is his novel *Arabesques*.

Ephraim Kishon is perhaps Israel's best-known author on the international stage. Born in Hungary in 1924, he emigrated to Israel in 1949, shortly after the state was founded. Kishon has written novels, plays for radio and for the stage, and screenplays. However, his real claim to fame are his masterly satiric works about modern Israel. English titles include *New York Ain't America* and *The Funniest Man in the World*.

JERUSALEM – HOLY CITY OF JEWS, CHRISTIANS AND MUSLIMS

JERUSALEM

JERICHO / QUMRAN

BETHLEHEM

WEST OF JERUSALEM

JERUSALEM

Jerusalem – in Hebrew *Yerushalayim*, in Arabic *Al-Quds*, "The Holy" – is the holy city of the Jews, Christians and Muslims. The most important shrines of the three great monotheistic religions of the world are situated here.

The Jews pray at the Wailing Wall, all that remains of the Second Temple; above this, the magnificent Dome of the Rock is a reminder that the prophet Mohammed rode from here to heaven on his horse Buraq, and in the adjacent Al-Aqsa mosque the faithful prostrate themselves in prayer five times a day beneath the black dome. Not far away, pious or historically inclined tourists walk down the Via Dolorosa, following the route of Christ's passion as far as the Holy Sepulcher. In the Old City of Jerusalem, the holy shrines of all three faiths are crowded next to each other, calling for a level of religious tolerance higher than anywhere else in the world; Jewish, Christian and Muslim neighborhoods, with synagogues, churches and mosques, run seamlessly into one another.

Preceding pages: Temple Mount with the Dome of the Rock in Jerusalem. In the Judaic Desert. Left: Women and men pray separately, even at the Wailing Wall.

6,000 Years of History

Around 6,000 years ago, Semitic nomads settled around the Gihon spring in the area south of the present-day Old City, put down roots and gradually became farmers. 2,000 years later the Amorites, better known as the Canaanites moved into Palestine, displacing the original population. Around 1650 B.C., the Hyksos whirled in from the east in their speedy chariots; based in Egypt, they ruled these northern regions as well for a hundred years. At the beginning of the New Kingdom in Egypt, Jerusalem again came under the sway of the pharaohs, who appointed a city king as the local authority on their behalf. When the so-called "heretic pharaoh" Akhnaten neglected foreign politics, instead concentrating his attention on his religious reforms (with the god Aten, he promulgated the world's first monotheistic religion), the vassal rulers in the Canaanite city-states seized the opportunity to become independent and proceeded to spend their time invading or attacking each other. It was during this era that the Israelite tribes began to acquire land; but they were not strong enough to conquer the city of Jerusalem, which they knew by the name of Jebus (which may have meant "dry rock"), inhabited by Jebu-

57

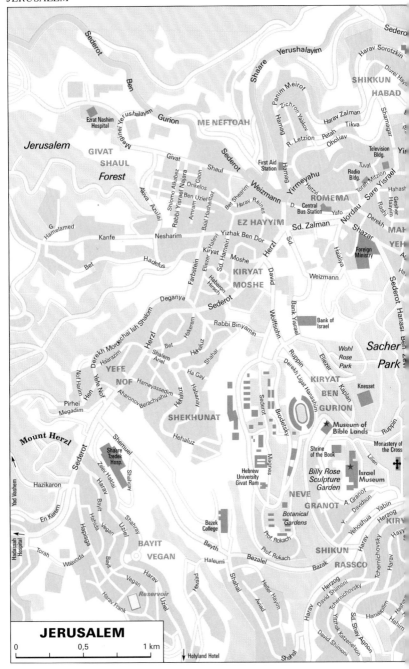

JERUSALEM

0   0,5   1 km

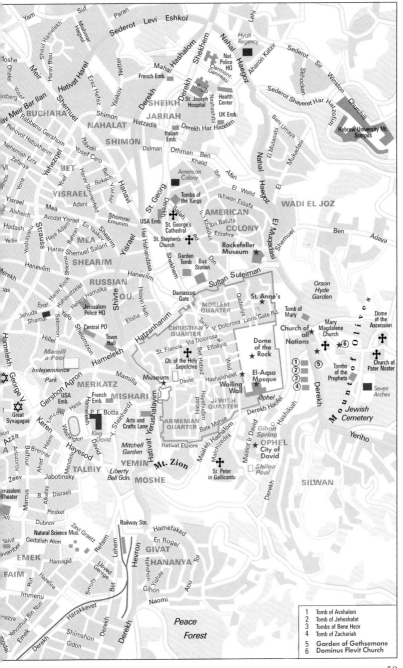

1	Tomb of Avshalom
2	Tomb of Jehoshafat
3	Tombs of Bene Hezir
4	Tomb of Zachariah
5	Garden of Gethsemane
6	Dominus Flevit Church

sites. Only after David had defeated the Philistines was he able to move into Jerusalem, around 998 B.C. It is he who gave the city its present name. (The name Jerusalem is commonly supposed to mean "foundation of peace," but probably means "foundation of Shalem," the latter being a West Semitic deity).

David's successor, Solomon, had the first Temple built during his reign (ca. 968-930). In 587, Babylonian armies under King Nebuchadnezzar II stormed into Palestine, razed the sacred edifice to its foundation walls and led the Jews off into slavery. Barely a century later, the Babylonian captivity came to an end and the returning Jews started to rebuild their city and began the construction of the second Temple. In 332, Jerusalem came under the control of the Greek Ptolemies. In 198 the Seleucids marched into the

Above: Model of the Second Temple, displayed in the district of Bet Vegan. Right: The city walls of Jerusalem by the Jaffa Gate.

city, desecrated the Temple and outlawed the Jewish religion. Judas Maccabaeus succeeded in taking over Jerusalem with his troops in 165, and the Temple was reopened for Jewish worship.

In 69 B.C., the Romans incorporated Palestine into their empire. With the help of Roman troops, Herod the Great captured Jerusalem in 37 B.C. and built a new Temple and a magnificent residence for himself. In 66 A.D. the uprising against the hated Roman occupiers blazed up in Jerusalem and spread throughout the country. It took four years for the Romans, first under Vespasian, then under Titus, to retake the city with their troops, and Jerusalem was completely destroyed in the process. 60 years later, emperor Constantine visited the Holy Land and ordered reconstruction to begin. In 132 A.D., there was a second rebellion – the Bar Kochba revolt, named after its leader. This time, it took the Romans three years to suppress the uprising. From that point on, Jews were forbidden to set foot in Jerusalem.

Under Constantine the Great, the first churches were built in the city, but they were all destroyed after the Persian invasion in 614 A.D. Worse still was the Persians' wholesale slaughter of the Christian population, with the cooperation of the Jews and Samaritans. Around 30,000 people were killed, and just as many led off into slavery. In 638, the Muslim army arrived, conquered the city after a lengthy siege, and changed its name to *Al Quds, the Holy*. In 691, caliph Abd al-Malik built the most beautiful shrine in Islam, the Dome of the Rock. When the Turkish Seljuks took the city in 1071, they prevented Christian pilgrims from visiting the holy places. In 1095, Pope Urban proclaimed the crusade at the Council of Clermont and on July 14, 1099, the Christian army, led by Godfrey of Bouillon, stormed through the city's streets, massacring Jewish and Muslim inhabitants in a terrible bloodbath. The Turkish conquest of Jerusalem in 1244 marked the end for the Crusaders; henceforth, the city was under Muslim rule.

In the 16th century, the Ottoman emperor Suleiman II had a new city wall built, and lived up to his nickname "the Magnificent" by commissioning a series of ornate palaces, mosques, public fountains and Koran schools.

In 1917, towards the end of World War I, General Allenby's troops expelled the Turks from the city and then from the rest of Palestine. After 1920, Jerusalem was the headquarters for the British high commissioner for the mandate territory of Palestine; and it was in this city that the state of Israel was proclaimed in 1948. One year later, as stipulated in the armistice agreement, the western part of Jerusalem was allocated to Israel, the eastern part, including the Old City, to Jordan.

During the Six-Day War of 1967, the Israelis occupied the eastern part of the city; in 1980, they declared "reunified" Jerusalem to be the "eternal capital of Israel," a status which neither the U.N. nor Arab and Palestinian politicians recognize even today.

The Old City

The **Old City** in the east of Jerusalem is still completely surrounded by the wall built in the 16th century by the Ottoman emperor Suleiman II the Magnificent, atop Byzantine and Roman foundations.

A stroll through the Old City is, above all, an uncommonly sensory experience. Stepping through the Jaffa Gate, you enter a colorful and lively oriental world, and soon lose all sense of time. The Arab shops along David Street and in the maze of alleyways leading off it exert an almost magical force of attraction. Spread out as a feast for your eyes are beautiful leather goods and brassware, colorful rugs and carpets, glazed Armenian tiles, genuine and fake antiques, Bedouin jewelry and embroidered Bedouin clothes, backgammon boards and little chests with mother-of-pearl inlay work and, of course, plenty of unspeakable

Above: In the atmospheric alleyways of Jerusalem's Old City.

tourist kitsch. Bargaining is absolutely essential and will often turn into a sophisticated form of choreography – you show interest, then retreat; the merchant follows; first offers are exchanged; hands are thrown skyward in feigned horror; you share a tea or coffee; and both sides pretend indifference until finally a price is agreed on to the satisfaction of both parties. Not everything should be haggled over, however: exceptions are second-hand items, foodstuffs, and anything in elegant stores with their fixed prices.

In the hurly-burly of the alleyways you will often have to press against the wall to let a donkey go by, tottering under its load. Arab women in their embroidered robes balance baskets and bundles on their heads with ease, while boys bearing trays of mint tea pass through the jostling crowds without spilling a drop. The coffeehouses are the domain of the men; this is where they sit reflectively, gazing at the world passing by outside, sipping at tiny cups of Arab coffee flavored with cardamom, and puffing on their hookahs.

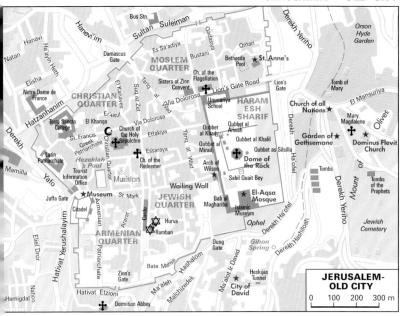

or water pipes. Many men still wear the traditional long robes, with the *keffiyeh* (Arab head-dress) wound casually around their heads. Backgammon players click the pieces over the boards, while ceiling fans swish lazily above them.

In Arab bakeries (which are particularly good in the Suq Khan al-Zait), anyone with a sweet tooth will be in seventh heaven: Arab pastries are sweet and exquisite, especially *baklava*, flaky pastry filled with nuts and dripping with honey. Everywhere, you will find stalls purveying sesame rings and *falafel* (fried dumplings made of chickpea puree with sesame paste served in warm flat loaves of *pita* bread). Or you can venture into an unsophisticated-looking restaurant to bolster your energies with *shish kebab*, topped off with an Arabic coffee.

A good place to start a walking tour through the Old City is the western Jaffa Gate, once the terminus of the caravan road to the coast and the port of Yafo (Jaffa). At the beginning of the 20th century, the Turks filled in the moat around the citadel in order to allow their ally, Kaiser Wilhelm II of Germany, to enter the city in his state carriage, in a dignified manner.

From the Jaffa Gate, David Street leads into the Old City. Immediately on your left, next to the Tourist Information Office, there are two inconspicuous Muslim tombs. These supposedly contain the bones of the two architects who designed the wall at Suleiman's command. The sultan, it is said, had them hanged because they had ommitted to include Mount Zion and David's Grave within the ramparts. Another version of this story is that the pair had to die because Suleiman was so impressed by the mighty city walls that he wanted to make sure the architects could not work for anyone else.

On the left rises the mighty old **Citadel**, also called the Tower of David. In 24 B.C., Herod the Great had a magnificent palace built a little further to the south which he protected with the citadel. In 70 A.D., the Romans used the citadel as a

63

garrison, and later still it was used by the Crusaders and Saracens.

Today's fortress dates from the 14th century and houses the excellently thought-out **Tower of David Museum** (Museum of the History of Jerusalem), where holograms, films, maps, scale models and photographs display the history of Jerusalem from the earliest days up until the present, in an entertaining and educational way. Every evening (apart from Fridays) an impressive sound and light show is held here. There is a wonderful view from the highest point of the Citadel over the Old City, the Mount of Olives, and also modern Jerusalem.

After the Museum, return to the Jaffa Gate: inside the city walls and on the left, you can climb up to the ramparts of the walls and walk along them as far as the Damascus Gate in the north or to the Zion Gate in the south. From there one can

Above: The Old City is subject to different laws of time than the rest of the world. Right: Deep in prayer at the Wailing Wall.

walk along the walls to the **Dung Gate**. The name of this gate dates from the time of Nehemiah (5th century B.C.), and one theory has it that it indicates an old tradition of dumping the city's sewage over the wall at this point; the Arabs know it as the Gate of the Moors. Whatever the name, it leads you back into the Old City.

At the Wailing Wall

To your right extends the **Ophel Archaeological Park**. In the 1970s and 80s, some important excavation work was done here; the discoveries included remnants of walls from the days of Herod and the remains of a two-story palace of the Mesopotamian queen Helena, who lived in Jerusalem around 70 A.D.

On the southwest side of the Temple area is the western wall, or **Wailing Wall**, so named because it is here that the Jews lament the destruction of their Temple by the Romans in 70 A.D. Once cramped, the area in front of the wall was expanded into the spacious plaza we see today by the demolition of the entire Moor's Quarter in 1967. You can only enter the area, which is itself counted as a synagogue, after going through a security check by the army.

This object, so holy to the Jewish people, is 18 meters high and 48 meters long; the lower course of stones date back to the time of Herod. The blocks vary in length, but are all about 1 meter high and hewn with such precision that they fit together without benefit of mortar. The Wailing Wall stands by its own weight alone; it once formed part of the western boundary wall of the Second Temple (as it is called, although it was in fact the third one).

Like most synagogues, the Wailing Wall has separate areas for men and women. Visitors may enter this holy place and even touch the wall, but must cover their heads before doing so (small cardboard caps are available for men at

he entrance). The spaces between the stones are crammed with small notes bearing prayers and wishes (there was a recent report of a man whose customers from all over the world faxed him their notes which he then inserted into the wall for a fee). Particularly in the late afternoon, before and after sundown, you will see many of the faithful sunk in prayer; on Fridays, Jews welcome their Sabbath here.

At the northeast corner of the Wailing Wall is **Wilson's Arch**, through which passed a road to the Temple in Herod's times; here, you can look down into a deep shaft to see the 14 layers of stone which once formed the Temple walls.

Solomon began construction of the First Temple around 964 B.C. By all accounts, it was extraordinarily magnificent, but was destroyed in 587 B.C. by the troops of Nebuchadnezzar. After his return from Babylonian captivity, a certain Zerubbabel set about building a new but less ornate temple on the same spot. When Herod was appointed king by the

Romans, he attempted to ingratiate himself with the Jews (he himself was of Edomite descent) by planning the erection of a sacred building which would put Solomon's temple to shame. But the rabbis were afraid that what Herod really intended was to tear down the Temple without building a new one. They demanded that he stockpile the entire building material for the new temple before demolishing the old one. The king agreed to this, as well as to the Jews' second request that only priests should be allowed to work on the temple's construction. Work began in 19 B.C., and the temple was finally completed in 64 A.D., only to be destroyed by Titus six years later.

In his *Jewish War*, Flavius Josephus described Herod's construction thus: "Viewed from without, the Temple had everything that could amaze both mind and eyes. Overlaid all round with stout plates of gold, in the first rays of the sun it reflected so fierce a blaze of fire that those who endeavored to look at it were forced to turn away as if they had looked

On the Temple Mount

Above the Wailing Wall, on the temple plateau of **Haram ash-Sharif** (which means "noble sanctuary"), the golden dome of the Dome of the Rock glints in the sun against the blue sky; the smaller, black dome of the Al-Aqsa mosque rises beside it. Between the Wailing Wall and the Ophel Archaeological Park, a ramp leads up to Bab al-Maghariba or the Moors' Gate, currently the only entrance to the Temple Mount, which is under Muslim administration.

As an Islamic holy place, the Temple Mount is considered second only to the Qa'aba in Mecca and Mohammed's sepulchral mosque in Medina. But the Mount is also a holy place for Christians and Jews alike: Christ preached here, and the first altar of Abraham and the first two Jewish Temples stood here.

It is particularly important not to wear any "immodest" clothing when you visit the Temple Mount – this means no short skirts or shorts, and keeping your arms covered.

The name of the **Al-Aqsa Mosque** goes back to the Koran where it is referred to in Sura 17 (called "The Night Journey" but also titled, in many manuscripts, "The Children of Israel") as *al-masjid al-aqsa*, which translates as "the furthest mosque," in other words, the one most distant from Mecca. Tradition has it that one night the angel Gabriel appeared to Mohammed and had him mount the winged horse Buraq, which bore him first to the al-Aqsa mosque and then from the Holy Rock to heaven, where God himself instructed him. The prophet returned to earth before the night was over.

Between 705 and 715, the caliph al-Walid had a magnificent mosque built here; a few years later, it was demolished by an earthquake, but had been restored by the end of the century to all its former splendor. This mosque in turn was levelled in 1033 by another earthquake.

straight into the sun. To strangers, as they approached, it seemed in the distance like a mountain covered with snow; for any part not covered with gold was dazzling white."

Large signs were set up to warn Gentiles of the danger the Temple could mean to them: "No foreigner is permitted to cross the barrier surrounding the Temple. Anyone apprehended in the Temple will only have himself to blame when death follows instantaneously." To be on the safe side, this announcement was written in numerous languages. A tablet of this type was discovered during excavations in 1935, and is today housed in the Rockefeller Museum.

When Vespasian's son Titus conquered Jerusalem in 70 A.D., the Temple went up in flames and burned right down to the ground.

Above: View of the gilded cupola of the Dome of the Rock. Right: Marble columns and granite pillars support the roof of the Dome of the Rock.

Shortly after this disaster another, smaller mosque was built, used first by the Crusaders and then by the Knights Templar. A few months after the battle of Hattin in 1187, Saladin had driven all the Franks out of Jerusalem and the building was restored to its old function as a mosque. In the 16th century, Suleiman II the Magnificent made extensive aesthetic improvements to the mosque.

In 1951, the Jordanian king Abdullah ibn Hussein, the great-grandfather of the present king, was assassinated as he entered the mosque. In 1967, the building was damaged by shellfire and in 1969, a Christian fanatic set it on fire.

The exterior of the mosque is of a simplicity that belies the enchanting interior. Seven naves are separated from one another by rows of elegant columns, and the light streaming in gives the interior, carpeted with rugs, a feeling of extreme spaciousness. The mosque is 80 meters long and 55 meters wide. Adjacent on the left is the White Mosque, or Women's Mosque, reserved for the use of women only. In the 12th century, sultan Saladin had the drum of the dome decorated with mosaics, donated a pulpit made of cedarwood (which was unfortunately destroyed by arson in 1969) and built a wonderful prayer niche or *mihrab*.

To the east of the mosque is a small Isamic Museum which includes among its exhibits fragments of stone and wood from the earlier mosque buildings.

Upon leaving the al-Aqsa mosque, you pass a purification spring called *al-Qa'as* in Arabic ("the chalice") before going up steps leading to the terrace of the Dome of the Rock. The arches spanning the steps date from the Mameluke period and were called the Scales of the Last Judgement. The Muslims believe that the scales will be suspended here at the Last Judgement and the faithful weighed.

The **Dome of the Rock**, *Qubbat al-Sakhra*, is one of the most beautiful examples of Islamic architecture in the

world. The shining dome made of gilded aluminum arches over the Holy Rock. According to Jewish tradition, this was where Abraham was to have sacrificed his son Isaac (Genesis 22:1-19); Islamic tradition adds that Mohammed ascended to heaven from this rock on his steed Buraq. Between 687 and 691, the caliph Abd al-Malik had the Dome of the Rock built with the assistance of Byzantine master builders, and inscribed in the interior: "This dome was built by God's servant Abd al-Malik, the Prince of the Faithful, in the year 72 (691 A.D.). May God have mercy on him." In the 9th century the caliph al-Ma'mun had the name of his predecessor erased and his own inserted, but the workmen forgot to change the date.

The Qubbat al-Sakhra is octagonal, and the peak of its dome measures a height of 55 meters. The external walls of the octagon are decorated at the bottom with marble and at the top with shiny colored faïence tiles, blue for the most part, which the Ottoman emperor Suleiman

added in the 16th century. A door at each of the four cardinal points admits visitors into this shrine. The ceiling of the Dome of the Rock is supported by an outer ring of eight marble pillars and 16 slim columns, while the inner ring of four granite columns and 12 marble columns surrounds the Holy Rock, which is 18 meters long, 13 meters wide and about 2 meters high, and protected by a wooden grille dating from the 1960s. The ceiling is made of wood and richly decorated, while the floors are of marble slabs. In the arcades and inside the dome gleam glorious mosaics. In the southeast corner, with a little imagination, you will be able to see the footprint of Mohammed, which the prophet left during his ascent to heaven. This is also the location of the reliquary, which contains some hairs from Mohammed's beard. Steps lead down to a small cave beneath the rock. Tradition has it that the cave was formed because

the Prophet's ride to heaven was at such a speed that the rock was sucked up out of the ground, and the angel Gabriel only just managed to hold it back at the last moment. The impression made by his fingers gripping deep into the rock can be seen on its eastern edge. In a hollow below the floor of the cave is the **Well of Souls** where, according to Muslim belief, the souls of the dead gather to pray.

The Dome of the Rock is not, as it happens, a mosque, and no public services take place here. Qubbat al-Sakhra is a jewelry case, as it were, for the holy rock it encloses.

The Dome of the Rock is surrounded by a series of smaller buildings from different epochs. To the east is the Qubbat al-Silsila or **Dome of the Chain**, an open pavilion where on the day of the Last Judgement a chain (in Arabic *silsila*) will separate the good from the evil-doers; for the Jews, this marks the site of David's place of judgement. To the northwest, on the edge of the terrace of the Dome of the Rock, is the octagonal **Dome of the As-**

Above: Under the shady trees in the garden of the Temple Mount.

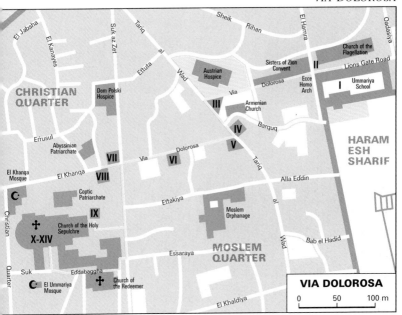

:ension, the Qubbat al-Mi'raj, which is where Mohammed is supposed to have prayed before his journey to heaven. Also in the northwest corner is the **Dome of the Spirits**, the Qubbat al-Arwah, where the souls of the blessed meet each night. Here too is the **Dome of Hebron**, the Qubbat al-Khalil, and the **Dome of St. George**, the Qubbat al-Khadir. Near the western entrance there was once a beautiful fountain, now sadly dry, called the **Sabil Qa'it Bey**, named for its donor, a 15th-century Egyptian Mameluke sultan called al-Ashraf Saif al-Din Qa'it Bay.

Along the Via Dolorosa

Leave the Temple Mount via the northern gate and turn right in the direction of St. Stephen's Gate or the Lion's Gate. After a few minutes you will come to **St. Anne's Church** on your left, and the pools of Bethesda. The church of St. Anne is associated with the birthplace of Mary; according to Christian tradition,

this was the site of the house of Mary's parents, Anne and Joachim. In 1150 A.D., the church was built here at the command of Queen Arda, the widow of the first Crusader-king of Jerusalem, Baldwin I. After re-conquering Jerusalem, Saladin had the church turned into a mosque and the convent into a Koran school or *madrasa*. Above the main gate you can still see today the dedicational inscription placed there under Saladin's orders. In the 19th century, the Ottoman sultan Abd al-Majid gave the church to Napoleon III in thanks for his help during the Crimean War; the French emperor had the church restored to its original appearance. This Romanesque basilica with three aisles is a nice example of a Crusader church, built of heavy blocks of stone and provided with small windows. Should a group of Christian tourists break into a psalm, you would have a chance to marvel at the church's excellent acoustics.

Directly beside St. Anne's Church stretches an excavation site with the

69

Pools of Bethesda, two enormous cisterns about 10 meters deep and 120 x 60 meters in length and width. In the course of construction of the new Temple, Herod had these water reservoirs renovated and enclosed the area on all four sides with columned halls; he also had a fifth hall built over the wall separating the two cisterns. The sick gathered by the pools to obtain relief from their ailments, as the waters were regarded as curative; the place was accordingly called *Beth Hesda*, meaning "house of mercy". Excavations have also revealed the remains of a Byzantine church with mosaics and the columns of a Roman shrine to Aesculapius.

Leaving the St. Anne complex turn right and walk west along Lion's Gate Road or Tariq Bab Sitti Maryam. This area was the location of the **Antonia Fortress** which Herod built at the time of

Above: The Via Dolorosa – both a bazaar street and a route for pilgrims. Right: Good Friday procession, Via Dolorosa.

Christ, naming it after his Roman protector Mark Antony. Even today, it is open to question whether or not Christ really was condemned to death here by Pontius Pilate; during his visits to Jerusalem, Pilate often stayed in Herod's palace near the Citadel by the Jaffa Gate. However, Christian tradition regards it as a certainty that Christ was condemned in the Antonia Fortress, and here began his path to the hill of crucifixion, Golgotha. The fortress is thus the starting point of the Via Dolorosa, which follows the route of Christ's passion. At three o'clock every Friday afternoon, the Franciscan monks move in a great procession along the 14 stations of the Via Dolorosa as far as the Church of the Holy Sephulchre, and anyone may join the procession. Stations I to IX are actually on the Via Dolorosa, while Stations X to XIV are within the church – in other words, above Golgotha and the Holy Sephulchre. Today, of course, the Via Dolorosa looks very different from the way it did at the time of Christ. At that time, for one thing, the

street was a lot deeper. The route of the crucifixion party has been changed many times until it finally arrived at its present form in the 18th and 19th centuries.

Station I, where Christ was condemned by Pontius Pilate, is on the left in the al-Umariyya Koran school. A flight of steps leads up to a door which opens onto a courtyard. This is the site of the old Antonia Fortress, where Christ is supposed to have heard the judgement on him. **Station II**, where Christ took up the cross, is on the other side in the Franciscan Monastery of the Flagellation. The monastery houses a rewarding museum with archaeological findings and an exhibition of the flora and fauna of Israel. In the Chapel of the Flagellation, three stained-glass windows depict the relief of the pardoned criminal Barabbas; Pilate washing his hands of guilt; and the flagellation of Christ. The dome of the chapel is decorated with the crown of thorns.

Spanning the Via Dolorosa a few steps beyond the Franciscan monastery is a part of the **Roman Ecce Homo arch**.

Built around 135 A.D., it alludes to the words of Pilate who, according to the Gospel of St. John, called out to Jesus as he came forth wearing the crown of thorns, *Ecce homo*, or in English "Behold the man!" (John 19:5). It was with these words that Pilate presented Jesus to the public after he had been scourged and mistreated.

The other part of the arch has been integrated into the Ecce Homo Basilica, which along with the adjoining **Convent of the Sisters of Zion** was founded in the last century at the instigation of a French priest. In the convent, you can view a model of the Antonia Fortress. Another exhibit, but in the crypt, is the "lithostrotos," a large section of pavement that supposedly comes from the courtyard of the fortress. John says: "When Pilate therefore heard that saying, he brought Jesus forth, and sat down in the judgement seat in a place that is called the Pavement, but in Hebrew, Gabbatha" (John 19:13); in the original Greek of the Gospel, the word translated as "pave-

71

VITTORIA GISMONDI PELLEGRINA IV T.S. A' RICORDO DEI SUOI GENITORI

ment" is *lithostrotos*. What you now see, however, is not in fact the original pavement from the time of Christ, but rather the remnants of a Roman street dating back to the reconstruction projects of the emperor Hadrian. You can quite clearly see where bored Roman sentries scratched boards for their games into the paving stones. From the crypt you come to the Struthion Pool (or Sparrow Pool), a huge cistern which was part of the defensive ditch of the Antonia fortress.

The Via Dolorosa now runs into a north-south street, Tariq al-Wad, where the Austrian Hospice is located. Turn left and left again to reach **Station III**, where Christ fell under the weight of the cross; the event is depicted above the entrance to a small chapel on the spot. A few meters further on, also on the left-hand side of the street, is **Station IV** (where Christ met his mother). This encounter is

Above: Via Dolorosa, Station III. Right: Someone in this house has made a hajj to Mecca. Far right: Bazaar, Muslim quarter.

commemorated in a small chapel with a relief. In the crypt of the adjoining Armenian church, a mosaic floor marks the spot where Mary supposedly was standing. At the point where the Via Dolorosa now turns to the right, on the corner, is **Station V**, where Simon of Cyrene helped Christ carry the cross. This was where the Roman soldiers realized that Jesus would not be able to manage the steep path up to the Mount of Calvary, grabbed Simon of Cyrene out of the crowd, and forced him to help the condemned man carry his cross.

This narrow alleyway is lined with shops; halfway along on the left is **Station VI**, where Veronica handed Jesus a cloth to wipe away his sweat. The cloth was marked with an impression of Jesus' face; the purported original has been in St. Peter's in Rome since the 8th century. At the junction of Suq Khan az Zait street (oil market) is **Station VII**, where Christ fell for the second time; it is marked with a small Franciscan chapel. The route turns left and immediately right into the

alley; a stone set in the wall on the left with the inscription ICXC NIKA indicates **Station VIII**, where Jesus spoke to the weeping woman accompanying him: "Daughters of Jerusalem, weep not for me, but weep for yourselves, and for your children. For, behold, the days are coming in which they shall say, Blessed are the barren, and the wombs that never bore, and the paps which never gave suck. Then shall they begin to say to the mountains, Fall on us; and to the hills, Cover us" (Luke 23:28-30).

The route now leads back to the Suq Khan az Zait and continues to the right. Roofed over in places, narrow and crowded, the alleys in the heart of the Muslim bazaar quarter are illuminated with a mysterious light filtering down from above which creates a chiascuro around the pyramids of fruit and vegetables, meat, spices, fabrics, and household goods offered for sale on every side. Brightly-painted houses proclaiming that one or more of their residents have completed a *hajj*, or pilgrimage to Mecca,

crowd against façades with elegant arched doorways, fragments of Roman columns, house entrances decorated with old Arabian stone carvings, and roofed arcades where roving street vendors have spread their wares in a veritable carpet across the ground. With its Arabian atmosphere, the quarter forms a strange setting for the passing groups of psalm-singing Bible tourists.

After about 100 meters, a ramp on the right leads up and into an alleyway which brings you to a Coptic church. At the end of this little street, a column marks **Station IX**, where Jesus fell for a third time under the weight of the cross.

Continuing on in the original direction along Suq Khan az Zait, you will come to a right-hand turn which will lead you past the Lutheran Church of the Redeemer and bring you to the entrances of the Church of the Holy Sepulcher.

An alternative route is to go through the gate to the left of Station IX and onto the roof of the church, where there is a small and picturesque Ethiopian cloister.

From there, one can arrive at the square before the Church of the Holy Sepulcher by proceeding through two Ethiopian chapels.

In the Church of the Holy Sepulcher

The **Church of the Holy Sepulcher** is the most sacred place in Christendom, as its walls enclose Calvary or, as it is also known, Golgotha, the "place of the skull," where Christ was crucified and died. Close by is also the place where he was buried and from where he rose again.

As part of his urban renewal project, Hadrian had a temple to Aphrodite erected above the site of the crucifixion and grave, first of all sealing off the entire area, including the rock of Golgotha and the grave, with one enormous base structure which covered everything. In 313, Constantine the Great had the first mag-

Above: A pilgrim in the Christian quarter seeks lodging. Right: The Church of the Holy Sepulcher.

nificent Church of the Holy Sepulcher erected over the holy places. The Persians, who conquered Jerusalem in 614, destroyed this building. After the emperor Heraclius defeated these invaders in 628, a second church was built on the site, which was not quite so magnificent and was also smaller than its predecessor. In the 10th century, Muslim troops set this building on fire, but no great damage was done – this privilege was reserved for caliph al-Hakim, who completely destroyed it. The Crusaders were the next people to rebuild the church, which was consecrated in 1149 on the 50th anniversary of the taking of Jerusalem. 38 years later, Jerusalem was in the hands of Saladin; however, he respected the Christians' church and kept it from being destroyed. The church withstood the ravages of time until the year 1808, when it was set on fire by a pilgrim's candle and had to be rebuilt yet again. At the beginning of this century, the edifice that was now the fifth Church of the Holy Sepulcher suffered severe damage from an

earthquake. The joint owners of the church, the Latins, Armenians and Greeks, could not come to an agreement on the restoration of the church and the British mandate power had to secure the building as best it could. The three parties were eventually able to reach a compromise, and restoration work on the church started in the 1960s. The work was at last finished in January of 1997, after continual interruptions of jealous squabbling between the three religious groups; and the rotunda is now free of scaffolding and flooded with light for the first time in about 70 years.

The bickering between these three parties has unfortunately gone on since time immemorial. Back in the middle of the 19th century, the Turks decided they had had enough of it, and issued the so-called "status quo" decree, which was taken over by the state of Israel. The decree simply froze the ownership situation of the time; the Turks also specified the precise times at which services could be held, and forbade the introduction of any new religious observances. This did not, however, put an end to the very unchristian squabbling at the most holy places in Christendom. Each of the three groups is embarrassingly insistent that its claims be fulfilled to the very letter of the law, and lodges a bitter complaint if it believes any other group has a different interpretation of the situation.

The Latins, Armenians and Greeks each carry out work on the parts under their control after little or no consultation with the others; in some areas, you can only shake your head at how little the sections go together, and some of the decoration seems to be the product of an aesthetic taste which, to put it politely, takes a bit of getting used to.

The Church of the Holy Sepulcher is a labyrinth of chapels and side-chapels on top of and beside each other, an unplanned chaos of shrines and altars, tombs and memorials, in which it is very hard to find your way around. Many visitors simply stumble in lost bewilderment through this enormous house of God.

In front of the entrance there is a small paved forecourt, and during the main tourist season this is crammed with people, as is the church inside.

The façade of the church, decorated with masonry work, dates back to the days of the Crusaders. You enter through the left-hand portal – as Saladin bricked up the right-hand one in 1187 – and are immersed in dusky gloom. On your left is the Muslim doorkeeper's place – a Muslim family has looked after the keys to the church for centuries. Straight ahead, there is a long, flat block of marble: this is the **Stone of Unction**, where Joseph of Arimathea and Nicodemus rubbed the body of Christ with fragrant oils and then wound him in his linen shroud. Today many of the faithful still rub precious oils into the stone.

To the right of the Stone of Unction, a steep flight of stairs leads up to the 5-meter high mount of Calvary, and the

Above: Christians believe that Jesus was anointed for burial on the Stone of Unction.

Chapel of Golgotha with its three altars This is the location of **Station X** of the passion, where the legionaries stripped Christ of his clothes; of **Station XI** where Christ was nailed to the cross; of Station **XII**, where Christ died on the cross; and **Station XIII**, where the dead Messiah was laid in the arms of his mother. Above the altar of the Nailing to the Cross with its copper reliefs dating back to 1588, a mosaic depicts the crucifixion on Golgotha. On the Greek Orthodox Stabat Mater altar stands a statue of the Mother of God, who according to belief, stood on this spot watching her son's slow death. The Greek Orthodox altar of the crucifixion displays the hole in the rock in which the cross allegedly was inserted; you may reach beneath the altar and touch the rock. To the right of the altar is a 20-centimeter crack in the rock which supposedly split at the moment Christ died.

To the right of the exit from the chapel is the **Catholicum**. This Greek Orthodox church consists of the domed central nave of the earlier Crusaders' church. Exactly beneath the dome, in a chalice, is a wickered ball which in Christian belief is supposed to be the omphalos, or navel of the world.

Alongside the Catholicum is the great Rotunda. At its center is the small **Chapel of the Holy Sepulcher**, always with a long line of visitors waiting at its entrance. This is **Station XIV**, where Christ's body was laid in the grave. According to the Bible, Joseph of Arimathea put Christ in the tomb which he had originally hewn for himself out of solid rock.

The entrance to the Rotunda brings you into an anteroom which today goes by the name of the **Chapel of the Angels**. This is where an angel announced the resurrection of Christ to three women: Mary Magdalene, Mary the mother of Jacob, and Salome. Kept in a shrine here is a fragment of the stone which was rolled across the tomb to close it.

Behind a low doorway is the burial chamber itself, only 4 square meters in size. On the right is the marble tomb slab on which Christ is said to have lain. At the back of the chapel, the Copts have a tiny sacred room in which another fragment of the tomb rock is kept.

As Joseph of Arimathea had given his tomb to Jesus, he had to have a new one made for himself; this tomb is located beside the Rotunda's tiny west apse.

Near the Church of the Holy Sepulcher, the 50 meter tower of the Luthern **Church of the Redeemer** soars heavenwards. From the top of the tower, there is a wonderful view over the Old City and modern Jerusalem. The church was consecrated in 1898 in the presence of Kaiser Wilhelm II.

In the Jewish Quarter

Before the Crusades, the Jews lived in the northeast part of the city, where the Muslim quarter is today. But the crusading Franks so utterly destroyed the Jewish quarter that when the Sephardic rabbi Moses Namanides (also known as the Ramban) came to Jerusalem in 1267, he found it as good as defunct. He and his companions began to lay out a new settlement around the Ramban synagogue. The number of Jews swelled in 1492, when Jews whom the Catholic monarchs Isabella and Fernando had had expelled by decree from Spain began to arrive; while in the 18th and 19th centuries Ashkenazy Jews streamed in from Eastern Europe. By 1865, the Jewish residents of Jerusalem already represented more than half of the population. By now, the Jewish quarter was cramped and crowded, and the new arrivals started building their houses outside the city walls.

During the war of independence in 1948, this city district had to be given up. According to the armistice agreement, east Jerusalem went to Jordan: the people who lived there moved out, and the quarter remained a ghost town for more than a generation. In the Six-Day War, the Israelis captured this part of the city. Since then, archaeologists have been conducting extensive excavations, and architects are carefully rehabilitating the area. This work has already paid off: there is a friendly atmosphere to the Jewish quarter, and its yellow sandstone houses gleam warmly in the sun. Keep in mind, however, that the Israeli occupation of this part of the city does not comply with international law, and is therefore not recognized by the U.N.

As you come into the Jewish quarter from the direction of the Church of the Redeemer, you will see, to the left of the street Suq al-Husur, the 8-meter wide main street of Jerusalem, lined with colonnades, full of shops and dating back to Byzantine Jerusalem of the 6th century. In those days the **Cardo**, as it is called, was twice as wide as it is now; today, its surface is 5 meters lower than the level of the other streets in the quarter. When you feel the old paving stones under your

feet, you can, with a little imagination, get a feeling for what things might have been like on this street in the old days in Jerusalem. Just as in those days, sophisticated and elegant stores have sprung up along one section of this Israeli Fifth Avenue; here, too, is the excellent restaurant Culinaria.

Opposite the steps which lead down to the business area, a narrow passage brings you to the **Broad Wall**, the remains of a part of the city walls almost 7 meters wide and 2,700 years old. If you take a right turn, you will soon reach the heart of the Jewish quarter, **Hurva Square**, lined with inviting small cafés. Here, too, are the remains of the **Hurva Synagogue**, which Ashkenazy Jews from Poland started building in the 18th century. It was destroyed in the hostilities between the Jews and Arabs in 1948; but the domed central edifice has been left as

Above: In the Jewish quarter of the Old City. Right: Children in orthodox Jewish families already wear temple locks.

a ruin (the Hebrew word *hurva* mean ruins) to serve as a memorial against war

Nearby is the **Ramban Synagogue** built in 1267 as the first synagogue o Jerusalem's Old City. In 1585, it wa converted into a mosque; after man cycles of destruction and rebuilding, i took on its present form in 1967.

Also at Hurva Square is the **Herodian Quarter** archaeological site and th **Wohl Archaeological Museum**. Here you can see house foundations, frescoes mosaics, ceramics, glassware and ritua baths from the time of Herod the Grea (40-4 B.C.), all excavated here. The building remains found here were probably once the extensive residence of high priest. When the temple wa stormed in 70 A.D., the Romans probably destroyed this complex as well.

Around the corner from the Wohl Museum is the **Burnt House**, a basemen workshop which was among the buildings belonging to the Bar Kathros family of priests, whose house also went up ir flames during the conquest of Jerusalem

1 70 A.D. An audiovisual presentation explains the excavation work and familiarizes you with the findings and the layout of the the cellar.

If you turn left after leaving the Burnt House, a few steps will bring you to a wonderful panorama; from here you can let your gaze wander over the Wailing Wall and the golden cupola of the Dome of the Rock. This is a favorite backdrop for tour guides as they deliver their commentary.

On Mount Zion

If you leave the Old City by the Dung Gate, a street to the right leads up to Mount Zion; a shorter route is to go through the **Zion Gate** directly up Mount Zion. Ahead of you, the steep spire and high bell tower of the Catholic **Church of the Dormition** thrust into the sky. When the German Kaiser visited the region in 1898, the Turkish sultan presented him with the area on Mount Zion, as a gift, and Wilhelm passed it on

to the archbishopric of Cologne. Architect Heinrich Renard designed the church in a Neo-Romanesque style; it was consecrated in 1908. According to Christian belief, this was the spot where the mother of Christ did not die as such, but rather fell into an eternal sleep (Latin: *dormitio*). The mosaics on the floor inside the church symbolize the Trinity, the apostles and the zodiac; Mary with the infant Jesus is depicted on a mosaic in the apse, while the crypt contains a statue of the sleeping Mary beneath a mosaic dome. The church and its monastery are run by German Franciscan monks.

South of the church, on the first floor of a mosque complex dating from the 14th century, is the **Hall of the Last Supper** (also known as the Coenaculum or Cenacle). Its vaulted ceiling is borne by two Gothic columns, and a fragment of stone opposite the Muslim prayer niche marks the spot where Christ sat at the Last Supper. After the resurrection of Christ, the disciples returned to this "upper room," and it was here, according

to the Acts of the Apostles, that the miracle of the Pentecost took place, when the Holy Ghost descended upon the apostles in the form of tongues of fire (Acts 2:1 – 4). Even today, no one knows the actual location of the "upper room" where Jesus and the disciples made their farewells. It is probable that the room was in a house within the city walls.

The lower story of the same building contains the "Hall of the Washing of the Feet," today a synagogue, as well as **David's Tomb**. Since the time of the Crusades, this place has been venerated as the burial place of the great king, although he was actually buried elsewhere in the city. The massive sarcophagus is covered with an embroidered silk cloth whose Hebrew inscriptions read, "David, King of Israel, lives eternally," and "If I forget thee, O Jerusalem, let my right hand forget her cunning" (Psalm 137,

Above: A rare sight – snow before the Zion Gate. Right: "David's Tomb" is now a synagogue.

"By the waters of Babylon..."). If the Bible report is true – and historians believe it is – the uniter of the Israelite tribes cannot be buried here, as he was interred in the so-called City of David on Mount Ophel east of Mount Zion (1 Kings 2:10, "So David slept with his fathers, and was buried in the city of David"). Since the Bible also calls the City of David the "stronghold of Zion" (2 Samuel 5:7), and this name was transferred to the hill in the Byzantine era, believers in the Middle Ages looked for the City of David on Mount Zion, and believed they had found it too.

Next to the building which houses "David's Tomb," there is a small memorial, the Chamber of the Martyrs (or "Chamber of the Holocaust"), which commemorates the murder of 6 million Jews, with exhibits from the concentration camps and memorial tablets for those Jewish communities which were completely wiped out by the Nazis.

The Mount of Olives and East Jerusalem

Begin your visit to the Mount of Olives – which rises 120 meters straight from the plain and is named, as one might expect, for the many olive groves there – at **St. Stephen's Gate** (also known as the Lion Gate). Through this, you leave the Old City; bearing right, you will soon reach the **Tomb of the Virgin** with the Cave of Gethsemane.

The façade and the wide marble steps down to the crypt date back to the Crusader period. In a side chapel half-way to the crypt you can see, on the right the tombs of Mary's parents, Joachim and Anne, and on the left the tomb of St. Joseph. In the actual crypt, which dates from the Byzantine period, is the tomb of Mary herself, hewn from the living rock. It is flanked by a Christian-Armenian altar on one side and an Islamic prayer niche on the other. Since Jesus – under

the name of Isa Ben Miriam (Jesus son of Mary) – is counted as one of the five prophets of Islam, the Muslims do, of course, also venerate his mother. The other four prophets of the Muslims are Noah, Abraham, Moses and Mohammed.

From the courtyard in front of the church, a passage leads to the **Cave of Gethsemane**, which contains fragments of a mosaic floor from the Byzantine period. According to a Christian belief, this is where Jesus was betrayed by Judas and arrested by the Romans.

Leaving the Tomb of the Virgin, you run the gauntlet of a double line of street traders to reach the **Garden of Gethsemane**. The name comes from the Aramaic *gat shamna* or the Hebrew *gat hemanim*, both of which signify "oil press." The area was very probably once an olive grove with an oil mill. In this peaceful and shadowy place, some ancient and gnarled olive trees, supposedly from the time of Christ, still flourish. After the Last Supper, Christ came with his disciples into the garden of

Gethsemane where they intended to spend the night. He was then overcome by deadly fear and stepped a little way apart from the disciples, and "kneeled down, and prayed, saying, 'Father, if thou be willing, remove this cup from me: nevertheless not my will, but thine, be done.'" He then "prayed more earnestly: and his sweat was as it were great drops of blood falling down on the ground" (Luke 22:40-44).

The present **Church of Gethsemane**, also known as the Church of the Agony, was designed by the Italian Antonio Barluzzi and built between 1920 and 1924; many countries donated money for its construction and magnificent interior. The twelve domes were painted by artists from different countries; hence the church's other designation, the Church of All Nations. In front of the main apse is the rock where Christ in his agony prayed to God, and this theme is depicted in the mosaic and the apse. In the side apses are depictions of the betrayal of Judas and the arrest of Jesus.

81

The next stop further up the hill is the **Church of Mary Magdalene**, which is readily identifiable as a Russian Orthodox church by its seven golden onion domes and the cross with two crossbeams on the top. Czar Alexander III had the church built in 1888 as a memorial to his mother, Maria Alexandrovna. In the crypt is the tomb of the Russian Grand Duchess Elisabeth Feodorovna, who was murdered by the Bolsheviks in 1918 with the Tsar and the imperial family.

Continuing on the steep path up the Mount of Olives, you will come to the **Church of Dominus Flevit** (Latin for "the Lord wept"). Also under the supervision of Italian architect Antonio Barluzzi, construction on this harmoniously proportioned, tear-shaped church started in 1955. Standing on Byzantine foundations, it is surrounded by a small, shady

Above: View of the Mount of Olives with the Church of Gethsemane and the Russian Orthodox Church of Mary Magdalene. Right: Jerusalem by moonlight.

grove. To the left of the entrance are part of a mosaic floor which dates back to the 5th century. As Christ rode on a donkey down the Mount of Olives on Palm Sunday, followed by a mass of people, and saw the city shining in the sunlight, he wept, having seen in a vision its coming fall (Luke 19:41-44). From this point you still have a wonderful view of the Old City of Jerusalem.

Steps carry you farther up the Mount of Olives; soon you will see on your right, in the Jewish cemetary, the **Tomb of the Prophets**, where Haggai, Zechariah and Malachi, three of the so-called twelve minor prophets of the 6th and 5th centuries B.C., are supposedly buried. This appears to be rather less than probable, since this particular type of grave was only developed after the time of Christ. Two semicircular passages contain a total of 26 loculi or burial places.

Above the catacombs, there is a large communal grave holding 48 people. They all lost their lives in the fighting around the Jewish quarter in 1948, and

hey were hastily buried inside the quarter where they had fallen. After the army had occupied East Jerusalem in the Six-Day War, the bodies were exhumed and reburied here. The grave houses not only soldiers but also the bones of a little boy who had served as a runner during the fighting. Every year the army holds a memorial service for the fallen.

A little way further on foot and you come to the top of the Mount of Olives. This is the location of the Seven Arches Hotel (formerly the Intercontinental), from where you can enjoy the famous picture-postcard view of the Holy City. For a good photograph, you really need to get here early in the morning so that you have the sun at your back and the scenery appears in its most attractive light. The only flies in the ointment here are the ceaseless pestering of souvenir sellers and the blandishments of the camel men intent on talking you into a camel ride.

However, the view is a lovely distraction from such concerns. The mountain slopes gently down into the Kidron valley; on Temple Mount, the gilded dome of the Dome of the Rock gleams over the roofs of the Old City; in the distance the skyscrapers of modern Jerusalem reach into the sky. To the right of the Dome of the Rock you can see in the city walls the (closed) Gate of Mercy, also known as the Golden Gate. According to Jewish belief, the Messiah will one day pass through this gate into the city (Christian teaching holds that this has in fact already happened). Almost the whole hillside is taken up by the **Jewish Cemetery**, where for almost 2,000 years the Jews have been burying their dead. It is the oldest cemetery in the world still in use.

About 150 meters north of the Seven Arches Hotel is the **Chapel of the Ascension**. This small octagonal building dates back to the time of the Crusades; its dome is of Islamic origin. It was here that Christ supposedly started his ascent to heaven, pressing so hard on the earth with his sandaled foot that it left an impression on the rock.

Only a few meters away is the **Convent of the Paternoster**. According to a Christian belief from the time of the Crusades, it was here that Christ taught his disciples the Lord's Prayer ("Our father..." or, in Latin, *Pater noster...*). Faïence tablets reproduce the text of the most famous prayer of Christianity in more than 70 languages, including one version in braille on a metal plate to the left of the entrance. In 1868, the French Princesse de la Tour d'Auvergne purchased the site and on the Byzantine and Frankish foundations had a convent built for Carmelite nuns. She is buried in the grave chapel to one side of the entrance.

The Kidron Valley

We now return to the foot of the Mount of Olives. At the Tomb of the Virgin, the road forks; take the right-hand fork down into the Kidron valley. A short walk will bring you to a series of impressive sepulchres, among them the so-called **Tomb of Absalom** (the son of David), which, unfortunately for the attribution, dates from as recently as the 1st century A.D. An almost perfect cube carved out of the rock, it is decorated with columns and a round roof and is almost 15 meters high. Behind it, under the name of the **Tomb of Jehosaphat** (fourth king of Judea, 873-849), there stretches another large burial complex with numerous burial chambers hewn out of the rock. A few meters further on is the oldest of the tombs, the **Tomb of the Bene Hezir**, built by a Jewish family of priests in the 2nd century B.C.; the balcony-like façade is decorated with columns, and behind it is a tomb cut out of rock with numerous burial chambers. After James, the brother of Jesus and first bishop of Jerusalem, was killed by the high priest Hananias, his body is supposed to have been buried

Right: The Rockefeller Museum is worth a visit.

here, which is why the burial chamber i also known as the Tomb of St. James Also impressive is the square **Mauso leum of Zachariah** (father of John th Baptist), which was cut entirely from th living rock in the 1st century A.D.; it i crowned by a pyramidal roof and dec orated with Iconic columns.

A little way on, on your right at th bottom of Mount Ophel, is the **Giho Spring**, the only spring in Jerusalen which supplies water all year round an where the Virgin Mary fetched wate from. Here, the excavation team from th Hebrew University uncovered the **Cit of David**. Around 1000 B.C., David lai out his city on Mount Ophel and brough the Ark of the Covenant here too. Parts o the city fortifications, remnants of build ings, a sewage system and terraces con nected by steps have been excavated.

King Hezekiah (727-698 B.C.) had a underground water conduit laid from th Gihon spring to the Pool of Shiloah to en sure that Jerusalem would have an ade quate supply of water in the event of siege. You can actually walk along th 500 meters of **Hezekiah's tunnel** as fa as the Pool of Shiloah, although in som sections you will have to go at a crouch.

You can also reach the **Pool of Shiloa** above ground; you will find it 500 meter away, on your right. At this pool, Chris is supposed to have healed a blind ma (John 9:7). From the pool a stepped pat from the Roman period leads to the Cath olic church of **St. Peter in Gallicantu** built in 1931 on the eastern slopes c Mount Zion. Its strange name is Latin fc "where the rooster crowed." This is sup posedly, but probably not actually, th site of the palace of the high priest Cai phas, where Peter denied Christ thre times before the cock crowed. Inside th church you can view cisterns and cellar from the Roman period as well as a fairl impressive dungeon reputed to b "Christ's prison cell." Jewish and earl Christian finds are on view in the churcl

North of the Old City

Suleiman Street leads from the Damascus Gate or Herod's Gate to the northeast corner of the Old City. Located here is the **Rockefeller Museum** or **Archaeological Museum** with its unique collection of archaeological exhibits. Founded in 1927 with generous donations from the American industrial magnate John D. Rockefeller, the museum exhibits finds from the prehistoric period up to the 18th century. Among the oldest items are a fragment of skull from neolithic Jericho, carved ivory from Canaanite Megiddo, a statue of the Egyptian pharaoh Ramses III, and a stele of his predecessor Seti I.

A little way back down Suleiman Street, Saladin Street turns off right. At the junction of this street and Nablus Road is the burial complex known as the **Tombs of the Kings**. For a long time, the inhabitants of Jerusalem regarded the catacombs as the burial place of the kings of Judea. However, in the middle of the

last century the French archaeologist Félicien de Saulcy established that the tombs were of a considerably more recent date: Queen Helena of Adiabene (a small vassal kingdom in present-day Iraq) had the catacombs hewn from the rock in the 1st century A.D. She had come to the holy city and converted to Judaism. If you plan to visit the tomb, bring a flashlight; it will light your way from the large, rectangular vestibule through a gate into a square main chamber which is the center of a complex of niche burial chambers.

A short distance further north is the **American Colony Hotel** (which has an excellent restaurant), located in a former pasha's palace of the 19th century. The American Colony is favored by journalists working in Jerusalem; it was also the place of the first secret meetings between Israelis and Palestinians on the road to peace negotiations.

Turn off Saladin Street onto Nablus Road. Passing the Anglican St. George's Cathedral and St. Stephen's Church with the French Bible Institute, you will come

85

where Yiddish is predominantly spoken. The men still wear Hasidic costume: black clothes, fur-trimmed hats and temple locks (*peiyot*). On the day before the Sabbath, there is a lively market in the center of Me'a She'arim (which means "one hundred gates"). Notices advise visitors on their comportment: driving on the Sabbath is forbidden, as is photography and the wearing of "indecent clothes" (shorts and clothes which expose the arms and legs). Northwest of the Me'a She'arim quarter is the **Buchara** (or Bokharan) quarter, established in 1892, whose inhabitants can often still be seen wearing the picturesque folk costumes of Central Asian Buchara.

West Jerusalem

Walking down Jaffa Street towards the Old City, you will come right into the main business center of Modern Jerusalem, centered around the pedestrian zone of **Ben Yehuda Street**. In the heart of the new city you can while away the hours in elegant boutiques, shopping centers with a wide range of goods, street cafés and restaurants.

King George V Street branches off south from Ben Yehuda Street. The Monastery of the Pères de Sion, founded in 1874, is here, as well as **Independence Park**, with a cistern from old Jerusalem. The buildings of the **Jewish Agency Building** are the headquarters of the Jewish Agency, founded in 1897 by Theodor Herzl, where the Zionist archives are housed. A little to the south is the magnificent **Great Synagogue** of the Chief Rabbinate, consecrated in 1982. Also housed in the synagogue is a museum of Jewish sacred and popular art.

A little way further west, on the right-hand side of Ben Zevi Street, is the 11th-century **Monastery of the Holy Cross**, a defiant fortified monastery surrounded by walls, with courtyards and terraces, at the center of which is a domed church.

back towards the Old City. Just before the Damascus Gate, Conrad Schick Lane leads left to the **Garden Tomb**. Here, it is very easy to imagine how Christ's tomb might have looked. The tomb was discovered by the British general Charles Gordon (1833-1885) in 1883. Since the rock resembled a skull, he believed that he had found Cavalry, or Golgotha (which both mean "the place of the skull"). When a tomb was also brought to light here, the euphoria was extreme – until archaeologists established that the tomb dated from around the 4th century. Because of this story, the place is also known ironically as *Gordon's Golgotha*.

Go along Shivte Yisrael Street and Me'a She'arim Street to reach the **Me'a She'arim quarter**, which ultra-orthodox Jews founded in the northwest of the city in 1875. Here, there are countless Talmud schools, ritual baths and synagogues

Above: An orthodox Jew in Me'a She'arim.
Right: Relaxed atmosphere in the sidewalk cafés of the New City.

Take bus number 9 or 99 to the government district – the Qiryat Ben Gurion – and the **Knesset**. This is the home of Israel's single-chamber parliament whose name and number of seats (120) goes back to the *Haknesset Hagedolah*, the Great Assembly of the period of the Second Temple. The floor mosaic and the bright, colourful tapestries were designed by Marc Chagall. In front of the building is a 5 meter-high *menorah* or sacred seven-branched candelabrum presented to the young state of Israel by the British Parliament. Southwest of the Knesset is one of the most important exhibition buildings in the country, the **Israel Museum**, actually comprised of four separate museums. The outstanding attraction here is the dome-shaped **Shrine of the Book**, which imitates the shape of the pottery vase in which the Qumran (or Dead Sea) scrolls were discovered between 1947 and 1956 in a cave above the Dead Sea. The original documents are on display here. Next to the shrine is the **Billy Rose Art Garden**, an open-air ex-

hibition of the sculptures of many artists, including Auguste Rodin, Henry Moore and Pablo Picasso. The **Samuel Bronfman Biblical and Archaeological Museum** displays exhibits from the time of the Old Testament, while the **Bezalel National Art Museum** houses a large collection of Judaica from all over the world, including such items as Moroccan festival clothes and bridal adornments.

Between the Knesset and the Israel Museum is the recently-opened **Bible Lands Museum**. It owes its existence to Canadian multimillionaire Elie Borovsky, whose collection of antiquities forms the museum's core; exhibits cover the periods of both the Old and New Testaments.

Ruppin Street leads on westwards to the **Hebrew University**, which was laid out in 1948 and also houses the Jewish National and University Library. The entrance hall to the university is decorated with a mosaic from the 5th-6th centuries.

Ruppin Street leads onto Herzl Boulevard and to Mount Herzl, the highest

elevation in Jerusalem, at 890 meters. The mountain takes its name from the founder of Zionism, Theodor Herzl (1860-1904), who was buried here in 1949. Herzl, an Austro-Hungarian, worked as the Paris correspondent of a Viennese newspaper and reported on the Dreyfus affair. The outbreak of anti-Semitism and the racial hatred he witnessed in France shook him deeply, particularly as France had been considered a paragon of tolerance up to that point. In 1896, he published his book *The Jewish State*, in which he argued that the only solution would be for the Jews to establish their own nation. One year later the first Zionist Congress convened in Basel; responding to this event, Herzl wrote, "If not in five years, then in fifty years, a Jewish state may become reality." Exactly fifty years later, the U.N. ap-

Above: Yad Vashem commemorates the Nazi murder of six million Jews. Right: Chagall's stained-glass window in the Hadassah Synagogue.

proved the partition plans for Palestine, thus making his dream come true.

Buried nearby are members of Herzl's family as well as leading Zionists, the former prime ministers Levi Eshkol (died 1969) and Golda Meir (died 1978). The most recent grave is that of Yitzhak Rabin (assassinated on November 4, 1995). West of these graves is Israel's largest military cemetery. At the entrance to Herzl Park, a small museum displays an authentic reconstruction of Herzl's study and library in Vienna.

From Mount Herzl, Har Hazikaron Street leads to Memorial Hill (Har Hazikaron). Here, the **Holocaust Memorial**, or Yad Vashem, commemorates the 6 million Jews murdered by the Nazis and their abettors.

Yad Vashem, meaning "a place and a name," derives from a remark made by the prophet Isaiah in his "promise to the foreigners and childless" (Isaiah 56:4-5).

This huge complex contains a Holocaust archive with more than 50 million documents, a research and documentation center and a publications agency, as well as a synagogue, a youth and educational center, and an art museum which exhibits the work of concentration camp inmates. The Hall of Remembrance is built of heavy basalt blocks and concrete; the names of the concentration camps have been chiseled into the floor slabs. An eternal flame flickers in front of a large bronze dish which contains the ashes of the dead from every extermination camp. In front of the building stands the lofty column of remembrance (30 meters high) with the exhortation *Zkhor* (Remember!) at its top. In the Avenue of the Righteous, 5,500 evergreen carob trees stand as a memorial to all the Gentiles who worked to save Jews from the Nazis, for the most part at the risk of their own lives. Their names are inscribed on small plaques; a tree has recently been added for Oskar Schindler. The Holocaust Museum displays thousands and

ousands of documents and photographs, as well as videos, sound recordings and exhibits relating to the Final Solution the Nazi regime was pursuing for he Jewish question. Finally, there is also he terrible pathos of the **Children's Memorial** of Yad Vashem, commemorating the 1.5 million children who were also murdered by the Nazis.

Turning to the left upon exiting the Yad Vashem, one comes to a street leading to a vantage point where one of the rain's cars which transported Jews to Auschwitz is "ascending" to the heavens. Below this lies the **Valley of the Destroyed Communities**. Here, the names of about 5000 no longer existent Jewish communities have been chiseled into the several meter-high rock wall.

Rav Uziel Street descends from Herzl Boulevard and after 2 kilometers brings you to the **Holyland Hotel**, in the city district of Bet Vegan. Here, you can see an extraordinary model on a scale of :50, covering about 10,000 square meters and made of stone, metal and marble, which shows Jerusalem at the time of Christ. First conceived of by archaeologist Michael Avi-Yonah, the model presents a view of ancient Jerusalem according to the latest research. Whenever archaeologists or social historians make new discoveries or findings, the model is updated accordingly.

Back on Herzl Boulevard, take a left turn and go through the village of En Kerem to **Hadassah Hospital**, the university clinic of Hebrew University and the largest hospital in the Middle East. The hospital is world-famous for the twelve stained-glass windows in its synagogue designed by Marc Chagall, who was born in a Jewish community in Russia. The windows depict the founding fathers of the twelve tribes of Israel.

East and South of Jerusalem

Bethlehem, Hebron, the oasis city of Jericho and the caves of Qumran on the Dead Sea are all located in the West Bank, where the *intifada* – the Palestinian

popular uprising against the Israeli occupiers – made headlines, caused deaths, and kept emotions at a boiling point from 1987 to 1993. Since Jericho (in 1994) and Bethlehem (in 1995) became part of the autonomous Palestinian region, things have become quieter and it has become safe to visit these places. Still, it is best to consult one's consulate before visiting the West Bank (especially if travel in an Israeli rental car or in the direction of Ramallah or Hebron is intended), in order to hear the latest developments and find out about any potential dangers.

Basically, the inhabitants of the West Bank are pleased to see interested foreign visitors, welcoming them with proverbial Arabic hospitality.

Qumran can be reached by Israeli public buses, with several daily departures for Eilat or En Gedi from the Central Bus Station on Jaffa Street in Jerusalem. Buses and shared taxis (*sherut*) connect Jerusalem to Jericho and Bethlehem, departing from the bus station at the Damascus Gate in the Old City.

About 3 kilometers east of Jerusalem, on your way to Jericho, you will pass the village of **Eizzariya** on the eastern slope of the Mount of Olives, called Bethany in the New Testament. This is where Christ resurrected Lazarus; it was also the starting point of Christ's triumphal procession into Jerusalem. A favorite destination for pilgrims is the modern church of Lazarus, built on the foundations of two previous buildings and containing the tomb of Lazarus. Today, the population of the village is almost exclusively Arab.

Leaving the village, the road climbs steeply. Next comes the industrial settlement of **Ma'ale Adummim**. After the town, on the right, is the Khan al-Hatur or the **Inn of the Good Samaritan**. Archaeologists have excavated remnants of walls here, so it is indeed possible that

Above: Hisham's Palace in Jericho, a beautiful example of Umayyadin architecture.
Right: Bedouin children near Jericho.

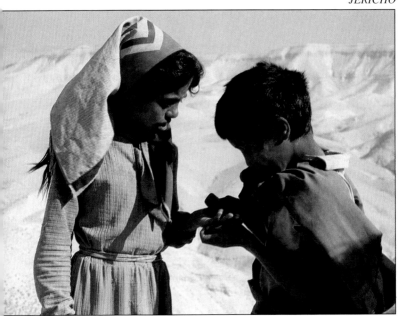

here was an inn here at the time of Christ. The Bible tells the story of a man who was attacked by robbers and left lying there half dead; two passers-by, a priest and a Levite, refuse him their help, but finally a man from Samaria comes along who pours oil and wine into the wounds of the unfortunate and brings him to an inn (Luke 10:30-37).

A few kilometers further, a red arrow points down into the Wadi Kelt to the **Monastery of St. George** which clings spectacularly to a rocky cliff. The road to it is very narrow and bumpy. Starting in the 3rd century, monks lived out here in the desert, praying in their caves which served as their cells. The first monastery was built 200 years later and dedicated to the Virgin Mary. The present building dates from the end of the last century, and is named after St. George of Koziba.

Jericho and Qumran

From the Monastery of St. George, it is not far to **Jericho**, supposedly the oldest city in the world and the first which the Israelites were able to conquer.

As long as 12,000 years ago, people started to settle here around the spring of Ain al-Sultan. Their settlements developed into permanent villages; they kept herds and, managing to domesticate an ancestor of modern wheat, practiced an early form of agriculture. Two thousand years later, the settlement had grown into a city, complete with defensive walls of stone and a tower. It is thought that three thousand or so inhabitants owed their wealth to trading in salt, asphalt and sulfur from the Dead Sea. On numerous occasions over the following millennia the town was destroyed, rebuilt, abandoned by its inhabitants and reoccupied. When the "Chosen People" advanced to Jericho's gates in 1300 B.C., it had declined into an insignificant little town with neglected defenses in a poor state of repair. One could almost imagine that the trumpets' blare and the Israelites' war cries were enough to bring the whole lot tumbling down.

For a long time the town remained un-inhabited. Around 900 B.C. there was re-settlement, and it was in this period that the prophet Elijah was here with his follower Elisha; it was here that a miracle was wrought with the waters, which is why the Ain al-Sultan spring is also known as the **Elisha spring**. One day, the spring suddenly began gushing out waters which caused sickness and miscarriages. The inhabitants begged Elisha for help; he scattered salt into the water, and the freshwater spring was healed (2 Kings 2:19-25).

Jericho underwent further occupations, destruction and rebuilding until Herod was given the city in 30 A.D. by the Roman emperor Augustus. Herod built as finely as his coffers allowed, and the magnificent winter palace soon became his preferred place of residence. In the year 4 A.D. the tyrant died here – to the great joy of his subjects.

It was here that Christ cured the blind Bartimaeus. Roman legionaries destroyed the city after the first Jewish uprising , and in 638 the Muslim armies arrived. During the era of the Crusades, the Franks held Jericho for a number of years, but Saladin captured the city in 1187, after which it fell into a long sleep of obscurity. In 1948 the town passed to Jordan; in 1967 the Israelis captured western Jordan, which they have occupied ever since. In the autumn of 1994, Yassir Arafat moved into Jericho in order to take the first steps – partial autonomy – towards a Palestinian state. Administrative buildings have sprung up since then; and the city, which was almost empty of tourists during the years of the *intifada*, now offers a casino, is building hotels, and even has a cable railway up to the Cloister of the Temptation.

Today, Jericho is a shady, lushly green oasis town with a predominantly Arab population of around 7,000. The lowest city in the world, its elevation is about 250 meters below sea level. Freshwater

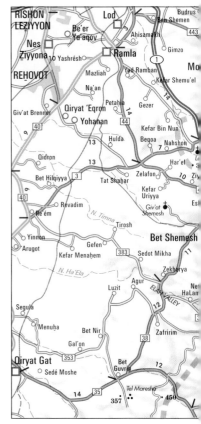

springs make good harvests of citrus fruits, dates and bananas possible. The market square is surrounded by attractive garden restaurants and cafés.

Do not expect to see spectacular excavated ruins at **Tel as-Sultan**; still, it is hard to remain oblivious to the fascination of looking at the oldest stone building on earth, a round tower which is about 9000 years old. Not far to the north there is a shrine erected by Mesolithic nomads around 8000 B.C. Also, the Elisha Spring still bubbles away here, as it has for so many centuries. Near the spring are the remains of a Byzantine synagogue with an attractive floor mosaic.

Rising to the west of Jericho is the **Mount of the Temptation**, 350 meters

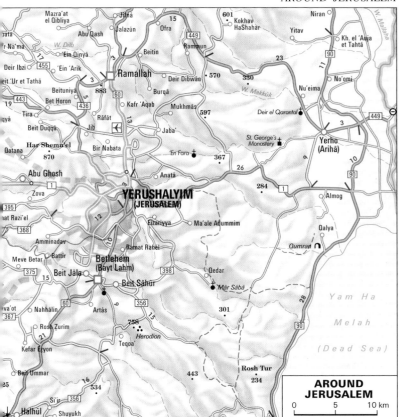

in height, on which Jesus fasted for 40 days. The devil then came to him and challenged him to turn the stones there into bread. Jesus replied with the famous words: "It is written, Man shall not live by bread alone, but by every word that proceedeth out of the mouth of God" (Matthew 4:3-4).

From the 4th to the 14th centuries, pious hermits lived here in the caves of the mountain. They called their abode *Mons Quarantus* or Mount of the Forty, in allusion to the 40 days Christ fasted. The locals somehow corrupted this into *Qarantal*, which is the name the mountain bears today. At the end of the last century a Greek Orthodox monastery was built halfway up to the peak.

One and a half kilometers northwest of the Tel as-Sultan, the ruins of the Khirbet al-Mafjir, better known in the region as **Hisham's Palace**, rises out of the sand. This magnificent building was probably not built by Hisham (ruled 724-743) but by his successor Al-Walid. The palace is one of the most significant examples of architecture from the period of the Ummayyid dynasty. Before it was even completed, however, it was so severely damaged in the great earthquake of 749 that building work was stopped. The outstanding attraction of the ruins, laid out on a square ground plan, is what were probably the most splendid baths in the Islamic world at that time. Particularly attractive are the depictions of plants, ani-

93

mals and people – despite the Islamic ban on figurative art – including a mosaic which shows gazelles beneath orange trees. Frescoes from the palace of Hisham can be seen in the Rockefeller Museum in Jerusalem.

Twenty kilometers south of Jericho in a rock massif on the banks of the Dead Sea are the **Caves of Qumran**, in which the Essenes, a particularly strict Jewish sect, settled during the 2nd century B.C. In 68 A.D., during the first Jewish uprising, the Romans destroyed the settlement, but the inhabitants had managed to seal their scrolls in pottery vessels and hide them in the nearby caves. In 1947 the young Bedouin Mohammed al-Dib ("the wolf") came across a pottery vessel containing scrolls in a cave. Archaeological investigations brought to light other scrolls in other caves. Their discovery was a sensation. They are, in fact, the old-est existing Bible texts and include one parchment with a total of 66 chapters from the book of Isaiah. There were also manuscripts dealing with the everyday religious life of the Essenes. After the discovery of the scrolls, the ruins of an extensive Essene settlement were excavated. Since no living rooms or bedrooms were found in this complex, it is thought that it served the Essenes who lived in the surrounding caves as a kind of monastery.

Today, at the formerly walled-in site you can see a ruined tower, the remains of a kitchen, an assembly room and refectory, and a scriptorium where the scrolls were probably written. Several cisterns and ritual washbasins supplied by an aqueduct have also been discovered, as well as a bakery. The finds from Qumran are currently on display in the Israel Museum in Jerusalem and in the Museum of Amman in Jordan.

Some distance away from the complex is the hill massif with the caves where the scrolls were found. They can only be visited as part of a conducted tour.

BETHLEHEM AND HEBRON

Eight kilometers south of Jerusalem and under Palestinian rule since 1995, the little town of **Bethlehem** lies in the midst of a hilly landscape. Christian Arabs, as well as Muslim ones, live here; and it was here that Christ was born.

In 7 B.C. the emperor Augustus ordered a census in order to obtain basic taxation information on Palestine. Everyone had to return to where he had been born and this meant Joseph of Nazareth had to return to Bethlehem, accompanied by Mary, who was betrothed to him. Since there was no room for them in the house of his kinsfolk, Joseph and Mary moved into a cave used for storage. This is where Jesus was born, an event which, according to historical research, actually transpired in the year 7 "before Christ"

Above: In front of the Church of the Nativity in Bethlehem. Right: Here, the Virgin Mary is said to have given birth to Jesus Christ.

The **Grotto of the Nativity** was already being venerated by the faithful in the 1st century A.D., and over the centuries numerous churches were built above it.

The most sacred spot in the **Church of the Nativity** on Manger Square is the Grotto of the Nativity, twelve meters long and four meters wide, reached by steps leading down from either side of the choir. The place where Jesus came into the world, beneath the Altar of the Nativity, is marked with a silver star with the inscription *Hic de virgine Maria Jesus Christus natus est* (Here Jesus Christ was born of the Virgin Mary). Adjoining is the small Grotto of the Manger, where, according to Christian belief, the shepherds came to worship the child; and indeed, opposite the altar of the Three Wise Men is a manger or feeding trough hewn out of the rock. There are more caves beneath the floor of the Church of the Nativity, such as the Great Cave with the Chapel of St. Joseph and the Chapel of the Holy Innocents, which commemorates the Herodian murders.

In the **Museum of Old Bethlehem**, you can see old furniture and costumes, as well as arts and crafts from the 19th century.

The townspeople of Bethlehem live from agriculture, animal husbandry and tourism, this last reflected unmistakably in the innumerable souvenir shops. Typical Oriental flair is present in the Arab market and in the narrow alleyways of the bazaar.

Eleven kilometers southeast of Bethlehem, in the midst of the yellow-gold desert of Judea, rises Mount Herodian, 758 meters high. Herod had the peak of the mountain removed and the resulting flat top surrounded with a wall. Here, he built a fortified palace, the **Herodian**, complete with gardens and baths. A winding footpath or else a labyrinth of subterranean tunnels gets you to the top. Once there, you can see the remains of the palace complex, with towers and defensive walls, a refectory and thermal baths; there is also a breathtaking view out over the surrounding desert.

95

Serious disturbances between Arabs and Jews flare up again and again in the city of **Hebron**, 37 km south of Jerusalem, as the **Grave of Abraham** (Haram el-Khalil) is located here. This is an important holy site for both religions, as both regard Abraham as their patriarch. In the rock-tomb of Machpela, Abraham, his wife Sarah, their son Isaac and daughter-in-law Rebecca, together with Abraham's grandson Jacob and Jacob's wife Lea, found their final resting place. In the 6th century A.D., Caesar Justinian built a church over the grotto; it was changed into a mosque about a century later. After the Six-Day war, Jews were again able to visit this massive edifice, which is crowned by two minarets; and in 1968 the Jewish settlement of Qiryat Arba came into being northeast of Hebron. The town of Hebron radiates a definite Arabic charm with its Islamic university and colorful bazaar streets.

Above: Impressive stalactite formations in the Sorek Cave by Nes Harim.

WEST OF JERUSALEM

Leaving Jerusalem along Herzl Boulevard towards the suburb of En Kerem (location of the Hadassah Hospital), turn left at the Kerem Junction onto Route 386, then right onto the smaller street 3866. Just after the village of Nes Harim is a sign to the Nahal Sorek Reserve and the **Sorek Cave**.

In 1967, an explosion at a nearby stone quarry caused the entrance to the Sorek cave to be exposed. A steep path leads up from the parking lot to the cave entrance and a safe pathway leads amateur explorers around the huge grotto and back to the entrance. Since the humidity is extraordinarily high, you start a visit by watching a video about the history of the cave, giving you a chance to acclimatize. Those with heart or circulatory problems should avoid visiting here.

A few kilometers further on Route 3866, a sign directs you south to the village of Beth Shemesh, where you join Route 38 to head south. Then take Route

83 to the west 10 kilometers after Bet Shemesh; 500 meters further on in the original direction, you come to the **Elah Valley** and a bridge spanning a *wadi* (a dry river bed). If you stop and look east here you will see the hill of Judea in the distance, and a path winding halfway up the steep rocks. This is the path Saul took with his army; he pitched camp to the left, above where you are now standing. The Philistine enemy had their camp to your right on the hill. The wadi separated the opponents.

It was here that the Philistine giant Goliath challenged one of the Israelites to single combat. The young David gave battle by seeking out five smooth pebbles from the brook, approaching Goliath and whirling his sling. The pebble struck the giant on his forehead and he fell. David drew Goliath's sword and cut off his head. When the Philistines saw that their strong man was dead, they fled and were pursued by the Israelite army, which then achieved a great victory.

Route 38 continues on southwards. About 1.5 kilometers past Elah Junction, on a terrace on the right-hand side of the road, are some **Roman milestones** under the shade of cypresses; found nearby, they date back to approximately 210 A.D. On the second milestone from the left is a Latin inscription; the last line reads: "Col[onia] Ael[ia] Cap[itolina] Mil[le]," followed by the numeral 24. This stone once stood on the road from Ashkelon to Jerusalem, which was called by this long Latin name under Roman rule. From this stone, it was 24 Roman miles to the capital. The Roman mile is equivalent to 1,000 double paces, which was about 8 stadia (1 mile/1.5 km).

A few kilometers further south, Route 38 meets Route 35, where you should turn off right. This is the location of the Beth Guvrin kibbutz. Very soon, a sign points left to the ancient **Beth Guvrin** and to **Tel Maresha**. The area of Beth Guvrin is honeycombed with some 800 bell-shaped caves. Archaeological investigations have shown that the area was used as a quarry, to which the caves owe their origin. The quarrymen who worked here between the 7th and 10th centuries made a small hole in the hard rock and then hollowed out the softer limestone beneath, thus creating a bell shape of the caves. The caves are generally between 12 and 15 meters in height, but some of the domes rise to a height of 25 meters.

A short distance further on is **Tel Maresha**, an ancient city which was inhabited by the Canaanites as early as the second millenium B.C. and existed right down into Hellenistic times. There is a series of interesting subterranean vaults, such as the Columbarium or "dovecote," which has more than 2,000 small niches. It was once thought that doves were bred here, but it is actually a large burial complex, and the niches were once occupied by urns. In another cave there is an olive press, and steps lead down to a water cistern and further tombs.

Ramla

Around 40 kilometers west of Jerusalem is the small, typically Arab town of Ramla. The most important architectural attraction is the **White Tower**, also called the Tower of the Forty Martyrs, which was completed in 1318 as a minaret. In front of the square tower (nearly 30 meters high) the 40 companions of the Prophet are buried, according to Muslim belief. The Christians say that 40 martyrs lie here. Beneath this lofty structure is the **White Mosque**. About 1 kilometer to the east in the bazaar quarter is the **Great Mosque** which was set up in the old crusaders' cathedral of St. John (12th century) after the expulsion of the Franks. Do not neglect to visit the gigantic system of subterranean **cisterns** laid out in the 9th century, which has supplied the townspeople with precious water ever since, even in the driest summers.

JERUSALEM

Getting There

Israel's international airport, **Ben Gurion Airport**, is 45 kilometers from Jerusalem. The most convenient way into town is to take a *Sherut*. These are shared taxis which can be found right in front of the airport building exit; they are available around the clock, depart as soon as they are full, cost about $10, and bring you right to your door. Bus numbers 423, 428, 945 and 947 (*Egged* line) run every 30 minutes between the airport and the central bus station on Jaffa Road. Between Friday evening and Saturday evening, as well as on religious holidays, there is no bus service; at these times, you have to rely on taxis and share-taxis (*Sherut*).

If you rent a car at the airport, you can reach Israel's capital in around 45 minutes on Route 1, which runs into Jaffa Road and leads into the city center.

Accommodation

LUXURY: **King David**, 23 King David St., tel. 02-6208888, one of Israel's best hotels, with a great historic tradition, as important politicians and other notables have been staying here since 1931; and with a lovely garden and view of the Old City; **Hyatt Regency**, 32 Lehi Street, tel. 02-5331234, located on Mount Scopus on one of the loveliest squares of Jerusalem, with fabulous views and an elegant interior. Less expensive than these two are the following: **American Colony**, Nablus Rd., tel. 02-6279777, going strong in a former pasha's palace for more than 100 years, with an oriental twist, traditionally the hotel of international journalists, UN officials, and politicians, with a good restaurant; **Lev Yerushalayim**, 18 King George St., tel. 02-5300333, good value for money in the heart of Jerusalem; **Mitzpeh Rachel**, Kibbuz Ramat Rachel, Zefon Jehuda, tel. 02-6702555, not far from the city center in the south of Jerusalem, marvelous hotel in a kibbutz, with good views out over the region (Mitzpeh means "observation point"), highly recommended; **Seven Arches**, Mount of Olives, tel. 02-6277555, formerly the Intercontinental and still called this by taxi drivers, on the peak of the Mount of Olives with a wonderful view.

MODERATE: **Eyal**, 21 Shamai Street, tel. 02-6234161, good value for money; **Zion**, 10 Dorot Rishonim, tel. 02-6259511, in the pedestrian zone of Ben Yehuda Street in the center of Jerusalem, not far from the Old City, surrounded by sidewalk cafés; **Hanagid**, 7 Schatz Street, tel. 02-6221111, new hotel in the center of Jerusalem, a short walk from the Old City; **Palatin**, 4 Agrippas Street, tel. 02-6231141, near the intersection of King George Street/Jaffa Rd., in the center of Jerusalem, a short walk from the Old City.

GUEST HOUSES AND HOSTELS: **Jerusalem Inn**; the hostel is located at 6 Histadrut Street, tel. 02-6251294, the guest house at 7 Horkonos St., tel. 02-6252757; **Lark Hotel**, 8 Latin Patriarchate, tel. 02-6283620, no-frills hotel; **Louise Waterman-Wise**, 8 Hapisga St., tel. 02-6423366, Jerusalem's largest youth hostel with guest house offering private rooms. Accommodation is cheapest in the many hostels and guest houses in the Old City: Accommodation near the Jaffa Gate: **Lutheran Youth Hostel**, 7 St. Mark's Rd., tel. 02-6282120; next to this is the **Lutheran Guest House**, with reasonably-priced private rooms, great views from the roof terrace; **New Imperial Hotel**, David Street, tel. 02-6282261, just behind the Jaffa Gate, former Grand Hotel where Kaiser Wilhelm stayed when he visited Palestine one hundred years ago; **New Swedish Hostel**, David Street, at the Jaffa Gate; **Citadel Youth Hostel**, 20 St. Mark's Rd., tel. 02-6247375, with a lovely, quiet atrium, great views of the Old City from the roof.

IN THE AREA: *CAMPING:* **Beit Zayit Camping**, Beit Zayit, tel. 02-5346217, 6 km west of Jerusalem, take bus 151 from the central bus station to the last stop, Beit Zayit.

BETHLEHEM: *MODERATE:* **Bethlehem Star**, Al Baten Street, Bethlehem, tel. 02-2743249.

Restaurants

Darna, 3 Horkanos Street, tel. 02-6245406, Moroccan cuisine, decor is also authentic; expensive. **Pasha**, 13 Simon Hatzadik Street, near the American Colony Hotel, tel. 02-5825162, typical Arabic cuisine, terrace, reasonable; free shuttle service from all hotels. **Armenian Tavern**, 79 Armenian Orthodox Patriarchate Road, Old City near the Jaffa Gate, tel. 02-6273854, typical cuisine in an old vaulted room, reasonable. **Strudel**, 11 Monbaz Street, Russian Compound, tel. 02-6232101, internet café-bar, cheap. **Eukalyptus**, 4 Safra Sq. (City Hall complex), tel. 02-6249331, authentic Israeli-oriental cooking, unusual, reasonable. Cheapest of all are the numerous *falafel* stands; tasty and filling, the small chickpea-burgers with lettuce and sauce in pita bread cost only a few pennies. Notable is **Felafel King**, King George St./corner of Agrippas St. There are several cheap and typical fast food places on Agrippas Street (behind the Mahane Yehuda market); they also stay open late. **Mamma Mia**, 38 King George Street, hidden behind a parking lot, good Italian food, reasonable. **Yemenite Step**, 12 Salomon Street, good, unusual (to a traveler) Oriental food, cheap.

Bars and Pubs

The bar in the **King David Hotel** (see above) is reputedly the best one in Jerusalem; equally well-known is **Fink's Bar** (with adjacent restaurant), frequented by journalists; King George Street/corner Histadrut Street. **Egon**, Ma'aleh Nahalet Shiva 9, pub with a courtyard and a large TV screen which shows music videos.

The Tavern, Rivlin Street, a few steps further on, sometimes offers live music.

Sights and Museums

Al Aqsa Mosque, Dome of the Rock and **Islamic Museum**, Old City, Temple Mount, Sat-Thu 8:00-11:30 am, 12:30-2 pm (opening times often change); **Burnt House**, Sun-Thu 9 am-5 pm, Fri 9 am-1 pm; **Chamber of the Holocaust**, Mount Zion, Sun-Thu 8 am-5 pm, Fri 8 am-1 pm; **Franciscan Monastery of the Flagellation**, Lions Gate Road, Mon-Sat 8-11:30 am, 1-6 pm; **Garden of Gethsemane**, at foot of Mount of Olives, daily 8 am-noon, 2-5 pm; **Gethsemane Grotto**, at foot of Mount of Olives, Mon-Wed, Fri/Sat 8:30-11:45 am, 2:30-4:30 pm, Sun/Thu 8:30-11:45 am, 2:30-3:30 pm; **Church of the Holy Sepulcher**, Old City, daily 5 am-7 pm; **Hadassah Hospital**, Qiryat Hadassah, Bus 19; hourly guided tours in synagogue, with film about hospital, Sun-Thu 8 am-1:15 pm and 2-3 pm, Fri 8-11:30 am; **Holyland Hotel** with model of ancient Jerusalem, Rav Uziel Street, Bus 21, 21A; Mon-Thu 8 am-9 pm, Fri, Sat 9 am-5 pm; **Israel Museum**, New Shaanan, Bus 9, 17, 24; Mon, Wed, Thu 10 am-5 pm, Tue 4-10 pm, Fri and Sat 10 am-2 pm; **David's Tomb**, Mount Zion, Sun-Thu 8 am-5 pm, Fri 8 am-2 pm; **Dominus Flevit Church** ("The Lord wept"), on the Mount of Olives, Sun-Thu 8 am-noon, 3-5 pm; **Church of Gethsemane** (also called Basilica of the Agony and Church of the Nations), in the garden of Gethsemane, open daily 8 am-noon, 2:30-5 pm; **Notre Dame of Zion**, Old City, Lions Gate Road, Mon-Sat 8:30 am-12:30 and 2-5 pm; **Knesset**, Derekh Ruppin Bus 9, 99; Mon/Thu 8:30 am-2 pm; **Tombs of the Kings**, Saladin Street, Mon-Sat 8 am-12:30 and 2-5 pm; **Tomb of the Virgin**, at the foot of the Mount of Olives; 6:30 am-noon, 2-5 pm; **Church of Mary Magdalene**, at the foot of the Mount of Olives, Tue/Thu 10-11:30 am; **Pater Noster Monastery**, Mount of Olives, Mon-Sat 8:30 am-1:45 pm, Sun 3-4:30 pm; **Hall of the Last Supper**, Mount Zion, Sun-Thu 8:30 am-4:30 pm, Fri 8:30 am-1 pm; **Rockefeller Museum**, Suleyman St., Sun-Thu 10 am-5 pm, Fri and Sat 10 am-2 pm; **St. Anne's Convent** with the pool of Bethesda, Old City, Lions Gate Road, Mon-Sat 8 am-noon, 2-5 pm; **Tower of David Museum**, Old City, Jaffa Gate, Sun-Thu 9 am-5 pm, Fri and Sat 9 am-2 pm; **Wohl Archaeological Museum** (Herodian Quarter), Old City, Hurva Square, Sun-Thu 9 am-5 pm, Fri 9 am-1 pm); **Yad Vashem**, by Mount Herzl, Herzl Boulevard, Bus 6, 8, 27, 99; Mon-Sun 9 am-4:45 pm, Fri 9 am-2 pm; **Mount Herzl**, Herzl Boulevard, Sun-Thu 8 am-5 pm, Fri 9 am-1 pm; **Bible Lands Museum**, Givart Ram, Sun-Tue, Thu 9:30 am-5:30 pm, Wed 9:30 am-9:30 pm, Fri 9:30 am-2 pm and Sat 11 am-3 pm.

IN THE SURROUNDING AREA: Bet Guvrim and **Tel Maresha**, Sat-Thu 8 am-4 pm, Fri 8 am-3 pm; **Church**

of the Nativity in Bethlehem, daily 6 am-6 pm; **Saint George's Monastery**, in Wadi Kelt, daily 8 am-12 pm; **Caves of Qumran**, Sat-Thu 8 am-4 pm, Fri 8 am-3 pm; **Tel as Sultan Excavation Site** , Jericho, Sat-Thu 8 am-5 pm, Fri 8 am-3 pm; **Sorek Cave**, Sat-Thu 8:30 am-4 pm, Fri 8:30 am-1 pm.

Markets

Mahaneh Yehuda, the largest market on Jaffa Road, offers fruit and vegetables, meat and fish; ideal for self-caterers. You can find all manner of foodstuffs every day in the bazaar streets in the Arabian quarter of the Old City.

Hospitals, Pharmacies, Emergencies

Bikur Holim, Strauss Street, special first-aid service for tourists; **Hadassah**, Ein Kerem and Mount Scopus; dental emergency service: **The Jerusalem Emergency Dental Centre**, 7 Eliash Street, Rejwan Square; **Superpharm** (pharmacy/chemist), 5 Burla Street and 3 Histadrut Street; **Ambulance**: 101.

Public Transportation

BUS: The Central Bus Station is on Jaffa Road. Buses depart from here for destinations throughout the country. For short distances within the city, bus 99 (*The Jerusalem Circle Line*) passes all of the major sights and stops at more than 30 stations: the route runs around the Old City with stops at Jaffa Gate, Mount Zion, Dung Gate (the Wailing Wall), Damascus Gate, Israel Museum and Knesset, Mount Herzl and Yad Vashem, the Holyland Hotel (Model of the Temple) as well as various hotel districts, and takes nearly two hours. Bus 99 departs from the bus station on Mamilla Road (on King David Street) at 10 am, noon, 2 & 4 pm, Fri at 10 am & noon.

SHERUT: *Sherut* taxis can be found at the following locations: **Habira**, 1 Harav Kook Street, near Zion Square, Sherut to Tel Aviv. **Ha'ooma**, at the Ram Hotel behind the central bus station, to Tel Aviv. **Aviv/Kesher**, at 12 Shammai Street, to Haifa. **Yael Daroma**, 12 Shammai Street, to Be'er Sheva and Elat.

TAXI: You can hail taxis on the street, or find them in front of large hotels. There are taxi stands at the Israel Museum and at Yad Vashem. You should bear in mind that the driver is legally obliged to turn on the meter; do not let yourself get involved in discussions about the price unless you are a true expert at the art of bargaining.

Tourist Information

Tourist Information Office, Safra Sq. (City Hall complex), tel. 02-6258844.

Christian Information Centre, David Street, at Jaffa Gate, behind the citadel, tel. 02-6280382.

Franciscan Pilgrims' Office, in the same building as the Christian Information Centre, tel. 02-6272697.

Jewish Student Information Centre, 5 Beit El, in the Jewish Quarter of the Old City, tel. 02-6288338.

TEL AVIV – COSMOPOLITAN CENTER

TEL AVIV

YAFO

ASHQELON

TEL AVIV – YAFO (JAFFA)

If you make sure, at check-in, that you are given a seat on the left-hand side of the plane, the final approach as you come in to land at Ben Gurion Airport can be truly stunning. You will look down over the blue sea flecked with whitecaps, kilometers of white sand beaches, and the modern thicket of skyscrapers that characterize the skyline of Tel Aviv. Israel's largest city, founded around 100 years ago, is a modern, rather westernized metropolis which, as a result of many successive waves of immigration, has expanded rather haphazardly along the coast and quite a way back into the interior. In 1910, the numerous individual districts were given the collective name of Tel Aviv, "Hill of Spring." On the eve of independence in 1948, a quarter of a million people were already living in the city, and this number has swelled to around 1.8 million today. Tel Aviv has developed into Israel's economic, as well as its cultural, center.

Yafo or Jaffa, the Arab part of Tel Aviv, can look back on three thousand years of history. It may well be the oldest

Preceding pages: Tel Aviv's beach and skyline. Left: Night owls prowl the coastal road of Tel Aviv.

working port in the world and, if the Roman historian Pliny the Elder (23-79 A.D.) is to be believed, was founded 40 years after the end of the Flood. Its name is supposed to go back to Japhet, the third son of Noah. Archaeological excavations have exposed the remnants of city fortifications from the time of the Hyksos, that is to say, around 1600 B.C. during the Middle Bronze Age. Six hundred years later the city, now known as Yapu, was an important Phoenician port; cedar from Lebanon was shipped here to be used in the new temple of Solomon. It was from here, too, that the prophet Jonah set sail, disobeying God's express command that he go to Nineveh and speak out against its wickedness; as punishment, Jonah was swallowed by a whale, which vomited him out on dry land three days later.

In 332 B.C. Alexander the Great captured the city for the Greeks and its name was changed to Joppe. About a century later, 200 Jews perished when the Greeks forced them to put to sea in boats and then sank them. This crime was avenged by Judas Maccabaeus when he stormed the harbor with his troops and destroyed every Greek ship he found. Under the Romans, Jews were permitted to move back into Yafo, whose official name had become Flavia Joppe. Then in 636 when

Muslim armies captured Joppe, they renamed it Jaffa. 1099 saw the arrival of the first ships bearing Crusaders from Europe; after this, the city's rulership changed many times between the Christians and the Muslims. The Crusaders were finally driven out of the city for good in 1268, and over the following centuries Yafo turned into a small, sleepy fishing port. Not until the beginning of the 19th century did Yafo resume its role as a commercial port, exporting such goods as cotton and citrus fruits to Europe on a large scale. Today's Tel Aviv was established in 1887; in 1950, the two towns were administratively joined under the name of Tel Aviv – Yafo.

TEL AVIV

A good place to begin a tour of Tel Aviv is on the promenade in the north of

Above: A street artist at work. Right: Dining on the beach promenade of Tel Aviv.

the city, at the marina, where many international hotels and a plethora of more modest establishments are located. Branching off from the heavily-traveled north-south artery of the Tayelet Promenade is **Ben Gurion Boulevard**; number 17 was the residence of Israel's first prime minister, David Ben Gurion (1886-1973), and his wife, Paula. The small house has been left exactly as it was when the Gurions lived there. Twenty thousand books are scattered throughout all the rooms in the house, while Ben Gurion's identification papers and a number of letters to various international politicians are on display in glass cases.

If you stroll south along the promenade, you will come, after a considerable walk, to Allenby Road, branching off to the left. This street is named for the British field marshal Edmund Henry Allenby (1861-1936), the supreme commander in Palestine during World War I, who, in 1917, captured Jerusalem from the Turks, and soon after the rest of Palestine. After a curve to the right, you will see **Bialik**

Street leading off to the left, a quiet residential street in the center of noisy Tel Aviv: here, there are a number of buildings from the days of the city's foundation. At the end of the street you can see a fountain designed by the painter and children's book writer Nahum Gutmann. Mosaics depict the history of Yafo from Antiquity up to the founding of Tel Aviv.

Number 22 was once home to the Israeli national poet, the "father of Hebrew poetry," Chaim Nachmann Bialik (1873-1934). This Russian poet was not able to emigrate to Palestine until 1924; three years later this white, two-story house with its decorative arches was complete, and soon became a meeting point for the Jewish intelligentsia. Today, European-Oriental furniture, thousands of books, paintings and other memorabilia are on display.

A few doors down is number 14, Bet Rubin or Rubin's house, where Israel's great painter Reuven Rubin (1893-1974) worked. In his will he left the house, together with its complete furnishings and 45 paintings, to the city of Tel Aviv; the city has now put it to use as a small gallery hosting a range of changing exhibitions. The pictures of young artists often contrast sharply to Rubin's works, which adds an interesting angle to many of the exhibitions.

Walk back to Allenby Street and turn left, or south. A few meters on you will come to Kikar Magen David, Star of David Square, with the *shuk*, or market, called **Carmel Market**. Every day of the week from 9 a.m. on, this square is filled with a pushing, shoving crowd of people shopping for fruit, vegetables, groceries and household goods. On Tuesdays and Fridays, the vendors are joined on the Nahalat Binyamin by craftsmen and artisans who have brought their wares to the market. Since this small street is lined with cafés, you can peacefully observe the surging chaos from over a cup of tea or coffee.

From Magen David Square, an underpass leads you safely beneath busy Allenby Road – with Dizengoff Street, one of the principle shopping streets in Tel Aviv; on the other side, you can continue on into King George Street.

At the corner of King George Street and Bet Leichem Street there is a clothing market; a few blocks further on there is a cul-de-sac on the right-hand side called Simtat Plonit. You cannot miss this little street, as its entrance is flanked by a pair of obelisks. This is another place where you can study the buildings of the city's earliest years, even if these historical buildings are not exactly in the best state of preservation and are furthermore surrounded by impersonal high-rises. The entrance to one house is guarded by a mighty stucco lion.

Further down King George Street, on the left, extends Meir Park or **Gan Meir**, which can make a very parched impression in summer. Occasionally, street musicians gather here in the evenings and present their repertoires to the best of their abilities. Opposite the park entrance is the second-hand bookshop Pollak's, where bibliophiles can pass the time happily browsing the store's extensive range of titles.

At the next corner, turn right into Ben Zion Boulevard; the writer Simcha Ben Zion was the father of the painter and poet Nahum Gutmann (who designed the fountain in Bialik Street). This wide street, lined with shady trees, leads to Kikar Habimah, **Habimah Square**, where there are three buildings worth examining.

One of these is the **Habimah Theater**, the national theater of Israel, whose origins go back to the Russian Revolution. In those days of social upheaval a group of Russian Jewish actors founded a theater in Moscow which presented exclusively plays in the Hebrew language. The group was so successful that as early as the 1920s they were touring Europe and the U.S.A. Many of the actors came to Palestine in the emigration waves of the late 20s and early 30s and set up the national theater here. The building's cornerstone was laid in 1935, while its extensive glass façade dates from the 1970s.

For those interested in art, the **Helena Rubinstein Pavilion**, next to the Habimah Theater, is noteworthy; this branch of the Tel Aviv Museum exhibits contemporary art. Between the museum and the theater is a small, shady, and inviting garden, called Gan Ya'akov. At its center stands a large mulberry tree, and the story goes that even before Tel Aviv was founded the Bedouins enjoyed the shade of this tree as their camels drank from the spring nearby.

The **Frederick Mann Auditorium**, also located on Habimah Square, is Tel Aviv's concert hall and home of the outstanding Israel Philharmonic Orchestra (IPO); seating 3,000 people, the building is famous for its excellent acoustics. Since Israel does not have any hang-ups about keeping serious or "classical" music rigidly separate from popular music, the auditorium is also a venue for rock concerts.

From Habimah Square, Rothschild Boulevard runs south. As its name perhaps already indicates, this is the richest part of the city. Tall, shade-giving trees line a street sporting offices and residential buildings with the occasional restaurant, such as the Rothschild, which offers good French cuisine, or the Yin Yang, one of the best Chinese restaurants in the country.

Another ten minute walk will bring you to the **Haganah Museum**, on the right. *Haganah* means "self-defense." After World War I, Jews who had fought in the British army founded this paramilitary organization in order to protect the Jewish settlements in Palestine. After the declaration of independence, the Haganah emerged with the Israeli army. This small museum presents the history of this self-defense force.

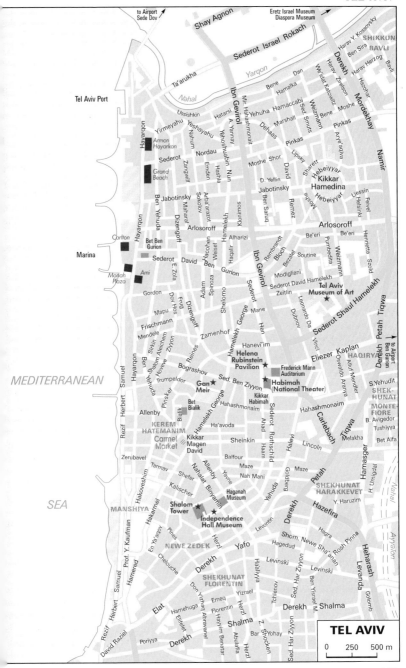

TEL AVIV

0   250   500 m

On no account should you neglect to visit the **Independence Hall Museum**, diagonally across the street. This large residential building was for years the residence of the best-known mayor of Tel Aviv, Meir Dizengoff; in 1930, he bequeathed the building to his city, and the first Tel Aviv Museum was set up here. In the great hall visitors with an interest in history can inspect the original furniture, including the bulky microphone with which, on May 14, 1948, the political leader of the Jewish population, Ben Gurion, proclaimed the state of Israel and thereby declared the nation's independence: On that momentous day, the message was broadcast over the radio to the whole world. Only a few hours later, tanks from five Arab armies began rolling towards the infant country of Israel. Many other exhibits in the building also document the first heady days of independence.

Above: Modern architecture: the new opera house in the Performing Arts Center.

On the central median of Rothschild Boulevard, the birth of the state of Israel is commemorated by a founders' memorial and a fountain. You cannot overlook the nearby **Shalom Tower**, Israel's first skyscraper. From its roof, you have a wonderful view of the city.

There are three museums not included on our walking tour which also merit a visit. First, there's the **Eretz Y'Israel Museum** (2 Lavanon Street, University, bus nos. 24, 25, 45) which has a number of pavilions with exhibits devoted to daily life in Israel. At the center of the museum grounds is the excavation site of Tel Qasile, where archaeologists have uncovered 12 layers of settlement.

The second museum is the **Museum of the Diaspora** or Beit Hatfusot (University Campus, Gate 2, Klausner Street, bus nos. 24, 25, 45) whose historical brief begins with the destruction of the second Temple and goes on to provide information on 2,500 years of Jewish life in the diaspora, giving some idea of what it means for people to be scattered over the entire world.

The last museum of the three is the **Tel Aviv Museum of Art** (27 Shaul Hamelech Boulevard, bus no. 24), which houses a large exhibition of both Israeli and international art: for example, there is a large wall painting by Roy Lichtenstein, as well as a collection of French Impressionists.

Tel Aviv's newest temple of culture is the **Performing Arts Center** at 28 Leonardo da Vinci Street. Home to the New Opera, it also accommodates modern dance and musicals.

YAFO (JAFFA)

With its narrow streets and renovated old town, Yafo, the ancient Arab harbor city, has a lot of atmosphere to offer. It is much more interesting than Tel Aviv, which is rather lacking in charm due to having been built so recently. You can

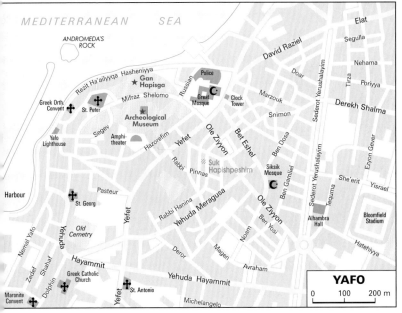

walk to Yafo from Tel Aviv along the beach promenade or take a bus (bus nos. 3, 10, 25).

As you come into town, you can see the police station of old Yafo on your right; the building was used by the Turks when they had the Palestinians under their thumb. During the British mandate which followed the defeat of the Turks, English troops were stationed in this police station, and the cells were used to incarcerate both Arabs and members of the Zionist underground organization, Irgun. Nowadays, the Israeli police establishes order from the historically laden building.

In the center of a small square – whose official name, Jewish Agency Square, hardly anyone will have heard of – stands a clock tower, erected in the year 1906, to commemorate the 30th anniversary of the reign of Turkish sultan Abdul Hamid II.

Next to the clock tower is the **Grand Mosque** or Mahmudiye Mosque, which dates back to 1810. In order to decorate the rooms inside, ancient columns were brought in from Caesarea and Ashqelon, but somehow they ended up being installed the wrong way around – with the capitals at the bottom.

From this small square, follow Bet Eshel Street; at number 11, you will see the arched entrances of a former *wakala* or **caravanserai**. As was typical of such inns, the lower floor provided stalls for the camels and storage rooms for goods, while the upper floor had accommodation for the guests.

A little further along Bet Eshel Street, roads branch off left to the Shuk Hapishpeshim, a large **flea market** which offers everything from silver jewelry, clothes and leather goods to fans, second-hand televisions and just about anything else you could want. The main street of the bazaar, the Olei Zion, runs parallel to Bet Eshel. The market is the last holdover of a large Turkish *suq* held daily in the 19th century in the area around today's clock tower. Anyone who is planning to make a purchase here needs plenty of time and patience, as bargaining or haggling is the

109

order of the day, in the time-honored oriental fashion.

Back at the clock tower, go along Yefet Street to the excellent **Abulafiyya bakery**, which offers sugared cakes, tasty rolls, filled flat bread and a variety of other baked goods.

Walk up the gently sloping Mifratz Schlomo Street to reach an overlook with an excellent view over the expanses of sandy beaches, the blue sea and the sky-scraper skyline of Tel Aviv. On your left is the **Jaffa Museum**, devoted to the old harbor city and containing many archaeological finds excavated in the region. Parts of the building date back to the era of the Crusades. Around 200 years ago, Ottoman Turks renovated and expanded it, and used it as a government building until 1897; it went on to serve as a soap factory until finally being set up as a museum in the 1960s.

Above and right: Tel Aviv's European flair and the old Arab harbor of Yafo contrast vividly.

To the left of the museum is an Otto man fountain from the early 19th cen tury. The arched passage nearby once le to a *hamam*, or Turkish bath; today, yo face a nightclub, beneath whose founda tions archaeologists discovered remain of walls 3,500 years old, relics of earlies Jaffa.

The Mifratz Schlomo continues it slow ascent, presenting you the whol time with wonderful views over Te Aviv; soon you arrive at **Kikar Ke dumim**, Kedumim Square, center of th excellently renovated harbor area of ol Yafo and a frequent venue for music per formances. Steps lead down to some ex cavations directly beneath Kikar Ke dumim: the foundations exposed ther tell the story of earlier settlements. Thi part of Yafo was once the red-light dis trict for Tel Aviv.

The pink church on the square belong to the **Monastery of St. Peter**, which th Franciscans built on the foundations of Crusaders' citadel in the 17th century; was extensively renovated in 1894. T gain entrance, tug on the bell rope next to the door, and the doorkeeper will open the door for you.

From a small terrace café on Kikar Kedumim, your gaze will sweep out over the port and the sea. The rolling waves break on **Andromeda Rock**, projecting from the sea foam, which takes its name from a myth of classical Antiquity. Cassiopoeia, the vain wife of king Cepheus, had boasted of her beauty to the Nereids, or daughters of Poseidon, maintaining that she was lovelier than anyone else. This kind of vanity infuriated the sea nymphs, who joined forces with their father, the sea god Poseidon, and sent a flood and an all-devouring shark into Cepheus' realm. The only way to put a stop to this plague was to sacrifice Andromeda, the beautiful daughter of Cepheus and Cassiopoeia, to a sea monster. Accordingly, the young, blonde woman was tied to Andromeda rock and left helplessly awaiting her death. Just then, however, the hero Perseus arrived, borne by his winged sandals, and was immediately enchanted by the beauty of the princess. "Speak, beautiful maiden," he cried, "why are you bound here in chains? You deserve a very different kind of adornment." Hardly had Andromeda recounted her story when the huge sea monster burst out of the water with gaping jaws. Perseus sprang into the air and darted like an eagle at the monster, stabbing it repeatedly with his sword until it was dead. He then married the beautiful Andromeda.

From Kikar Kedumim, walk up a small hill and then over a wooden bridge to the Gan Hapisga, or Peak Gardens. Archaeologists have exposed a total of 7 layers of settlement here, including fortifications from the Hyksos period (1600 B.C.), the remains of a city gate from the 13th century B.C. which bears an inscription concerning Ramses II, more Canaanite masonry, the remnants of Jewish settlements and relics from the Hasmonean

period (2nd century B.C.), and finally Roman foundations. From here, too, there is a wonderful view of the skyline of Tel Aviv.

Back at Kedumim Square, you can reach the harbor in no time at all along the narrow stepped streets. Fishing boats bob alongside the quays, fishermen take midday siestas on piles of fishing nets, and instead of Hebrew, everywhere here you hear only Arabic. The harbor basin is surrounded by restaurants; they are all good and serve freshly-caught fish. On summer days, gourmands sit under umbrellas directly at the water's edge, an arm's length from the fishing boats, and watch the finned cargoes being unloaded from the small boats; other men are busy repairing nets, while buyers from the restaurants stand close by, haggling over the wholesale prices. All of this local color gives the seafood you eat here a very special flavor.

Through a large gateway, you leave the harbor area; follow the steps leading up to the left to Louis Pasteur Street.

111

Here, a bronze sculpture of a fat and friendly-looking whale recalls the story of the prophet Jonah, who spent three days in the beast's belly before it spat him out. This particular whale is a creation of the sculptress and goldsmith Ilana Goor.

From here you should plunge into the labyrinth of small alleys of **Old Yafo**: in the renovated houses here art galleries have opened, craftsmen exhibit their products, and goldsmiths and jewelers offer individually designed pieces.

Back at the bronze whale, continue on down Louis Pasteur Street as far as its junction with Yafet Street. The corner here was once the location of the **St. Louis French Hospital**, named after Louis IX, who sailed into the harbor of Yafo in 1251 as leader of the seventh Crusade. Roman Catholic nuns set up Yafo's first modern hospital in this neo-Gothic building in the late 19th century; today it houses a health center.

On the other side of the street are three houses of some significance. In number 21, the Presbyterian Church of Scotland opened the **Tabitha School** in 1863. In the small graveyard behind the house lies Dr. Thomas Hodgkin (1798-1866) who, while he was working at Guy's Hospital in London, was the first to describe Hodgkin's disease (a malignant, painful and progressive enlargement of the lymph glands). On a visit to the Holy Land he fell ill and died. Number 23 was once a Catholic school for the French, and still bears the inscription **Collège des Frères**; today, the building houses administrative offices of the French embassy. The "Tudor fortress" of number 25 was once the home of the **Urim School**, which started its life in 1882 as a grammar school and was run by the very same nuns who looked after the hospital. Next to number 51 is the Roman Catholic

Right: Soldiers help to bring in the autumn harvest.

Church of San Antonio, which was dedicated to St. Anthony of Padua in 1932.

If you go back down Yafet Street, you will soon find yourself back at the clock tower where you started out. Early in the evening, Arab food stalls and cook-shacks open up in the narrow side streets here.

ASHQELON

Early Egyptian texts mention the city of Ashqelon (50 km south of Tel Aviv) as early as 2000 B.C. From the Amarna letters, dating from the time of the pharaoh Akhnaten (1400 B.C.), we know of the existence of written correspondence between the pharaoh and the local ruler. The Pharaohs bloodily repressed, however, any and every attempt to throw off the yoke of Egyptian rule. In the temple of Karnak in Luxor, in Egypt, there is a relief which depicts one of the many successful Egyptian stormings of Ashqelon.

At the beginning of the 12th century B.C., the Philistines established a firm foothold in the city, and used it as a base from which to plague the tribes of the Israelites.

Due to the diplomatic skills of the local rulers, Ashqelon survived with virtually no ill effects the attacks of the Assyrians and Scythians in the 6th and 5th centuries B.C., and even the occupation of Alexander the Great did the city no damage. During the Seleucid period, the city became one of the leading centers of learning in Palestine due to the influx of Greek scholars.

In the 2nd century B.C., in order to avoid being occupied by the Maccabaeans, the townspeople called on the Romans for assistance. Herod the Great was born in Ashqelon, but the city never formed part of his kingdom. After Muslim armies conquered the city in the 7th century A.D., Ashqelon was expanded into a fortified trading center. During the

me of the Crusades, the Muslim ªatimids had one of their important bases ere, and for a long time the Franks were ªnable to conquer the city. They resorted ⊃ building a ring of blockading castles round the city as a way of stopping the ity's dominance of the pilgrims' route ³etween Jaffa and Jerusalem. Finally, fter a siege which lasted more than half ⋅ year, Baldwin III managed to capture ⋅shqelon.

A few years later, the Muslims were ³ack in the city, to be followed again by ¹e Christians shortly thereafter. With the nd of the last Crusade, Ashqelon lapsed ¹to oblivion. In 1951, South African im- ¹igrants founded the settlement of Afri- ³ar near the abandoned Arab village of Vligdal, whose erstwhile inhabitants now ¹ve in the refugee camps of the Gaza trip. Harking back to Biblical times, the ¹ew settlers gave both places the name ⋅shqelon.

Ashqelon was one of the members of ¹e Philistine pentopolis, or five-city al- ¹ance, and even in those early days was already a major port as well as a station on the Via Maris, a caravan route leading from Egypt to Syria. Ashqelon was con- sidered a bulwark against the Israelite tribes; when Saul was killed by the Phil- istines, David cried out in his grief that people should keep quiet about the disas- ter, otherwise the news would reach Ashqelon and be the cause of rejoicing in that city.

In the Barnea district, the remains of a 6th-century Byzantine church were un- covered during building work; nearby, there's a **floor mosaic** from the same era.

At the center of the Afridar district with its large commercial center, there's a small **open-air museum**. Its exhibits include two Roman sarcophagi which were found by chance in the 1970s dur- ing construction of a house.

The **Painted Tomb** in Hatayasim Street dates from the Roman period (3rd century), and its wonderful frescoes are enchanting. They depict naked nymphs at a brook, a gazelle hunt, the head of the Gorgon and Pan with his pipes.

Migdal, the old Arab settlement, has considerably more character and atmosphere than modern Ashqelon. This quarter is also the shopping district for the city: on Mondays and Wednesdays there is a large fruit and vegetable market, and a general market for clothes, silverware and leather goods on Thursdays.

The new **Ashqelon Museum** was once a caravanserai. Its exhibits document local history from Roman times until the present.

On the southern outskirts of Ashqelon, directly by the sea, the remains of the ancient city, enclosed by the walls of the old Crusaders' city, spread out on land that today forms a **national park**. Like cannons aimed out over the sea, Roman columns project from the fortified walls; in the sea, the remains of other columns, battered by the waves, mark the site of the old harbor. Trench excavations by archaeologists have demonstrated the existence of settlement here since the Bronze Age.

The center of the area is the *Bouleuterion*, or council-house; it is more than 100 meters long and once consisted of colonnaded halls around an inner courtyard. Whether the complex actually served as a seat of government is dubious. The buildings, which were commissioned by Herod, could in fact have served as an agora.

Reliefs decorating the backwalls of the colonnaded halls depict the Egyptian goddess Isis with her son Horus; the Greek goddess of victory, Nike, waving a palm frond; and Nike sitting on a globe supported by Atlas.

The national park is also an ideal place to relax, with a camp site, picnic area, restaurant and bathing beach.

The Ashqelon coast has many kilometers of sandy beaches. But the waves often throw lumps of tar up onto the beach, as a little further to the south, at the quays of the Zikim kibbutz, oil tankers unload their cargo.

TEL AVIV

Getting There

Israel's international airport, **Ben Gurion**, is about 15 km east of Tel Aviv. United Bus Nr. 222 runs regularly between the airport and the city, with stops at the train station, the youth hostel (Weizmann Street) and the beach promenade, where most of the hotels are concentrated.

There are buses to Tel Aviv from Jerusalem and from Israel's other major cities every 10 minutes. From Jerusalem and the cities along the northern coast trains also run to Tel Aviv every hour.

Accommodation

LUXURY: **Carlton**, 10 Eliezer Peri Street, tel. 03-5201818, best address in Tel Aviv. **Sheraton Moriah**, 155 Hayarkon Street, tel. 03-5216666, nearly all rooms with ocean view. **Grand Beach**, 250 Hayarkon Street, tel. 03-5433333.
MODERATE: **Ami**, 4 Am Yisrael Hai Street, tel. 03-5249141, near the beach. **Armon Hayarkon**, 268 Hayarkon Street, 03-6055271, good, family-run.
BUDGET: **Adiv**, 5 Mendele Street, tel. 03-5229141, near the beach. **Aviv**, 88 Hayarkon Street, tel. 03-5102785, not far from the beach. **Hotel Nes Tziona**, 10 Nez Tziona Street, tel. 03-5103404, reasonable hotel near the beach. **Miami Hotel**, 8 Allenby Street, tel. 03-5103868, near the beach.
HOSTELS: **Youth Hostel**, 36 Bnei Dan Street, tel. 03-5441748, in the north of the city. **Old Yafo Hostel**, Olei Tzion Street, tel. 03-6822370, in the middle of flea market at the center of Old Yafo, one of the best hostels in the city. **Nr. 1 Hostel**, 84 Ben Yehuda Street, 4th floor, tel. 03-5237807, near the beach. **Gordon Hostel**, 2 Gordon Street, tel. 03-5229870, large, near the beach.

Restaurants

Casba, 32 Yirminyahu Street, tel. 03-6042617, one of the city's best restaurants for more than 30 years. **Boccaccio**, Hayarkon Street/corner David Frishman, tel. 03-5246837, popular with the lunchtime crowd. **Chimney**, Hayarkon Street/corner Mendeli, tel. 03-5235114, low-priced little restaurant. **The Chicago Pizza Pie Factory**, 63 Hayarkon Street, tel. 03-5100560, American pizza. **Catch 21**, Hayarkon Street/corner Bograshov, tel. 03-5232170, affordable lunchtime specials. **Bistro Picasso**, Hayarkon/corner Mapu, tel. 03-5175486, affordable small restaurant. **Via Maris**, Kikar Kedumim, tel. 03-6828451, good restaurant in old Yafo. **Toutoune**, Kikar Kedumim, tel. 03-6820693, fresh seafood, stylish ambience. **Yin Yang**, 64 Rothschild Boulevard, tel. 03-5606833, best Chinese restaurant in the country. **Shaul's Inn**, 1 Eliashiv St., tel. 03-5173303, excellent oriental cuisine.

Cafés / Bars

The best places for people-watching are the cafés along **Dizengoff Street**, which is lined with expensive shops; **Dizengoff Square** is also a good spot. In the cafés on **Nahalat Binyamin Street** you can observe the artisans setting up their stands for the **Carmel Market** on Tuesdays and Fridays. **M.A.S.H.** (More Alcohol Served Here), 275 Dizengoff Street, popular bar. **The Whitehouse**, 108 Hayarkon Street, large Israeli clientele. **Gordon's Pub**, 17 Gordon Street, quiet pub. **The Happy Casserole**, 344 Dizengoff Street, live music several times a week, including Israeli folk music.

Sights and Museums

Ben Gurion House, Ben Gurion Boulevard 17, Sun-Thu 8 am-2 pm, also Mon/Thu 5-7 pm, Fri 8 am-1 pm, Sat 11 am-2 pm. **Diaspora Museum**, University Campus, Gate 2, Klausner Street, Sun-Tue and Thu 10 am-5 pm, Wed 10 am-7 pm. **Eretz Israel Museum**, 2 Lavanon Street, University, Sun, Wed, Thu 9 am-2 pm, Tue 9 am-5 pm, Sat 10 am-2 pm. **Hagana Museum**, Rothschild Boulevard, Sun-Thu 8:30 am-4 pm, Sat 8:30 am-12:30 pm. **Chaim Nachmann Bialik House**, Bialik Street 22, Sun-Thu 9 am-5 pm, Sat 10 am-2 pm. **Reuven Rubin House**, Bialik Street 14, Sun-Thu 9 am-5 pm, Sat 10 am-2 pm. **Helena Rubinstein Pavilion**, Tarsat Street, a branch of the Tel Aviv Museum, Sun-Thu 10 am-8 pm, Fri 10 am-2 pm, Sat 10 am-3 pm. **Independence Hall Museum**, Rothschild Boulevard, Sun-Thu 9 am-2 pm. **Jaffa Museum**, Yafo, Mifratz Shlomo Street, Sun-Thu 9 am-2 pm, Tue also 4-7 pm, Sat 10 am-2 pm. **Monastery of St. Peter**, Yafo, Kikar Kedumim, daily 8-11:45 am, 3-5 pm. **Tel Aviv Museum of Art**, 27 Shaul Hamelech Boulevard, Sun-Thu 10 am-9:30 pm, Fri 10 am-2 pm, Sat 10 am-2 pm, 7-10 pm.

Shopping and Markets

The main shopping streets are Allenby Street, Dizengoff Street (international shops and all kinds of boutiques, especially at the northern end) and Ben Yehuda Street. Additional shops at the upper end of the price scale are concentrated around Hamedin Square in the north of the city.

The bookstore chain *Steinmatzky* has a large selection of English-language publications; there are two branches on Allenby Street and Dizengoff Street.

In the streets on Kikar Magen David, a large market is held every day; on Tuesdays and Fridays, artisans and craftsmen offer their wares in stands on Nahalet Binyamin Street. Nearby, at the corner of King George and Bet Leichem Streets, there's a market for inexpensive clothing of all descriptions.

In Yafo, *Shuk Hapishpeshem*, the huge flea market, is open every day on Olei Zion Street and the smaller side streets.

Hospital / Dental Clinics

Ichilow Hospital (dental clinic), Weizmann Street, 24-hour emergency service.

Transportation

BUS: The inner-city bus network is quite extensive, run by the two competing lines *Egged* and *Dan*. There's a single fixed price for all routes. Both lines also offer a multiple-trip ticket, called the *Kartisia*, which gets you 25 trips for the price of 20. The main lines, 4 and 5, service the entire city center and run on Ben Yehuda and Allenby Street as well as Dizengoff Street and Rothschild Boulevard. Bus 10 runs from City Hall along Ben Yehuda Street to Yafo and back along Hayarkon Street, which runs parallel to the beach promenade.

There are also privately-operated mini-buses, which come in handy on the Sabbath, when the larger lines do not run. From Tel Aviv's central bus station, as well as the bus terminal at the main train station on Arlosoroff Street, buses depart for destinations throughout the country, leaving every ten minutes for Jerusalem, several times an hour for Haifa and Be'er Sheva, and several times a day for Elat (advance reservations advised).

SHARE TAXIS: Share taxis, or *Sherut*, are stationed at the central bus station; these are Mercedes stretch-limousines, which take off as soon as their seven seats are filled. *Sherut* run on the same routes as buses, but they're faster and somewhat more expensive. (On the Sabbath, there's an additional surcharge of 20 %).

TRAIN: Trains to the north leave hourly from the Arlosorroff Train Station, stopping in all major towns, such as Netanya, Hadera, Haifa and Nahariyya. Trains run from Tel Aviv to Jerusalem several times a day. There are no trains on Saturdays.

Tourist Information

Tourist Information Office, New Central Bus Station, 6th floor, by platform 630, tel. 03-6395660, will make hotel reservations, offers city maps, brochures etc., Sun-Thu 8:30 am-5 pm, Fri 8:30 am-2:30 pm.

The tourist information office at Ben Gurion Airport is open round the clock.

ASHQELON

Accommodation

LUXURY: **The Shulamite Garden**, Hatayasim Street, tel. 07-6711261.

MODERATE: **The Samson Gardens**, Hatamar Street, tel. 07-6736641. **Ashqelon Hotel**, South Africa Boulevard, tel. 07-6734234.

Parks and Museums

Ashqelon National Park, daily 8 am-5 pm. **Ashqelon Museum**, Sun-Thu 9 am-1 pm, 4-6 pm, Fri 9 am-1 pm, Sat 10 am-1 pm.

THE NORTHERN MEDITERRANEAN COAST

HERZLIYYA / NETANYA HADERA / CAESAREA HAIFA / AKKO NAHARIYYA

HERZLIYYA

The seaside resort of Herzliyya Pituach – which would be Herzliyya-on-Sea in English – can be regarded almost as a suburb of Tel Aviv. It was founded in the 1920s as a farming settlement and named after the founder of Zionism, Theodor Herzl. Many foreign diplomats, Near East correspondents and foreign businesspeople have settled in the resort, enjoying its peace and quiet and the fact that it is only 10 kilometers north of the bustle and noise of the capital.

In addition, Herzliyya, with its many film studios, is the movie and television center of Israel. Luxury hotels stand shoulder to shoulder along the long beach, while a marina provides moorings for myriad yachts. Inexpensive restaurants and a number of cafés are clustered around two small squares in the town. A fast bus service, number 90, links Herzliyya and Tel Aviv.

In the north of the resort, off the main road, is the **Sidna Ali Mosque**, built in the 13th century and named for one of Saladin's army commanders who fought

Preceding pages: Fish has been landed here for 3500 years: the harbor of Akko.
Left: Kibbutz farmers provide even the city hotels with vegetables.

against the Crusaders. The mosque commands a beautiful view of the sea.

Arshaf Apollonia

Not far away, where the shore is steeper, rises the hill of **Tel Arshaf** with the remains of an old Canaanite settlement. The Greeks who came in the 4th century B.C. called the place Apollonia, and it remained an important harbor into Roman times. The Arabs called the town Arsuf, and during the time of the Crusades its townspeople had to suffer under the Franks.

One day the knight Gerard of Avesnes, a close friend of the commander of the Crusade, Godfrey de Bouillon, fell into the clutches of the Saracens. When the Christians attacked the town, the defenders took their captive, now mockingly bound to a cross, and hung him over the walls to catch the arrows. Gerard begged Godfrey, who was in earshot, to be careful, but the reply consisted of some remarks concerning eternal life, after which Godfrey gave the order to fire. Gerard was hit by ten arrows.

When the Muslims saw "how all compassion had died in the hearts of the Christians," they pulled the severely wounded knight back behind the walls. They nursed him back to health and then,

119

hard as it is to believe, they let him go free. In 1191, Richard the Lionhearted wrote military history when he, in the field, annihilated the superior forces of Saladin at Arsuf.

When the British put an official stop to further immigration into Palestine during the 1940s, the early medieval pier came to be used at night as a secret landing place for Jewish refugees.

NETANYA

The fine white sandy beach of Netanya is eleven kilometers long. Netanya is the largest seaside resort in the country, with 160,000 inhabitants, and is particularly popular on account of its pleasant climate. In the late 1920s the town was laid out at the center of extensive citrus groves and named for the Jewish American philanthropist Nathan Strauss. But Netanya does not yet feel comfortable, so

Above: Netanya is the country's largest beach resort.

to speak, since the many waves of immigration have meant that the town had to expand quickly without the benefit of much real planning.

Apart from the many vacationers who bring in money for the Netanyans, the second greatest source of income is the diamond and jewelry industry. During World War II, diamond-cutters fled to Palestine from the Netherlands and Belgium, settling and founding small businesses in Netanya.

Nowadays, you can visit some of the large production facilities, such as the **National Diamond Center** (90 Herzl Street) or **Inbar Jewelry** (31 Benyamin Boulevard); here, you can watch diamond-cutters at work and then purchase at relatively inexpensive prices. Other major employers are the citrus fruit packing plants and the local brewery (the only one in the country).

The main street of Netanya is the long shop-lined **Herzl Street**, which becomes a pedestrian precinct just before it reaches the sea, ending in Haazmaut

Square above the beach. There is a tourist information office here and a number of pleasant cafés.

All kinds of performances, including music concerts, are staged in the town's semicircular open-air theater, which faces the sea and, in the evening, the setting sun.

HADERA

The coal-fired power stations of Hadera give themselves away from a distance by thick columns of smoke rising into the sky. This small city is located a few kilometers from the sea; for visitors, its main attraction is its museum on the history of local settlement. In Israel, Hadera is also a kind of symbol for the endurance of the first Jewish settlers who fought against all kinds of resistance and obstacles to build a future for themselves in what would be their new country.

In 1891, a small group of Russian Zionists came to Palestine looking for land to settle. A rather shady Christian Arab sold the men around 3,000 hectares of land. The immigrants wrote and told the people back home in Russia that they had bought a lot of land with good water and that there was also a wonderful beach nearby.

As the immigrants began making the land ready for plowing, they came to the unpleasant realization that the moist meadows and ponds were ideal breeding grounds for the anopheles mosquito which carried malaria.

In order to dry out the land the immigrants planted countless thousands of water-consuming eucalyptus trees and laid kilometers of drainage pipes. Nevertheless, by the end of their first year at Hadera more than half of them had died of malaria.

This sad story is brought alive for the visitor in the **Khan Historical Museum**, once an Ottoman caravanserai (74 Hagiborim Street).

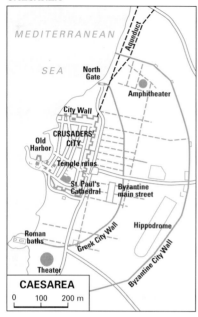

CAESAREA

One of the most important archaeological excavation sites in Israel is in
Caesarea, although the area is lacking in
spectacular ruins. Looking at the rubble-
strewn ground, you will need a lot of imagination to believe that these are the remains of what was once one of the most
magnificent cities in the region.

History

Phoenician traders from Sidon
founded the harbor settlement of Migdal
Sharshan here in the 4th century B.C. In
63 B.C. it was captured by the Romans.
About 30 years later, Octavian, who was
to become the emperor Augustus Caesar,
gave the city to Herod, who renamed it
Caesarea Maritima after his patron and
invested huge sums of money in developing it into a magnificent metropolis.

*Right: A beautiful view in the Roman amphi-
theater at Caesarea.*

The harbor was built under the mos
severe difficulties and inopportune conditions; the Jewish historian Flavius Josephus reports that even with a west wind
the swell was high and goes on to say
"But the king by lavish expenditure and
unshakable determination won the battle
against nature and constructed a harbor
bigger than the Piraeus, with further deep
roadsteads in its recesses. The site was as
awkward as could be, but he wrestled
with the difficulties so triumphantly that
on his solid fabric the sea could make no
impression, while its beauty gave no hint
of the obstacles encountered. Adjoining
the harbor were houses, also of limestone, and to the harbor led the streets of
the town, laid out the same distance apart.
On rising ground opposite the harbor
mouth stood Caesar's temple, of exceptional size and beauty; in it was a colossal
statue of [Augustus] Caesar, no whit in-
ferior to the Olympian Zeus which it was
intended to resemble..." (*The Jewish
War*, I, 407).

Herod's city and harbor building project extended over 12 years (22-10 B.C.)
In the 6th century A.D. Caesarea was
promoted to capital of the Roman province of Judea, and between 26 and 36
A.D. Pontius Pilate resided in Herod's
palace as procurator. As the New Testament reports, Peter came into the city in
those days and baptized a certain man in
Caesarea called Cornelius, a centurion of
the band called the "Italian band" (Acts
10:1). In 44 A.D. Agrippa, grandson of
Herod the Great, was "eaten of worms
and gave up the ghost" (Acts 12:23) a
punishment for the execution in Caesarea
of the disciple James. Paul spent some
time in prison in the city before being
sent to Rome for trial (this was his right
as a Roman citizen).

In 63, there was severe unrest in the region which was bloodily suppressed
Jews and Greeks were both striving for
control of the city. The situation became
more extreme, bordering on civil war

and Josephus writes that "the people of Caesarea massacred the Jewish colony in less than an hour, slaughtering more than 20,000 and emptying Caesarea of the last Jew" (*The Jewish War*, II, 467). Since the Romans had supported the Greeks, this led to the first uprising of the Jews against the Romans, three years later. King Herod Agrippa II, who was on good terms with Rome, was forced to flee with his sister Berenice from Caesarea to the safety of Tiberias. The Roman general Vespasian set up his headquarters in the city from where he directed the suppression of the revolt of Galilee. In the year 69 he was proclaimed emperor in Caesarea.

Under the long and impressive name of Colonia Prima Flavia Augusta Felix Caesarea Metropolis Provinciae Syriae Palaestinae, the city enjoyed a period of cultural and economic prosperity which began in the 2nd century. The church father Origen (185-254) founded a theological college here, setting up a large library which held 30,000 books (or rather, scrolls); here, he edited the *hexapla*, an edition of the Bible with the original Hebrew text and various translations into Greek. Between 314 and 339 the church historian Eusebius was bishop of Caesarea; the end of the 5th century saw the birth here of another historian, Procopius, who went on to write a detailed description of the Byzantine court of Justinian.

When, in 613, the Persians attacked and took Caesarea with the help of the local Jewish community, there were 50,000 Christians living in this sprawling city; many of them were slaughtered. 26 years later the Muslim Arabs captured the metropolis, after which its name was Arabicized into Qaisariyya.

The Crusaders were the next bringers of death and disaster. In 1101 under the leadership of Baldwin I they took the city after a brief siege and massacred its inhabitants. In this city, which they dubbed Césarée, in French fashion, the Frankish knights supposedly found the Holy Grail, which was identified as the cup from which Christ drank at the Last Supper.

123

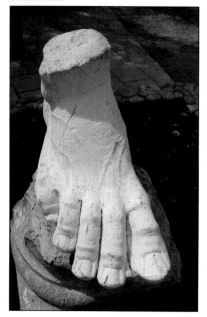

the story of the Grail until the late Middle Ages.

In 1187 Saladin recaptured the city and had the fortifications razed to the ground; four years later, Richard the Lionhearted arrived with his troops and had them rebuilt. In 1220, Caesarea was once more in the possession of the Muslims, but nine years later the Crusaders were back again behind its walls. In the middle of the 13th century, King Louis IX of France, also known as St. Louis, had the walls of Caesarea built higher still; it is these constructions that comprise the mighty walls we see today. However, his efforts were in vain, since the Egyptian Mameluke sultan Baybars took the city anyway in 1265. In order to prevent the Christian fleet from anchoring and possibly allowing the crusaders to refortify Caesarea, the Arabs destroyed the city and its harbor once and for all.

Sightseeing

The stout **city walls** from the era of the Crusades still stand in all their loftiness; in the old days three gates led into the city, vigilant guards stood atop the 16 towers, and further security was provided by a deep moat around the fortifications. At the southeast corner you can climb up onto the walls and enjoy the fine view over the ruins and the sea.

In the north, archaeologists have uncovered a small part of the city walls and two round towers which date back to the time of Herod the Great. The Crusader ships once moored in the **harbor** basin, which can still be clearly recognized; to build their docks and quays, the Crusaders made use of many stones from ancient Caesarea.

The huge Herodean port has now been reclaimed by the sea and lies under the waves about 200 meters out. In honor of the Roman emperor it was named Sebaste, in allusion to the Greek appellation for Augustus. Two piers once projected

The commander of the Italian fleet, which had made a significant contribution to the capture of the city, took the sacred vessel to Genoa.

The myth of the Grail, which is supposed to bring supreme bliss to its possessor, goes as far back as Celtic prehistory where it appears as a marvelous cauldron, another form of the Horn of Plenty. In Christian belief, Joseph of Arimathea, who took Christ down from the cross and buried him, is supposed to have come to the west of Britain in the year 60 or thereabouts in order to spread the Gospel. He had with him, so the story goes, the Holy Grail, which he buried at the present-day town of Glastonbury. The apparent rediscovery of the Grail in the Holy Land revived this early Christian legend, and Celtic poets and French writers turned out version after version of

Above: Feet of clay? An example of the size and magnificence of ancient Caesarea. Right: The Crusaders' Gate at Caesarea.

out into the sea, one some 200 meters in length, the other three times as long. Huge breakwaters were set up on the outside of the piers. Joseph gives a detailed report of the construction work: "[Herod] first marked out the area for a harbor of the size mentioned, and then lowered into 37 meters of water blocks of stone mostly 15.24 meters long, 2.75 meters deep and 3.05 meters broad, but sometimes even bigger. When the foundations had risen to water level he built above the surface a mole 60 meters wide; half this width was built out to break the force of the waves and so was called the Breakwater (*prokymia*); the rest supported the encircling stone wall. Along this were spaced massive towers [...]. There was a row of arched recesses where newly-arrived crews could land, and in front of these was a circular terrace forming a broad walk for those disembarking" (*The Jewish War*, I, 420).

Near the harbor, Herod had a platform 15 meters high built on massive arches; upon this, a **temple** and the **royal palace** were constructed. Some of these arches have survived; alongside them, you can also observe what is left of **St. Paul's Cathedral**, which dates from the time of the Crusades.

In the south of the city, Herod's building project provided for a **theater** which could accommodate several thousand spectators. But when at the beginning of the 5th century gladiatorial combat and the baiting of animals could no longer be reconciled with Christian ethics, the Romans converted the theater into a fortress. Today, however, the beautifully restored theater houses a summer music festival.

In the north of Caesarea, Herod had an **amphitheater** of gigantic dimensions built; however, it has not yet been excavated. After the conquest of Jerusalem, Titus held gruesome celebrations here for his brother's birthday, as Josephus describes: "...he celebrated his brother's birthday in the grand style, reserving much of his vengeance on the Jews for this notable occasion. The number of those who perished in combats with wild

beasts or in fighting each other or by being burnt alive exceeded 2,500. Yet all this seemed to the Romans, though their victims were dying a thousand different deaths, to be too light a penalty" (*The Jewish War*, VII, 44).

In the east of the city is the **hippodrome** which in Antiquity, according to various sources, could hold between 20,000 and 38,000 spectators and whose main straight was 220 meters long. The film *Ben Hur* gives a good impression of the breathtaking chariot-racing of the time.

At the main entrance to the Crusaders' city begins the 150-meter length of the **Byzantine main street** which was once decorated with marble slabs and mosaics. The street was lined with shops and workshops. Two large seated statues lacking heads are a puzzle: the red figure may have been made on the occasion of

Above: The High Aqueduct at Caesarea is supported by 28 arches. Right: Sunset near Dor.

the visit of the emperor Hadrian and depict the Roman ruler, while the significance of the white figure is open to all kinds of speculation as the archaeologists themselves have no idea. It is thought that the sculptures were not commissioned especially for this shopping street but rather came originally from Roman temples.

About one kilometer north of the Crusaders' walls, the sand of the dunes is crossed by the 28 arches of the **High Aqueduct**. During the Roman period cities needed vast quantities of water each day for their public wells and baths as well as for irrigating gardens and fields. Herod's engineers first built a flat water pipeline from the foot of Mount Carmel, 13 kilometers to the north, then bored a tunnel several kilometers long through the rock. From this tunnel, the water poured into the High Aqueduct which then brought it the rest of the way into the city.

South of Caesarea is the **Sdot Yam** kibbutz, which has a small archaeological

museum. This was once home to the Jewish poetess Hannah Sennesh, who later fought against the Nazis during World War II and was hanged. The kibbutz also maintains an attractive vacation village with a beach for bathing. The luxurious **Dan Caesarea Golf Hotel** possesses the only 18-hole golf course in Israel, and also offers riding and tennis.

In the Footsteps of the Rothschilds

From here, you can take either the busy multi-lane Route 2 straight through to Haifa without stopping, or you can proceed at a more leisurely pace through Israeli wine country at the foot of Mount Carmel.

Around 5 kilometers east of Caesarea, in the midst of extensive vineyards, is the settlement of **Binyamina**, founded in 1922 and named for the French baron Edmund James Rothschild (1845-1934), who had taken the Hebrew name of Benjamin and who had invested vast sums in helping Jewish families settle in Palestine. The single-story houses with their red-tiled roofs are reminiscent of Provence. North of Binyamina stretches **Jabotinsky Park**, named for Vladimir Jabotinsky (1880-1940), the right-wing Zionist and spiritual leader of the Irgun terrorist group. In the 1930s and 40s in this nearly-deserted area this underground organization trained the fighters who were to be such a problem for the British troops. The park also includes an Ottoman castle and a small Roman theater, both restored. The fortifications, which date back to the 18th century, were built on the older foundations. Excavations have revealed two bathing pools with Roman mosaics and also a statue of Aesclepius, the Greek god of medicine. The theater dates from the 2nd century.

Another 3.5 kilometers to the north, the **Ramat Hanadiv** or "height of the benefactor" is signposted in the Rothschild Memorial Garden. In the midst of a large park planted with cedars, cypresses and palms, there is a black mausoleum which holds the mortal remains

of Edmund and his wife Adelaide. A map in stone shows the settlements which were founded at Rothschild's instigation.

The Rumanian Jews who settled in the area did not manage to drain the land during the last century; only when the baron helped them out in the 1880s with drainage and viticulture experts did agriculture flourish here, and in 1893 the first Carmel wine was exported to Europe. Since the Rothschilds had expressed the wish that they would like to be buried here, an Israeli warship brought their remains from France to Israel in 1954.

After another two kilometers you come to the village of **Zikhron Ya'akov** (Jacob's Memorial) which the grateful settlers named for James or Jacob Rothschild (1792-1868), the father of Edmund. Make sure you get in a visit to the **Carmel Oriental Wine Cellars**, the second largest in Israel. The tour lasts an

Above: A mural painting commemorates the Rothschilds' activities in the region. Right: Unorthodox bathing beauty.

hour and a quarter, and along the way you are shown all of the stages in wine making, maturation and bottling, finishing up, of course, with wine-tasting at the end. Here you can stock up on the noble juice of the house of Rothschild, such a Cabernet Sauvignon, Sauvignon Blanc and Fume Blanc, rather more cheaply than elsewhere. Each year in autumn there is a three-day wine festival after the harvest.

You should not neglect to stop in at **Bet Aaronson** in Hamesyasdim Street. This is the house of the botanist Aaron Aaronson (1876-1919). Baron Rothschild financied his studies in France, and the knowledge Aaronson acquired there proved to be invaluable to the local farmers. The long rows of Washingtonia palms, for example, originated with him.

Aaronson became internationally known when during his botanical investigations in the area he came across an ancient form of wheat which had never been domesticated. He is also highly respected in Israel because during World

War I he and his sisters Sarah and Rebecca, as well as his assistant Absalom
Feinberg, joined the NILI secret organiz-
ation which actively resisted the Turks.
When Feinberg was caught in the Gaza
Strip trying to contact the British, he was
killed and buried there. About 50 years
later his grave was found: it lay, so they
say, under a palm which had sprouted
from a seed in his pocket. After the Six-
Day War he was reburied in Jerusalem.
Sarah Aaronson was discovered by the
Turks and tortured, following which she
committed suicide in her brother's house.
Aaronson himself came back to Zikhron
Ya'akov with the British in 1918. One
year later his airplane disappeared without a trace on its way from London to a
peace conference in Paris.

To the west of the city you can relax in
the quiet of **Beth Daniel**, blessed as it is
with a wonderful view of the Carmel
coast. In 1938 Lillian Friedlander had
this small complex of houses built in
memory of her son, Daniel, as a refuge
for musicians. Daniel was a gifted pianist

who studied music in New York, where
he took his life when he was just 18.
Music concerts are held here regularly
and the place has been honored with the
visits of great names, such as Leonard
Bernstein and Arturo Toscanini. But
quite ordinary visitors are also welcome,
as Beth Daniel is also a guesthouse.

Nearly 6 kilometers to the northeast,
towards Yoqneam, is another Rothschild
settlement, namely **Bat Shelomo**; it was
founded in 1889 and named after the baron's mother. You could almost believe
that time had stood still here: the locals
still farm their land very much as they
have always done. If fresh natural produce appeals to you, you can take the opportunity to pick up local cheese, olive
oil, and even honey.

The road carries on towards Yoqneam,
from where it continues northwards in
the direction of Daliyat al-Karmil. After
about 8 kilometers, take a right turn; and
after another 3 kilometers you will come
to **Muhraqa** and the **Carmelite monastery**. In 1886 the abbey was built on the

foundations of an older church. From its terrace there is another wonderful view of Mount Jezreel ("seedplot of God"). This place is of particular interest to Bible tourists, as it is here that the prophet Elijah is supposed to have challenged the priests of Baal to a competition. At that time, the Chosen People were wavering between Yahweh and Baal, and so Elijah proposed that both he and the priests of Baal should each "take a bullock, and cut it in pieces, and lay it on wood." They would each call on their god and the god who then brought fire to the wood, "let him be God." From morning to midday the priests of Baal called incessantly on their god to answer them with fire, but nothing happened. Elijah could not resist mocking: "Cry aloud: for he is a god, either he is talking, or he is pursuing, or he is in a journey, or peradventure he sleepeth, and must be awakened" (1 Kings 18:22-27). Finally, Elijah

Above: Member of the Druse minority at Deliyat el Karmel.

130

called on the Lord and He let fire fall; consumed the offering, showing th people who the real God was. Elijah ha the people seize the priests of Baal an ordered them to be slain on the spot.

The main road to the port of Haifa reached via the small Druse town of **De liyat el Karmel** and the smaller town c Isfiya, also inhabited by the Druses both are favorite destinations with fans c the local handicrafts.

HAIFA

Haifa, the "gate of Israel," is the thirc largest city in the country, and, at least i terms of its location, certainly the mos attractive. From the sea, there are house all the way up the spacious slopes c Mount Carmel, to elevations offerin visitors a glorious view of the dome c the Baha'i shrine and the city, the po and the blue sea with ships anchored c sailing in and out. On a clear day you ca see out over the bay as far as Akko. B from the sea front there are also enchan ing views of Haifa, particularly at dus when a constellation of lights is scattere over Mount Carmel.

History

The first documented record of the cit is in the 3rd century A.D. Four hundre years later, the settlement was overrun b Muslim Arabs who razed it to the groun In 1099, the Crusaders passed Haifa by for them Jerusalem was more important but the respite was brief. Once the ho city had been taken, the Franks turne their attention to the port city and lai siege to it. Haifa was captured muc more quickly than expected, and thos who did not manage to escape were sim ply cut down by the Christian soldier Together with Jaffa, and later with Acr as well, Haifa became one of the mai ports where reinforcements for the Cru saders landed. In 1187 Saladin recap

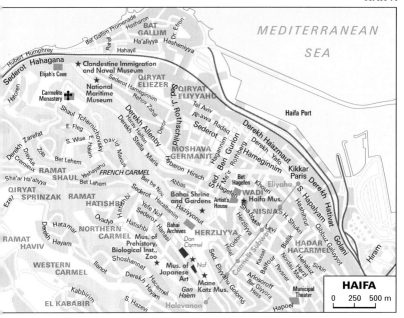

tured Haifa, but in 1191 Richard the Lionhearted was able to march right back into the city – albeit only because Saladin had demolished the city walls. In 1252, the French king Louis IX had the fortifications rebuilt – as he already had done in Caesarea – but in vain, as 14 years later the Mameluke sultan Baybars recaptured the city once and for all for the Saracens. Once Acre, the last stronghold of the Crusaders, had fallen, the Arabs rampaged along the coastal strip, destroying towns, villages, monasteries, fields, irrigation systems and quays in a medieval scorched-earth policy aimed at preventing the return of the Franks. For many centuries, Haifa remained a sleepy small fishing port, although it did have one holy spot of its own: the cave of Elijah, which was visited by Jewish, Christian and Muslim pilgrims. When, in the Ottoman period, the port city developed into the center of the wheat export trade, it slowly recovered in importance, and by the early 19th century Haifa was the most important port in the entire Near East.

In 1869 the religious reformers of the German Order of the Knights Templar established its own quarter in the city. Kaiser Wilhelm II began his visit to the Holy Land in 1898 in Haifa, and the Turks were compelled to build a new landing quay especially for his visit. With the opening of the Haifa-Damascus railway line in 1904, and the wave upon wave of Zionist settlers flooding into the country, Haifa continued to grow into what Theodor Herzl called the "city of the future." In 1912, German Jews established a technical college which today is one of the most important research institutes in Israel. In the 1930s, under the British mandate, the harbor was modernized and extended; furthermore, it became the terminus of an oil pipeline from Kirkuk in Iraq (which was shut down in 1948).

Today, Haifa is still Israel's most important port and industrial metropolis; more than a quarter of a million people live in this attractive city on the slopes of Mount Carmel.

131

Sightseeing

The city of Haifa can be divided into three parts. Along the narrow strip by the sea is the harbor complex with its loading docks and warehouses; then there is the middle city halfway up the slopes of Mount Carmel, called *Hadar Ha'Carmel*, which was once the focus of settlement for the immigrating Jews. Today, it is the bustling shopping area of the city with its many shops and department stores. Last, extending up to the peak which is called the Mercaz Ha'Carmel, are the finer residential districts and the big international hotels.

To get a first general view of the city, you should start in the port section at Paris Square (Kikar Paris) by taking the **Carmelit Subway** (as its name suggests, an underground railway) six stations up Mount Carmel as far as its terminus at

Above: "Two Torah students," painting by Mané Katz, 1943. Right: The Baha'i Shrine in Haifa.

Hanassi Boulevard. Here, you will find **Gan Ha'em** park, which has a small zoo, and the **Museum of Biology and Prehistory**. You should on no account miss visiting the enchanting **Tikotin Museum of Japanese Art** at 89 Hanussi Boulevard. Up here, behind the high towers of luxury hotels, runs Yefe Nof Street, which is also fittingly known as Panorama Street, as it commands sweeping views over the city, the port and the Mediterranean.

At 89 Yefe Nof Street is the **Mané Katz Museum**, the house and studio of the Jewish Expressionist painter Emmanuel Katz (1894-1962). Katz was born in the Ukraine but left his adoptive city of Haifa his home, together with a collection of paintings, sculptures and Judaica. Like Chagall, the main subjects of his work were taken from the daily village life of the Eastern European Jews.

If you walk along Yefe Nof Street you will soon come to **Sderot Hatziyonut**, the long Boulevard of Zionism. Originally this street was named for the United

Nations but when the U.N. passed a resolution in 1975 which, in Israeli eyes, equated Zionism with racism, the city administration reacted with anger and promptly renamed the street. There is a little garden of sculptures here where you can unwind for a while. The life-size bronze statues of children are the creation of Ursula Malbin, a refugee from Nazi Germany.

A few minutes on foot along the boulevard will bring you to the entrance of the Persian Gardens on your left. In the middle of the gardens is the snow-white **Baha'i Shrine** with its golden dome, which dominates the city and has in effect become its emblem. A whole series of illustrious founders of faiths, including Moses, Buddha, Zarathustra, Christ, and Mohammed, are considered by the Baha'is as prophets; another of these is their own founder, Mirza Hussein Ali, known as the Baha'ullah or "Glory of God." Due to the nature of his religious teachings, the Baha'ullah was forced to flee Persia and was held prisoner by the Ottoman

Turks for almost 40 years in the citadel of Akko. He spent his final years in a house in Akko where he died in 1892; and his grave is in Akko.

The Baha'i religion has adapted many passages from the Bible and the Koran, preaches the unity of God and his prophets, and in its teachings promotes friendship and harmony between men.

The center of the shrine is the mausoleum for Mirza Ali Mohammed, known as *al-Bab*, or "the gate." This martyr of the sect had preached the imminent arrival of the Baha'ullah and for this was executed in 1850 in Persia. In 1909 his remains were brought to Haifa. The Baha'i community in Iran is of a considerable size but is currently subjected to the most savage repressive measures by the Iranian authorities.

The shrine was erected between 1948 and 1953 by the son and successor of the Baha'ullah. It harmoniously unifies European and Oriental architectural styles. No expense was spared: the walls are clad in Italian natural stone; the 12,000

roof tiles were hot-gilded in the Netherlands; the splendid columns are made of rose granite. A short distance away from the shrine is the Baha'i archive and the domed House of Righteousness in which the supreme council of the faith presides. These two buildings are not open to the public.

Looking down from the Baha'i shrine, you can see Ben Gurion Boulevard running straight as an arrow from the port toward the point where you are standing. To the right and left of this busy thoroughfare is the **German colony**. A row of typical two- or three-story white buildings with red roof tiles is still standing, and these houses bear German names. This is where members of the Templar movement settled at the end of the last century, winning the affection of their neighbors on account of their hardworking habits. The community was self-supporting; German thoroughness and the well-known Teutonic industriousness meant that they enjoyed a high standard of living. Handicrafts businesses of all kinds sprang up, streets and gardens were laid out and the industrious Germans made their mark on the city.

If you walk on, down the Boulevard of Zionism, you will come, at the intersection of this street and Hagefen Boulevard, to **Beth Hagefen**, where for more than 30 years the Arab-Jewish Center has been striving for understanding between the peoples and cultures. All kinds of events are put on here; check out the information board and you are sure to find something of interest. The house is located at a kind of boundary in the city: to the northeast is Wadi Nisnas, the Arab quarter, and to the south are the Jewish residential districts on the slopes of Mount Carmel.

Around the corner, in the Boulevard of Zionism, the **Artist's House** is entirely given over to the artists of the city. Cross the street and go a short distance down Shabettai Levy Street: on your left is the Haifa Museum, which displays excavation finds from Egypt, local finds dating from the Canaanite to the Roman period, Greek ceramics, and Greek and Roman sculptures. Also on view are Jewish and Islamic objects, both religious and secular, as well as modern art.

In the **Chagall Artists' House** opposite the museum, contemporary Israeli artists display their work.

To the east, Shabbetai Levy Street becomes Herzl Street, one of the main shopping streets of the city. Parallel with it to the south, is Nordau Street, closed to traffic and lined with cafés, pubs and restaurants. It is a good place to hang out for a while.

In the northwest of the city, near the sea, where a funicular carries people up to the peak of Carmel in glassy globes, Allenby Road branches off to the right from the Sderot Hagana coast road. Right at the beginning of this street, Elijah's

Above: Visitors ascend in glass balls on the cable car to the peak of Mount Carmel.
Right: Fruit market in Haifa.

ave and the Clandestine Immigration
nd Naval Museum are located across
rom each other.

Elijah's Cave is sacred to Jews, Mus-
ims and Christians alike. This is where
he prophet is supposed to have sheltered
rom the wrath of king Ahab in the 9th
entury B.C. Further up the slope are the
uildings of the **Carmelite Monastery**,
vhich was built in 1827 on the remains of
Byzantine abbey. The church is located
ver the cave in which the prophet Elijah
upposedly lived. A stone pyramid com-
nemorates the Napoleonic soldiers who
vere killed by Ahmed al-Jezzar in 1799.
few meters away is the Stella Maris
ighthouse (meaning "light of the sea");
his part of the coast has been protected
y a lighthouse since 1821.

The rather dry name of the **Clandes-
ine Immigration and Naval Museum**
s deceiving: the museum in fact centers
round one of the most dramatic episodes
n the recent history of the region.

On the eve of World War II, the Brit-
sh, alarmed at the swelling influx of non-

Arab settlers into Palestine and the ensuing unrest, suspended immigration of
Jews into the country, which had been
under British mandate since the end of
World War I. Refugees from Europe,
which was fast being occupied by the
Germans, only managed to get through
the British maritime blockade secretly
and with a lot of luck. The museum's
central exhibit is an old military landing
boat with the name *Af-al-pi-chen*
("Nevertheless"), which had been converted into a blockade-runner and in
1947, with more than 400 concentration
camp survivors on board, attempted to
reach the coast of Palestine. The British
intercepted the ship and interned the passengers on Cyprus. Back in 1941, refugees on the *Struma* suffered a worse fate;
this leaky old tub was forced to put in at
Istanbul, but the Turks refused to allow a
repairs team to go on board; after weeks
of fruitless negotiations the *Struma* had
to put to sea, only to sink after just a few
hours – it is said that of the 700 souls on
board, only one survived. The British

showed a particular lack of sensitivity when, in 1947, they escorted back to Germany a ship whose passengers consisted of 4,000 former concentration camp inmates. Of the 63 blockade runners which tried to reach the coast of Palestine after the war, only 5 arrived – all the rest were intercepted by the Royal Navy. The intern camps on Cyprus were full of Jews who had survived the Holocaust. A gripping fictional treatment of these days may be found in Leon Uris' novel *Exodus*.

The **National Maritime Museum**, also on Allenby Street, has a great number of displays and ship models, nautical equipment and archaeological finds, which all combine to bring 5,000 years of seafaring alive in an interesting manner.

If you are interested in art, do not fail to make an excursion from Haifa out to **En Hod**, a few kilometers south on the coast. Formerly an Arab village, this small settlement is today an artists' colony. Painters and sculptors have come here to live and work, and the village now boasts 150 families. In the 1950s the Rumaniandadaist and painter Marcel Janco (1895-1984) discovered the abandoned village and was enchanted by the beauty of both the village and its surroundings. It did not take him long to resettle it with 20 of his fellow artists.

A large gallery exhibits the work of the local artists. The **Janco Dada Museum** houses paintings by Janco, and includes an audio-visual presentation on the Dada movement. Near the village, there's an open-air theater which presents concerts in the summer.

AKKO

One of the most atmospheric locales in Israel is the old city of Akko (perhaps better known to some as Acre). With its old and ancient buildings, its mighty ramparts and walls, its relics of the days of the Crusades, its small fishing harbor, the

Above: Haifa, Israel's industrial metropolis, is a modern urban capital.

streets of the bazaar, and the muezzin's call echoing over the cramped, dark alleyways, it calls to mind memories of the Arabian Nights, exactly corresponding to how you would imagine an Oriental city to be.

History

Akko is mentioned for the first time in Egyptian texts dating from 1500 B.C. The port was conquered or occupied during the following two centuries by the troops of the Egyptian pharaohs Thutmose III, Akhnaten, Seti I and Ramses II. After 100 years of turbulent history, during which Akko/Acre was frequently shuttled from ruler to ruler; Pompey, who had been appointed by the Roman senate to clear up any and all problems in the East, annexed Palestine in 65 B.C. and incorporated Akko into the Roman empire as a free city. 17 years later, Julius Caesar disembarked his troops here.

It was in Acre that, in 30 B.C., Herod the Great met with his patron, the emperor Augustus, presented him with costly gifts, and had a gymnasium opened in the city – at least this is what Josephus reports – to commemorate the imperial visit. For the next few hundred years, Akko remained an important port, its status not even being affected by the Arab conquest in 636. Akko became the principle port for the Ummayyid dynasty which was ruling in Damascus, and the harbor functioned as a point of departure for the conquest and Islamification of north Africa.

In 1099, the Crusaders simply ignored Akko: Jerusalem was for them infinitely more important. It was four years before they made their first attempts to gain control of this strategic port – but in vain, since the defenders were constantly being supplied with fresh troops and weapons by sea. In 1104, the city was finally taken after the sea supply route was effectively cut off by a blockade of Genoese galleys.

AKKO - OLD CITY

0   100   200 m

Akkon, as it was now called, became the principle port for the Crusader forces in the Holy Land. Almost all of their supplies and reinforcements were landed here, and most of the private commerce between Arab, Jewish and Christian merchants was negotiated here, as well. Many European city-states set up trading offices in Akkon in order to benefit commercially from this interface of the Orient and Occident.

In 1110, the Arabs made an unsuccessful attempt to recapture the city. Over the following years, Akko became not only the wealthiest trading metropolis in the region but also the unofficial residence of the Crusader kings. In 1187, all of this prosperity seemed lost when Saladin captured the city. Two years later, Christian troops under the command of Guy de Lusignan attempted to retake it, but they were not successful until 1191, during the Third Crusade. King Richard the Lion-Hearted, King Philip II of France, and the Austrian duke Leopold V captured Akko for Christendom thanks to

137

their united forces and heavy siege equipment; they used nearly 100 catapults, which threw heavy boulders against the walls for weeks on end. Richard the Lion-Hearted, who is regarded with affection by many – contrasting markedly with their opinion of his brother King John – completed the capture of the city by slaughtering almost 3,000 Arabs.

Here, too, as in Caesarea and Haifa, it was the French king Louis who had the fortifications strengthened and expanded. On two occasions, in 1263 and 1266, the Egyptian Mameluke sultan Baybars made unsuccessful attempts to take Akko. But when a Christian mob massacred a number of the Muslim inhabitants in 1920, the Arabs saw themselves forced to take vigorous action without compromise. The sultan Ashraf Khalil assembled a powerful army comprising 150,000 infantry and 65,000 mounted

Above: Akko is surrounded by a formidable-looking city wall. Right: A range of sweet temptations.

troops. The defenders with their mere 1,000 knights and 15,000 mercenaries must have gone pale when they first caught sight of this massive army. They were able to hold out for six weeks, but the Saracens finally stormed the city and with their sabers avenged their slaughtered brothers in faith. Only a few Christians managed to escape in galleys. The city was destroyed by its new masters and declined, during the ensuing centuries, until it was nothing more than a sleepy little fishing port.

In the middle of the 18th century, the Turkish pasha Dahr al-Omar initiated the revival of Akko, laying out new city walls. His murderer and successor, Ahmed al-Jezzar, known as "the butcher" and himself a particularly gruesome despot even by the standards of those bloody days, commissioned extensive building work, overseeing the construction of mosques, caravanserais, public fountains, Koran schools, and also the citadel.

In 1799, Napoleon came to the East with dreams of a French-controlled east-

rn empire which would extend from Egypt northwards to cover all of Turkey and eastwards to India. But the British soon knocked these imperial ambitions out of him. For almost three months, Napoleon besieged Akko, but the fact that it was under the protection of the Royal Navy kept the French troops from being able to capture it. The firepower of the British fleet and the nautical skills of Admiral Lord Nelson were the obstacles which ultimately resulted in the heavy French losses culminating Napoleon's Oriental adventure.

At the beginning of the 19th century, the Egyptians ruled Akko for a few years. Then up until World War I, the region made up a part of the Ottoman Empire. By that point, the port had completely lost its importance, as it was both too small and too shallow to accommodate freighters and steamships. Due to its more favorable harbor, Haifa had grown more commercially and strategically valuable. In May, 1948, the Israeli army marched into old Akko.

Sightseeing

Weizmann Street leads through the old gateway in the massive city walls into the **Old City** of Akko, of which the population is entirely Arab. On the left, you can climb the high defensive ramparts; your reward at the top is a view out over the bay as far as Haifa. The northwest corner of the ramparts is protected by the powerful tower of **Burj Kurajim**.

The Ahmed al-Jezzar Mosque in the center of the old city was built in 1781-83 in the "Turkish rococo" style on the foundations of the Crusaders' cathedral and bears the name of its founder. This imposing mosque is one of the largest and most important Muslim holy places in Israel. In front of its main entrance there is an enchanting garden with, at its center, an elegant purification fountain surrounded by columns supporting a copper roof. The mosque boasts a special shrine, a reliquary which contains a hair which reputedly comes from the beard of the prophet Mohammed. In an annex to the

mosque, Ahmed al-Jezzar is buried, together with his son.

Opposite the mosque is the entrance to the so-called **Crusaders' City**, once headquarters of the Order of the Knights of St. John of Jerusalem and today a monumental complex of subterranean buildings. In 1791, Ahmed al-Jezzar had its vaults demolished and built his citadel on top. Parts of the Crusaders' halls were uncovered in 1955-64. An entrance hall leads onto a courtyard and gives into the giant and lofty knights'halls which later probably served as stalls. Before these, a narrow alleyway leads you past the administrative halls which have been further excavated since 1993, and to the complex's central courtyard. From here, you can reach what is referred to as the "Crypt," although at the time of the Crusades it in fact served as the knights' refectory. Three colossal round pillars sup-

port ogival vaulting. A narrow underground passageway once led from the refectory to the harbor; this secret tunnel was intended to allow rapid flight in the event of a siege.

The **City Museum** opposite the Crusader's City has been set up in what was once the baths of Ahmed al-Jezzar, the Hamam al-Basha (Pasha's Bath) which date to 1780. The museum exhibits a collection of archaeological finds, as well as costumes, weapons and Islamic art.

The **Citadel** was also built at the instigation of Ahmed al-Jezzar on the ruins of the Crusaders' city. During the British mandate, it was used as a high-security facility where many Jewish activists were imprisoned, and some executed. According to one Israeli source, many of the condemned went like heroes to their premature deaths with the national anthem *Hatikva* on their lips. From the British point of view, however, they were terrorists and the murderers of innocent people. The ideological head of the *Irgun*, Ze'ev Jabotinsky, was also held prisoner here.

Above: The "Crypt of St. John," once the Crusaders' dining hall. Right: In the courtyard of the Khan al Umdan caravanserai.

In 1947 there was a spectacular mass breakout; in an ambitious and precisely planned action, Jewish underground fighters blew a hole in the massive walls and freed a number of senior terrorist leaders who had been condemned to death. One of these was Menachem Begin, a member of the notorious Stern Gang, who was later to become president of Israel. There is a gripping account of his escape in Leon Uris' novel *Exodus*. The **Israeli Museum of the Heroes** in the citadel is dedicated to the history of these days, with many photographs and other exhibits for the visitor to study.

There is a series of caravanserais near the port. The oldest of them is the Khan al-Afranji or **Caravanserai of the Franks**, which was built in 1600 or so for European merchants. It houses a small Franciscan monastery. Another one, the Khan al-Umdan or **Caravanserai of the Columns**, has been beautifully restored and was originally built by Ahmed al-Jezzar on the remains of a Dominican monastery from the time of the Crusades.

The building material was brought in from Caesarea: the granite and porphyry columns of the arcade of the inner courtyard come from the ancient ruins. The high clock tower was built in 1906 on the occasion of the festivities honoring the 30th anniversary of the rule of Ottoman sultan Abdul Hamid II.

At the **harbor** of Akko you can watch fishermen mending their nets, boats sailing in and out and a lot of hustle and bustle. There are two good fish restaurants here which serve various delicacies such as crabs in a garlic herb sauce and freshly-caught calamari deep-fried in batter. At night a lighthouse sends its beams far out to sea and makes for a feeling of security.

In the old days, the harbor pier was much longer, extending as far as the now destroyed Fly Tower, a tiny and once fortified island in the bay of Akko. To the south stretch the kilometers of white sand beach known as the **Hof Argaman** or "Purple Beach," with several hotels towering over it. If you plunge back into

141

the labyrinth of alleys in the old town and walk up Hagana Street, you will pass the **Baha'i House**, where Mirza Hussein Ali, the Baha'ullah, spent twelve years of his exile.

Friendly Akko is an ideal base for excursions to Galilee and the north. On the way north towards the seaside resort of Nahariyya, after about 3 kilometers, you will come to the Persian **Baha'i Gardens** of al-Bahji ("the pleasures"). For followers of the Baha'i sect, this is the holiest spot on earth. Here in the country house, surrounded by its beautiful gardens, the Baha'ullah spent the last years of freedom left to him after his release. In 1892 he was buried nearby. The main entrance is reserved for members of the sect; followers of other faiths have to use the side entrance.

About 1 1/2 kilometers further on, an **aqueduct** runs to the right of the road. As early as Roman times there was a water

pipeline bringing the precious liqui from the Kabri springs to Akko. The O toman pasha Ahmed al-Jezzar had th aqueduct restored in the 18th century.

The surrounding fields belong to th **Lochamei Hageta'ot Kibbutz**. Visito who are interested in modern histor should not neglect to call in here. Th community project was founded in 194 by German, Polish and Lithuanian Jew A documentation center has what is prol ably the most extensive collection of d cuments in the world dealing with th Jewish resistance in Germany, Lithuani and Poland. Photographs show everyd Jewish life in Eastern Europe, the upri ing in the Warsaw ghetto, and the depor ation to the concentration camps.

NAHARIYYA

Israel's northern seaside resort w founded in 1934 by Jews fleeing fro Germany. Even in those days, the settle recognized what the town's real asse were: the white sandy beaches. Nah

Above: The chalk cliffs of Rosh Ha Niqra near the Lebanese border.

riyya became an idyllic and friendly resort and has remained so even up to the present day, when its population numbers around 30,000. Its main street is Ha'-Ga'aton Boulevard, which is lined with eucalyptus trees and shops, cafés and restaurants.

Nahariyya takes its name from the Hebrew word for river (*nahar*); it is still considered Israel's "German town," although the German language is scarcely heard here any more. What with the most recent waves of immigration, you are much more likely to hear Ethiopian Jews speaking Amharic or Iranian Jews speaking Farsee.

In 1947, archaeologists excavated a Canaanite temple 3,500 years old and dedicated to Astarte, goddess of fertility; the temple was equipped with a workshop for making sacred objects. Hundreds of cult items which were found here are presently being exhibited in the Israel Museum in Jerusalem.

Five kilometers north of Nahariyya is the site of **Tel Akhziv**, which contains ruins from former civilizations and has become designated as a national park. Canaanites, Phoenicians and Crusaders all settled here, and what remains of their buildings are today open to visitors. Also, a private museum exhibits archaeological finds. For those who are just looking for an enjoyable vacation spot, there is a beautiful beach here, complete with a restaurant and a Club Med resort.

Seven kilometers north of Nahariyya is **Kefar Rosh Ha Niqra** and the border with Lebanon. The name of the village means "cave head," a monicker which alludes to its two main attractions. There is, first of all, an extensive system of caves here which the sea has washed out of the soft chalk over the course of millions of years. A lookout point, with an adjacent restaurant, commands a spectacular panorama of the rugged and deeply fissured coast. Since 1968, a funicular has lifted visitors up 100 meters to the caves at the

NORTH OF HAIFA

0   5   10 km

foot of the chalk cliffs. Rosh Ha Niqra is the name of the enormous snow-white chalk cliffs which gleam in the sun and drop steeply down to the sea.

Over the millennia, these cliffs have had a considerable influence on the town's transportation connections. Alexander the Great did not waste much time trying to scale the massif, but simply had steps cut into its chalk to facilitate the movements of his troops. This "ladder of Tyre" was used not only by his soldiers but also by the many armies of his successors: the Diadochi; the Seleucids; Roman legionaries; Muslim Arabs; and finally the Crusaders, panting under the weight of their heavy armor.

In 1918, the British laid a road here and you can still clearly see the tunnel they drove through the chalk in 1942 for the railway line which once connected Beirut with Cairo via Haifa and Tel Aviv. Within five years, however, the Israeli underground fighters had blown up the tracks to prevent Arab troops using them to invade from Lebanon.

143

HERZLIYYA

Accommodation

LUXURY: **Daniel**, tel. 09-9528282. **Dan Arcadia**, tel. 09-9597070. **The Sharon**, tel. 09-9575777.
MODERATE: **Tadmor**, 38 Basel St., tel. 09-9525000.
BUDGET: **Eshel Inn**, tel. 09-9568208.

NETANYA

Getting There

Buses run several times a day from Tel Aviv, Jerusalem and Ben Gurion Airport to Netanya. There are also trains several times a day to and from Tel Aviv, and there is plenty of *Sherut* traffic, as well.

Accommodation

LUXURY: **Blue Bay**, 37 Hamelachin Street, tel. 09-8603603, tennis, pool, private beach. **The Seasons**, Nice Boulevard, tel. 09-8601555, best address in the area with large rooms and a private beach.
MODERATE: **Margoa**, 9 Gad Machness Street, tel. 09-8624434, family-style ambience. **Palace Hotel**, 33 Gad Machness Street, tel. 09-8620222.
BUDGET: **Orit Pension**, 21 Chen Avenue, tel. 09-8616818, cheap and good.
There are no hostels in Netanya.

Restaurants

Lucullus, 2 Jabotinsky Street, best restaurant in the city, French cuisine with an African-Arabian twist. **La Taboon**, 5 Ha'atzmaut Square, Yemeni cuisine, good and cheap.
Patisserie Antverpia, 1 Eliyahu Krause, notably delicious cakes.

Hospitals and Pharmacies

Laniado Hospital, tel. 09-8604666. **Pharmacies** on Herzl Street and Weizmann Street, such as **Trufa**, 2 Herzl Street.

Tourist Information

Ha'atzmaut Square, near the open-air theater, tel. 09-8827286.

HADERA

Museum

Khan Historical Museum, 74 Hagiborim Street, Sun-Thu 8 am-1 pm, Sun/Tue 4-6 pm, Fri 9 am-noon.

CAESAREA

Accommodation

LUXURY: **Dan Caesarea Golf Hotel**, Caesarea 30600, tel. 06-6269111.

Sights

Excavation site, open Sat-Thu 8 am-4 pm, Fri 8 am-3 pm, admission fee.

ZIKHRON YA'AKOV

Getting There

Regular buses and trains from Tel Aviv, Netanya and Haifa as well as a *Sherut* service.

Accommodation

LUXURY: **The Baron's Heights and Terraces**, Box 332, tel. 06-6300333, new, expensive, and the largest hotel in town.
MODERATE: **Bet Daniel**, Box 13, 06-6399001.

Restaurants

The Well, on Route 4, at the turn-off to Zikhron Ya'aqov, at the bus station.

Tourist Information

Gidonim, at the bus station, tel. 06-6398811.

Museums and Sights

Bet Aaronson, Hameyasdim Street, open Mon-Thu 10 am-12:30 pm. **Carmel Oriental Wine Cellars**, open Sun-Fri 9 am-12:30 pm.

HAIFA

Getting There

Buses run several times a day from Tel Aviv, Jerusalem and Akko; there are also several trains a day from Tel Aviv, and a regular *Sherut* service.

Accommodation

LUXURY: **Dan Carmel**, 85 Hanassi Avenue, tel. 04-8306306, best and most expensive hotel around, atop Mount Carmel. **Dan Panorama**, 107 Hanassi Avenue, tel. 04-8352222, on Mount Carmel, fabulous views. **Haifa Tower**, 63 Herzl Street, tel. 04-8677111. **Nof**, 101 Hanassi Avenue, tel. 04-8354311, lovely view out over Haifa. **Shulamit**, 15 Kiryat Sefer Street, tel. 04-8342811, quiet.
MODERATE: **Dvir**, 124 Yefe Nof Street, tel. 04-8389131, on Mount Carmel, good view. **Vered Hacarmel**, 1 Heinrich Heine Square, tel. 04-8389236, friendly place with a nice outdoor terrace.
BUDGET: **Lev Haifa**, 61 Herzl Street, tel. 04-8673753. **Saint Charles Hospice**, 105 Jaffa Road, tel. 04-8553705. **Bethel Tourist Hostel**, 40 Hageffen Street, tel. 04-8521110. **Carmel Youth Hostel**, 4 km south of the city center on Carmel Beach, tel. 04-8531944.

Restaurants

Sampa and **The Bank Restaurant** are two of the many restaurants along Hanassi Avenue at the top of Mount Carmel.
Voila, 21 Nordau Street, tel. 04-8664529, is a small, inconspicuous restaurant with a conservatory and good food, offering low-priced business lunches at noontime but providing only expensive dinners in the evening. **La Chaumière**, 40 Ben Gurion Boulevard, tel. 04-8538563, in the area of the former German col-

ony, French cuisine. **Tai Wah**, 60 Ben Gurion Boulevard, at the upper end of the street, is a low-priced Chinese restaurant.

Hospitals and Pharmacies

Ramban Hospital, tel. 04-8543111. **Carmel Hospital**, tel. 04-8250211. **Shomrom Pharmacy**, 44 Yafo Street. **Merkaz**, 130 Hanassi Boulevard.

Tourist Information

48 Ben Gurion Blvd, tel. 04-8535606.

Museums and Sights

Baha'i Shrine, Sderot Hatziyonut, daily 9 am-noon, Garden 9 am-5 pm. **Clandestine Immigration and Naval Museum**, Allenby Road, Sun-Thu 9 am-4 pm, Fri 9 am-1 pm. **Haifa Museum**, Shabbetai Levy Street, Sun, Mon, Fri 10 am-1 pm, Tue-Thu, Sat 10 am-1 pm, 5-8 pm. **Mané Katz Museum**, 89 Yefe Nof, Sun-Thu 10 am-4 pm, Fri/Sat 10 am-1 pm. **National Maritime Museum**, Allenby Road, Sun-Thu 10 am-4 pm, Sat 10 am-1 pm. **Janco-Dada Museum**, En Hod artists' colony, Sun-Thu/Sat 9:30 am-5 pm, Fri 9:30 am-4 pm.

AKKO

Getting There

Buses and trains run along the coast from several towns, e.g. Tel Aviv, Haifa and Nahariyya; only buses from Zefat. There are also any number of *Sheru*ts.

Accommodation

LUXURY: **Palm Beach Club Hotel**, Purple Beach, tel. 04-9815815, best hotel in town.

MODERATE: **The Argaman Motel**, Purple Beach, tel. 04-9916691. **Nes Ammin**, tel. 04-89950000, 5 km north of Akko, a bit off of the Akko-Nahariyya road, a Christian hotel which aims to promote Jewish-Christian understanding.

BUDGET: **Walied's Gate Hostel**, Salah ad Din Street, tel. 04-9910410, at the Land Gate, a bit out of the Old City. **Akko Youth Hostel**, in the Old City near the harbor and lighthouse, Box 1090, tel. 04-9911982. **Paul's Hostel and Souvenir Shop**, opposite the lighthouse at the south end of Hahagana Street, tel. 04-9912857.

Restaurants

Ptolmais and **Abu Christo**, two restaurants by the harbor in the Old City, simple furnishings, excellent fresh fish dishes such as crabs in garlic herb sauce. There are other small restaurants around the harbor as well as a whole series of cook-shops at the entrance to the Old City around the Al Jazzar Mosque.

Tourist Information

35 Weizmann Street, opposite the Al Jazzar Mosque, tel. 04-9911764.

Museums and Sights

Baha'i Gardens, on the road between Akko and Na-

hariyya, gardens open daily 9 am-4 pm, tomb Fri-Mon 9 am-noon. **Crusaders' City**, Old City of Akko, Sun-Thu 8:30 am-5 pm, Fri 8:30 am-2 pm, Sat 8 am-3 pm. **Citadel** with **Museum of the Heroes**, Old City of Akko, Sun-Thu, Sat 9 am-4:30 pm, Fri 9 am-12:30 pm. **Kibbutz Lochamei Hageta'ot** with a documentation center about Jewish resistance in Germany, Poland and Lithuania, on the road between Akko and Nahariyya, shortly before Regba, Sun-Thu 9 am-4 pm, Fri 9 am-1 pm, Sat 10 am-5 pm.

NAHARIYYA

Getting There

Numerous buses and trains run every day from a number of towns along the Mediterranean coast, including Tel Aviv, Haifa and Akko. There are also plenty of *Sheru*ts.

Accommodation

LUXURY: **Carlton Hotel**, 23 Ga'aton Boulevard, tel. 04-9922211, and the **Pallas Athene Hotel**, 28 Ma'apilim Street, tel. 04-9828222, are Nahariyya's two four-star hotels and thus the best places in town.

MODERATE: **Erna**, 29 Jabotinsky Street, tel. 04-9920170, near the beach. **Rosenblatt**, 59 Weizmann Street, tel. 04-9820069. **Hotel Eden**, Mayasdim Street, tel. 04-9923246. **Hotel Frank**, Aliyah Street, tel. 04-9920278. **Kalman Hotel**, 27 Jabotinsky Street, tel. 04-9920355, a little way from the beach.

BUDGET: **Sirtash House**, 22 Jabotinsky Street, tel. 04-9922586. **Motel Arieli**, 1 Jabotinsky Street, tel. 04-9921076.

There are no hostels in Nahariyya, but the tourist office can reserve reasonably-priced private rooms for travelers.

Restaurants

Pinguin, 31 Ga'aton Boulevard, traditional, typically Israeli tavern. **Salaam Bombay**, 17 Jabotinsky Street, Indian food.

The Singapore Chinese Garden, Mayasdim Street/corner Jabotinsky Street, and **The Chinese Inn Restaurant**, 28 Ga'aton Boulevard, are two other places with good Chinese food.

There are a number of small restaurants and bars along the beach promenade.

Sights

Grottoes of Kefar Rosh Ha Niqra: Sun-Thu/Sat 8:30 am-4 pm, Fri 8:30 am-3 pm, 7 km north of Nahariyya.

Hospitals and Pharmacies:

Western Galilee Regional Hospital, tel. 04-9850505. **Szabo Pharmacy**, 3 Ga'aton Boulevard, at the bus station.

Tourist Information

19 Ga'aton Boulevard, tel. 04-9879800.

NORTHERN
GALILEE

MONTFORT / BAR'AM
MT. MERON / ZEFAT
ROSH PINA / TEL HAZOR
HULA / TEL HAY
TEL DAN / BANYAS
NIMROD'S CASTLE / QAZRIN

THE CRUSADER CASTLE
MONTFORT

Proceeding east from Rosh Ha Niqra along the Lebanese border, you will eventually come to a sign on the right indicating the way to Goren National Forest. In this nature reserve near the kibbutz of Elon, oak, laurel, and Judas trees have been planted, and there are also camp sites and picnic areas. After a short stretch of rough road, you reach a parking lot which commands a beautiful view of the Crusader castle Montfort in its spectacular setting. Separated from the nature reserve by a deep valley, the majestic fortress towers atop a mountain ridge, dominating the surrounding landscape.

The entire area is solitary and covered with dense forest. A footpath leads three kilometers to Montfort; allow at least two hours for the walk there and back.

You can also reach the castle from Nahariyya (on the road to Zefat), passing through the village of Mi'ilya. Mi'ilya is inhabited by Christian Arabs; at the center of the village are the ruins of the Crusader fort Chastiau du Roi. Another,

Preceding pages: The Galilean countryside decked out for spring – the land flowers after the heavy rainfall of winter. Left: Open Torah roll.

shorter footpath to Montfort (30 minutes) begins 3 kilometers north of Mi'ilya.

It is immediately obvious that Montfort was only of limited strategic importance, since there was never any important settlement or buildings worthy of defense in its vicinity. Originally, the 12th-century French knight Joscelin de Courtenay built a small fort in the middle of his property, first naming it Mons Fortis and later Montfort. Saladin conquered the stronghold in 1187, but soon recognized its limited usefulness for military purposes and gave it – amazing but true – back to its original owner.

In 1229, the Order of the Teutonic Knights bought the fortress, changed the name to Starkenberg, and began extensive rebuilding work. In 1266, the Egyptian Mameluke sultan Baybars tried in vain to take over the now mighty fortification. Five years later he returned with special siege weapons and a troop of experienced trench experts; the catapults were manned by warriors of outstanding physical size and strength, while the sappers dug a tunnel under the ramparts.

After seven days, the knights were on the brink of nervous exhaustion and began to negotiate. Baybars let them escape to Akko (Acre) with the archive of their order and all of their valuables; they only had to surrender their weapons.

149

Since then, the castle of Montfort has been deserted.

The first person to describe the fortification with the trained eyes of an expert was T. E. Lawrence, better known as Lawrence of Arabia. He had been there early in the century while working on his master's thesis about Crusader castles in the Holy Land; while he was at it, he spied on the local infrastructure of the Turkish occupying forces on behalf of his country's secret service.

In 1926, a team of archaeologists sent by New York's Metropolitan Museum of Art began excavation work. These experts found weapons, armor, coins, some ceramics, and all manner of everyday objects. They are displayed in the Rockefeller Museum in Jerusalem.

In the large and impressive excavation-site, you can see the walls and bulwarks as well as a water mill, the chapter hall, the order chapel, rooms for lodging, and a dungeon.

THE SYNAGOGUE OF BAR'AM AND MOUNT MERON

Back on the road, Route 99 continues on along the Lebanese border to the east. A sign points to **Bar'am**, the well-preserved remains of a synagogue, probably dating from the 2nd or 3rd century. According to Jewish legend, the prophet Obadiah and Esther, the wife of the Persian king Artaxerxes, are buried here.

The Bible story of the queen is especially interesting, since the Book of Esther is set in the period in which Jews were persecuted under the Persian empire. According to this text, the emperor Ahasuerus (presumably Artaxerxes) took Esther, the adopted daughter of Mordecai, as a bride, not knowing that she was a Jew. Her adopted father, Mordecai (who was actually her cousin), was one of the emperor's favorites, since he had once uncovered a conspiracy against him. But Haman, one of the most power-

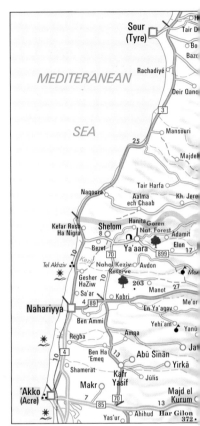

ful men at the court, was hostile to the Jews and hated Mordecai because of his privileged status. Through much plotting and intrigue, this villain was able to convince the king to decree a massacre of the Jews which was set, by drawing lots (*Pur*), for the 14th day of the month Adar.

Esther went to the king and revealed the truth about her Jewish heritage. The king was appalled, but a royal decree is a royal decree, and could not be retracted. With all the wisdom of Solomon, he added the amendment that the Jews should be allowed to defend themselves against their enemies. As a result, the schemer Haman was quickly caught and executed, and Mordecai assumed his of-

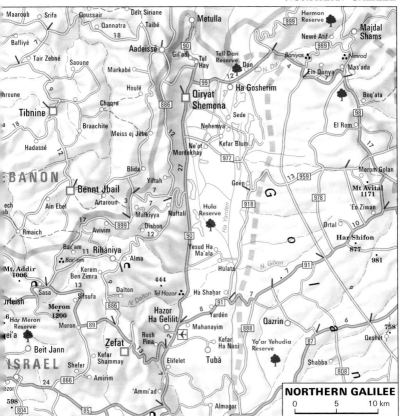

Maarqob · Srifa · Qoussair · Deïr Siriane · Metulla · Hermon Reserve 999 · Newé Atif · Majdal Shams · Qannatra · Taibé 18 · Bafliyé · Aadeissé · Gil'adi 90 · Tell Dan Reserve · Boniyas · Nimrod · Tair Zebné · Saoune · Markabé · Tel Hay 12 · Dan · N. Dan · Ein Qunya · Mas'ada · hroune · Houlé · Ha Gosherim · Qiryat Shemona 886 · Boq'ata · Tibnine · Chagra · Braachite · Sede · Nehemia · El Rom 98 · Meiss ej Jebe · Ne'ot Mordekhay · Kefar Blum 977 · Hadassé · LBANON · Blida · Yiftah 7 · Goën · Merom Golan 13 959 · Benit Jbail · Ain Ebel · Artaroun 3 7 · Malkiyya · Naftali · Hula Reserve 918 · Mt Avital 1171 · 'En Ziwan 978 · Rmaich · Avivim 899 · Dishon 12 · Ortal · Har Shifon 877 · Bar'am 11 Rihaniya · Bar'am · 'Alma · Hulata · N. Gibon 91 · Mt. Addir 1006 · Kerem Ben Zimra 13 · Dalton · 444 · Ha Shahar 91 · Irfeish · Sasa · Sifsufa · N. Dalton · Tel Hazor · 886 · Hazor Ha Gelilit · Yardén 8 · Meron 1200 · Meron 89 · Mahanayim 888 · Qazrin · Ya'ar Yehudia Reserve 87 · Qeshet 758 · 981 · Zefat · Rosh Pina · Kefar Ha Nasi · Shabba 808 · Beit Jann · Kefar Shammay · Elifelet · Tubā · ISRAEL · Shefer · Amirim 866 · 'Ammi'ad · Almagor 598 804 · 85

NORTHERN GALILEE
0   5   10 km

fice. Since that time, Jews have celebrated the joyful Purim festival every year on the 14th of Adar, in February or March.

What remains of the synagogue are parts of the façade and the row of columns from the entrance hall, both relatively well preserved. The most important find from this site is in the Louvre in Paris: a lintel from a door or a window with the inscription, "May peace be with this place and with all of Israel. This beam was made by Jose the Levite. Bless his work. Shalom."

The town of Zefat lies to the southeast of Bar'am; on the way, travellers pass 1,200-meter **Mount Meron**, which is northern Galilee's highest mountain. A road leads behind the SPNI Field Study Center (SPNI = Society for the Protection of Nature in Israel) until just below the summit; the peak itself is occupied by the army. When the weather is clear, the view to the north, far into the Huleh Valley, and to the south to the Sea of Galilee (Genezareth), is breathtaking. The mountain and its foothills are part of the 10,000-hectare Har Meron Nature Park.

ZEFAT

Zefat (or Safed), set at an altitude of more than 800 meters in the midst of magnificent landscapes, is the fourth holy city of the Talmud after Jerusalem, Tiberias, and Hebron in the West Bank,

and was once the spiritual center of Jewish mystics and cabalists. Its altitude and the resulting purity of its air, its completely restored Old City with its narrow, crooked streets, and its large artist's colony all combine to make Zefat a popular summer resort.

History

It was the year 66 A.D. when the historian Flavius Josephus, then barely 30 years old, was appointed commander-in-chief of the troops in Galilee in the Jewish uprising against the Romans. In his book *The Jewish War*, one of the most important sources of information about this period, he mentions that he ordered fortifications to be built around Zefat (which he calls Sepph) as soon as possible.

Above: There is a large population of orthodox Jews in Zefat. Above right: In Ha'Ari Synagogue. Right: The dome of Abouhav Synagogue in Zefat.

At the time of the Crusades, the town was called Safed. Early in the 12th century the Franks erected a first fortress on Hametzuda Hill; over the following years, this edifice was further developed and fortified. This was to protect King Baldwin who, pursued by the Damascene sultan Nur ad Din and his men, was forced to withdraw his men to the safety of Safed.

Ten years later, Amalrich I gave the fortress to the Order of Knights Templar and in 1188 Saladin managed to conquer it; a two-month long siege with heavy stoning from batteries of catapults finally drove the Crusaders from the fortress. The Arabs razed it to its foundations.

In 1240, the Order of Knights Templar initiated an alliance between the Crusaders and the Damascenes against the Egyptian sultan Aiyyub, and were given back the town as a reward. Yet they hesitated to accept it, knowing the high price of rebuilding, and were unwilling to pay for the reconstruction of the fortress. Still, the perilous times demanded safety

precautions, and eventually the castle again became a mighty defense that was even said to be invincible.

This hardly impressed the militarily successful Egyptian Mameluke sultan Baybars, who attacked in 1266. More than 2,000 people had fled to the safety of the fortress, and their provisions ran out three weeks later. The Christians wanted to surrender the castle and Baybars promised them that they could depart uninjured, but he then had all knights killed, as well as anyone who refused to convert to Islam. Many must have stubbornly remained true to their faith since, when cease-fire negotiations were begun a year later, the delegation of Crusaders were horrified to see the fortress walls decorated with human skulls. Even among his own people, Baybars had the reputation of a butcher, and was widely feared for his intimidating tactics.

When in 1492, in Spain, the so-called Catholic king and queen Ferdinand and Isabella formally decreed the banishment of the Jews, it started a wave of emigra-

tion of Spanish Sephardic Jews to Palestine; and many of these went to Zefat. Soon afterwards a school of theology opened there specializing in teaching the mystical practices and interpretations of the *cabala* (a mystical movement especially popular in the Middle Ages and in the modern period). Over the following centuries, the Jewish population of Zefat was severely tested; disastrous earthquakes devastated the city and surrounding countryside several times, the population was thinned by plague and typhus epidemics, or the Druses plundered and marauded among the inhabitants. On the eve of independence, only a few Jews still lived in the Muslim-dominated city. British troops left key strategic positions to the Arabs when they retreated, and it was clear that the few Jews qualified for combat, supported by some Hagana fighters, would not be able to hold their own for long. It was impossible to bring weapons, ammunition, or more soldiers to Zefat; and the situation looked so hopeless that the army actually advised

153

ZEFAT

0   100   200 m

the few Jews to surrender the town. But they were unwilling to give up, so the Israeli military commanders gave the defenders a single Davidka, a self-made, as yet untested howitzer (shell-launcher). In fact, the gun turned out to be so successful that the Jews could force the Arab soldiers to run for their lives, and from then on the inhabitants have spoken of "the miracle of Zefat." Leon Uris describes this event in great details in his novel *Exodus*.

Sights

The best place to start a tour of the city is the park of the **citadel**, where the remains of the Crusader castle, at an altitude of 834 meters, have defied the wind and weather for centuries. On Hativat Yiftah Road, which leads around the park grounds, the **Israel Bible Museum** is lo-

Right: Not only synagogues, but also galleries and crafts shops characterize Zefat's cityscape.

cated in the former house of the Turkish governor; here the Biblically-influenced sculptures, paintings and tapestries of the Jewish-American artist Phillip Ratner can be seen.

Zefat's main road is Yerushalayim Street, which turns into a pedestrian zone at its south end. From this peaceful part of town, steps lead down into the old but well-restored **Jewish quarter**, which is terrifically atmospheric. The first stretch of the narrow street is chock-a-block with souvenir shops and stores purveying religious items; you will soon reach the **Caro Synagogue**, named after Rabbi Yosef Caro, who came to Zefat in 1535 and was for many years the religious leader of the community.

A bit further on, you will find a small open-air theater in the shape of a semi-circle where plays and music are performed in the summer. A rewarding next stop on the left is the **Abouhav Synagogue** in the Sephardic (southern European) area of the Old City. The house of worship dates back to the time of Rabbi Isaak Abouhav, who taught here in the 15th century; it is painted in pale shades of blue, and religious images decorate the walls.

A few meters further down the street, a flight of stairs leads up to the right. Half way up you will find the **Ha'Ari Synagogue**, which marks the center of the Ashkenazy (Eastern European) part of old Zefat. The temple, named after Rabbi Ari, was built several years after his death in 1572; it was destroyed by an earthquake in 1837 but was rebuilt shortly thereafter. Hardly anyone had as much lasting influence in Zefat as Rabbi Ari. His real name was Isaac Luria, but he was called Ari, which means "lion" in Hebrew and is also an acronym for *Adoneinu Rabbeinu Itzhak*, "our master and teacher Isaac". During the few years he taught in Zefat, he wrote an interpretation of the cabala which is still used today. The Ha'Ari Synagogue is painted in light

olors, and the walls are only sparsely decorated.

The steps continue up further to Kikar Hameginim, the center of the Old City, its narrow streets paved with small, round tones. Its name, which means Square of the Defender, derives from a house on the quare where a commando outpost was tationed during the fighting in 1948. The group organized the neighborhood defense system for the entire Jewish quarter.

Today, you can take a relaxing break in the small restaurant-café Hakikar, have a cup of tea or bite to eat. Time, in short, has smoothed over all but the memories of the Jewish population's desperate situation in 1948.

If you follow the little street to the right out of Kikar Hameginim, you will soon reach the **Lubabinson Chabad House**, where you can learn more about Jewish customs in a study center or from the audio-visual show. Other noteworthy stops here include an art exhibition, as well as a book store.

Yerushalayim Street, Zefat's main street, eventually turns into a pedestrian zone and here – in the former Arab section of town – an **artists' colony** has grown up. The colony was founded in 1951 by six creative people who wanted to help breathe new life into the badly destroyed city. The pleasant climate and beautiful landscapes and countryside around Zefat soon attracted more painters, sculptors, and potters so that, after several years, as many as fifty artists lived and worked here. If you would like to get an overview of the artistic activity in the town, first peruse at your leisure the **General Exhibition**, which displays paintings, watercolors, paintings on silk, and sculptures. The show is housed in a former mosque.

At the southern end of the artists' quarter, the **Museum of Printing** is a reminder of the fact that the cradle of the book-printing industry was in Zefat. The first printing press was set up here in 1576, and it printed the first book in Hebrew one year later. Among other things, you

155

can see the first newspaper printed in Palestine, which dates from 1863.

ROSH PINA

Going northeast from Zefat, it is only a few kilometers to the small town of Rosh Pina, which was settled by Jews from Zefat in 1878. However, since they had little knowledge of agriculture and few tools, these settlers deserted the place soon after.

In 1882, Rumanian Jews arrived and named their new home Rosh Pina. Meaning "cornerstone," this name derives from Psalm 118, which says: "the stone which the builders refused has become the headstone of the corner." With the advice and financial support of Baron Edmund de Rothschild, the inhabitants began to raise silkworms in addition to cultivating cereals and tobacco; the

Above: The lovely and venerable city walls of Old Rosh Pina. Right: The excavations at Tel Hazor.

baron even donated the necessary mulberry trees. Production of the luxurious cloth started off well, but the settlers had little business sense and no effective marketing concepts. They were, therefore unable to sell enough silk, and one family after another left the settlement which had been founded with so much joy and hope.

Old Rosh Pina, the older part of town (follow the sign for the youth hostel), still looks very much as it did when it was founded toward the end of the 19th century. The street is paved with small round stones, a village bar is located at the town center, and a terraced cemetery stretches along the hillside.

The Schwartz Hotel, built in 1890 – at which time it was the first and only lodging available in Northern Galilee – still recalls some of the atmosphere of those early settlement years. Today, the old part of Rosh Pina is inhabited by about 60 artists whose work can be seen – and of course also purchased – at a gallery on Harishonim Street.

TEL HAZOR

About 8 kilometers north of Rosh Pina along Route 90 as you go toward Qiryat Shemona, the large excavation site Tel Hazor ("Hazor" means "farmstead") extends to the left of the road. For several centuries this was an important settlement. It was founded along the busy caravan route from Egypt to Mesopotamia via Palestine, a route known to the Romans as the Via Maris, in the early Bronze Age, around 2500 B.C.

The first written record of the settlement appears in old Egyptian texts dating from 1800 B.C., and from then on the name Hazor can be found regularly in various chronicles, often in association with the tin trade through which the city's inhabitants prospered. By around 1600 B.C., a lot of people wanted a piece of the city's wealth; the local population soared, and the lower plateau was also gradually settled.

In around 1200, a battle broke out at Merom, a lake north of the town, be-tween the Israelites, led by Joshua, and the Canaanites, led by Jabin, the king of Hazor. As the Bible recounts, the Israelites were victorious, and proceeded to massacre the population with typical Old Testament brutality. They plundered wherever they could and drove the stolen livestock out of the town. It was the end of Hazor.

The site remained uninhabited for a long time, until in the 9th century Solomon, and the kings Omri and Ahab after him, fortified the upper town once again. In 732 B.C., Hazor was again attacked, this time by the Assyrian ruler Tiglath-Pileser III and his troops, who took the surviving inhabitants back into their own empire as slaves.

Excavation projects have uncovered a total of 21 distinct layers of settlement. Corresponding to the town's original layout, the excavation site is divided into a narrow upper town and a lower town stretching to the north and east. In the upper town, you can still see massive stone casements and remains of buildings

157

as well as fragments of the citadel built by Ahab. Also dating from the time of Ahab (9th century B.C.) is the water supply system, which you can explore by descending a flight of stairs. A tripartite Canaanite temple was uncovered in the lower town. The various artifacts and finds that have been excavated here can be seen in the Israel Museum in Jerusalem and in the Hazor Museum, which is located in the nearby kibbutz of Ayelet Hashachar.

HULA NATURE RESERVE

Nine kilometers farther north on Route 90 towards Qiryat Shemona, a red sign directs you eastward to the **Hula Nature Reserve**, one of the last remaining marshlands in the country. When, at the beginning of the century, the newly immigrated Jews wanted to drain the area,

Above and right: Flocks of birds and extensive thickets of papyrus are typical features of the Hula Nature Reserve.

the British refused their request in orde to limit their arable areas as much a possible.

After independence, the Israelis did g ahead with draining the area in the 1950 But before they had completed the pr ject, they realized the significance of th ecosystem. Twice a year, thousands c migrating birds stop off here for a rest c their seasonal flight between Europe an Africa. Storks, pelicans, geese, duck herons, cormorants, ibises and man other exotic birds hatch their young in th refuge; insects that have already died ou in other regions buzz busily here; and th reserve's flora also includes man species of plants that are growing in creasingly rare in other parts of th world, such as large papyrus thicket There is plenty of other life as well: wate buffalo, beavers, wild boar, and wildca are also residents of the reserve, whic has a size of 323 hectares. A Visitors Center offers detailed information abou the national park and its plant and anima life.

TEL HAY

North of Qiryat Shemona is **Tel Hay**, "Hill of Life," where Israel's hero Josef Trumpeldor is buried. Inspired by the ideals of Zionism, Trumpeldor emigrated to Palestine from Russia in 1912 at the age of 32. Since he had served in the Czar's army, he entered a Jewish regiment of the British army when World War I broke out, and fought in the notorious battle of Gallipoli.

After the end of the war, he settled in the kibbutz Tel Hay. Back in those days, bands of Bedouins and Arabs regularly attacked the small settlement in the remote northern Hula Valley; Tel Hay and Metulla had already been preyed upon several times. Trumpeldor developed a defense strategy which was effective for some time. In 1920, he and seven other fighters in the kibbutz were murdered. Today, a museum in the kibbutz honors his memory as well as presenting more information about the history of settlement in the region.

Nearby is the Qiryat Shemona, in English "the town of the eight," named after Trumpeldor and his seven slain comrades.

TEL DAN NATURE RESERVE

From Qiryat Shemona, follow Route 99 to the east; 10 kilometers down the road you will come to Tel Dan Nature Reserve, a unique landscape of extraordinary beauty.

Ancient Egyptian texts already make mention of the Canaanite town Lais (given in the Bible as both Leshem and Laish), which was conquered by the Israeli tribe of the Danites several centuries later. Laish's citizens, a peaceful and gentle people, were completely wiped out by the warlike Israelites, who also burned down the town. Later, they rebuilt it and named the new settlement after the founder of their tribe, Dan.

When Jeroboam became king of the northern state after the division of the kingdom of Israel, he had a golden calf

159

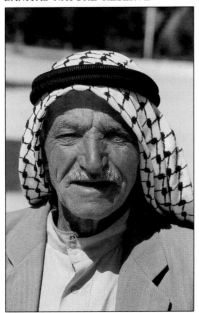

set up in the temples of Beth El and Dan as a symbol of God. The town finally met its end when the Assyrians invaded in 732 B.C.

In the shade of high ash, tabor oak, sycamore, pistachio, and laurel trees, you can walk along a churning, babbling brook, past streams and ponds; with a little luck you might spot a beaver. The Dan river is the largest of the three rivers that feed the Jordan, and also gave the latter river its name: "Jordan" means simply "comes from Dan."

Excavation work has been going on at Tel Dan since 1966. By now, archaeologists have uncovered the massive earth wall which once surrounded the town of Laish, a mighty town gate, the remains of a temple and other buildings, a paved road, and a large, paved plateau-like mound that must have been the place of

Above: Everywhere you go, you will encounter men wearing the traditional keffiyeh. Right: Remains of a fourth-century synagogue in Qazrin.

worship for the town – and was, perhaps the spot where the golden calf once stood.

The nearby kibbutz of Dan has a natural history museum to offer the visitor.

BANIYAS NATURE RESERVE

This Arab name is a bowdlerized derivative of the name *Paneas*, for that was the original name of the town here, which was dedicated to the Greek god Pan. Pan an Arcadian deity, was the son of Hermes and a nymph, and was worshiped as the patron of shepherds and their flock (which he was able to fill with *"panicked fear"* by playing his flute music). He is usually represented as half man, half goat.

Philippus, the son of Herod, named the town Caesarea Philippa, and it was here that Jesus spoke the fateful words to Simon Barjona: "And I say this to you Thou art Peter (*petrus*, in Latin, mean *the rock*); and upon this rock I will build my church, and the gates of Hell shall no prevail against it. And I will give unto thee the keys of the kingdom of Heaven and whatsoever thou shalt bind on earth shall be bound in Heaven: and what soever thou shalt loose on earth shall be loosed in Heaven" (Matthew 16:18-19) With these words, the institution of the papacy was established, and some time later Simon, now Peter, was the first to hold that office.

The main attraction of this enchanting region is the 10-meter Baniyas Waterfall from this point, signs point the way along a looping path that takes you beneath shade-giving trees to the Baniyas Spring and back.

NIMROD'S CASTLE

From Baniyas, the road leads through the Israeli-occupied Golan Heights to the vast castle complex of **Qala'at Nimrod** From up here, you can look out far over

he fertile Hula Valley. Even from a considerable distance, you can make out the mighty ramparts of this once strategically important citadel. The road up to it climbs steeply, with many hairpin bends. If you believe the legend, Nimrod – according to the Bible, "a mighty hunter before the Lord" (Genesis 10:9) and a great-grandson of Noah – was the first to build a fortress here. During the following millennia, it guarded the important caravan route from Damascus to the Mediterranean. More certain is that the Arab group of the Hashashin had one of their bases at the fortress at the beginning of the 12th century. Back then, this sect, a group which had developed from Shiite Ismaelites, was notorious and feared for committing politically-motivated murders while high on hashish; it is from the Hashashins – also called Assassines – that the English words *assassin* and *assassination* derive.

When the sultan of Damascus took action against the murderous sect members, they turned over their fortress to the Crusaders so that the Damascenes could not take it. But a few years later, the Arabs conquered the fort nonetheless. The Franks recaptured it some time after, and finally, in 1164, it was conquered again by the Saracens. At the beginning of the 13th century, the whole complex was destroyed right down to its foundations, to prevent the approaching forces of the Fifth Crusade from being able to take shelter in it.

In 1260, the Egyptian Mameluke sultan Baybars had Qala'at Nimrod rebuilt. With the end of the Crusades, however, the citadel lost its importance, and gradually, over the course of the centuries, it fell into disrepair and finally into ruin. This was one of the many sites the young T. E. Lawrence studied when researching his thesis on the Crusader fortresses.

The region around the castle is rough, rugged, but nevertheless impressive terrain. Characteristic of the area are steep slopes, deep valleys, and stony ridges sprinkled with only a sparse covering of vegetation.

QAZRIN

A spectacular stretch of road leads southwards from Nimrod's Castle, winding along the craggy slopes, and sometimes actually carved into the mountainside. Again and again, you are presented with extensive views out over the Hula Valley in the distance.

Continue on to the south towards the town of **Qazrin**, the administrative capital of the Israeli-occupied Golan Heights. The small town of 3,000 inhabitants was founded in 1977 and got its name from a nearby Jewish settlement from the 2nd century.

Ancient Qazrin Park contains the remains of this settlement; the daily life of its former inhabitants is vividly represented in a reconstructed house's furnishings. Objects found at this site can be seen at the **Golan Archaeological Museum** in Qazrin, which is also instructive about the history of the ancient town Gamla, known in Israel as "the Masada of the North." Remains of buildings, a synagogue, and a water supply system have been excavated there.

During the Jewish uprising against the Romans, a group of Jews entrenched themselves in Gamla (20 kilometers southeast of Qazrin) in a desperate fight for their lives. The Romans attacked the town in the year 67.

In *The Jewish War*, the Roman chronicler Flavius Josephus reported how tragically the affair ended for the defenders: "Trapped on every side, most of the men saw no remaining chance to save themselves and hurled their children, their wives, and finally themselves into the gorge."

The Golan Heighs Winery is to be found in Qazrin's industrial park; the wines produced here have won several gold medals at international exhibitions. By calling in advance (tel. 06-6961646), one can take a tour of the highly modern facility and enjoy some wine sampling.

ZEFAT

Getting There
Buses run several times a day from Tel Aviv, Akko Jerusalem, Haifa and Tiberias, and there is also a *Sherut* service.

Accommodation
LUXURY: **Rimonim Hotel**, Artist's Quarter, tel. 06 6994666, Zefat's best hotel, many rooms with grea views of the mountains of northern Galilee. Known fo its good restaurant with reasonable prices. **Ron** Chativach Yiftach, by Metzuda Park, tel. 06-6972590 **Rimonim Hotel**, Kiryat Omanimm, 069-920666, in a suburb of Zefat, known for its good and reasonably priced restaurant.
MODERATE: **Hotel Hadar**, Ridbatz Street, on Yeru shalayim Street, near the bus station, tel. 06-6920066 **Bet Nathan**, Yerushalayim Street, tel. 06-6920121.
BUDGET: **Bet Binyamin Youth Hostel**, at the Ama Trade School in the south of Zefat.
Ascent Institute of Zefat, 2 Ha'ari Street, tel. 06 6921364; this hostel is open only to Jewish travelers The tourist office arranges private accommodations.

Restaurants
Bat Ya'ar, north of Zefat in the Birya Forest, path i marked, tel. 06-6921788; rustic steakhouse with far tastic view over the Hula Valley as far as Hermor horse farm; day trips in the area possible. **Hamifgash** 75 Yerushalayim Street, tel. 06-6920510, popular res taurant with a large selection of Israeli wine (*Hami gash* means "meeting place").
Golden Mountain Cheese, Hameginim Sq., in the ol part of town, tel. 051-567504, home-made goat cheese, sandwiches, salads, tea and coffee.
Pinati, 81 Yerushalayim Street, tel. 06-6920855, ha won awards for its health-food menus; offers Italia cuisine with an Eastern European-Oriental twist.

Museums and Sights
General Exhibition of the Artists' Quarter of Zefa Sun-Fri 9 am-6 pm, Sat 10 am-2 pm.
Israel Bible Museum, Chativat Yiftach Road, Marc to September Sun-Thu 10 am-6 pm, Sat 10 am-2 pm October/November Sat-Thu 10 am-2 pm, Dec. Sun Thu 10 am-2 pm.
Museum of Printing, in the artists' quarter of Zefa Sun-Thu 10 am-noon, 4-6 pm, Fri/Sat 10 am-noon.

Hospital
Rivka Ziv General Hospital, Harambam Road, tel 06-6978811.

Tourist Information
50 Yerushalayim Street, tel. 06-6927485.

HULA VALLEY AND ENVIRONS

Getting There

Buses run several times a day from Zefat through the Hula Valley toward Qiryat Shemona. Buses to the Tel Dan Nature Reserve and the Baniyas Nature Reserve as well as Nimrod's Castle run several times a day from Qiryat Shemona through the Golan heights to Qazrin.

Accommodation

LUXURY: **Ayelet Hashachar Kibbuz Guest House**, Ayelet Hashachar Kibbutz at Tell Hazor, Mobile Post Hevel Korazim 12200, tel. 06-6868611, the first Israeli kibbutz to open a hotel; kibbutz tours, jeep and horseback tours of the area; an exceptionally nice place; the kibbutz is Israel's leading producer of honey.

Sea View Hotel and Health Farm, Rosh Pina, Box 37, tel. 06-6999666, hotel with adjacent health and beauty farm and a notably friendly atmosphere.

Amirim Holiday Village, Moshav Amirim, on Mount Meron, Mobile Post Carmiel 20115, tel. 06-6989571 (9 am-1 pm). The 300 members of the Moshav are vegetarians without exception, propagating and living out their back-to-nature philosophy. If you want to change your lifestyle or philosophy – at least temporarily – you have come to the right place.

Hagoshrim Kibbutz Hotel, east of Qiryat Shemona on Route 99, Upper Galilee 12225, tel. 06-6816000, the gentle Hermon River flows through this kibbutz, which has a friendly atmosphere and charming flair.

Kefar Blum Guest House, north of Route 977, near Qiryat Shemona, Upper Galilee 12150, tel. 06-6836611. One specialty of a stay at the kibbutz Kefar Blum are kayak trips on the River Jordan. From the end of July to early August, the kibbutz holds a chamber music festival.

Vered Hagalil, on Route 90 near Korazim, Mobile Post Korazim 12385, tel. 06-6935785, offers accommodation in little houses made of stone and wood, has beautiful views of the Sea of Galilee and a friendly atmosphere.

MODERATE: **Joseph's Well**, in the **Kibbutz Amiad**, near Korazim, Mobile Post Korazim 12335, tel. 06-933829; this kibbutz bottles wine.

Village Inn, in the kibbutz **Kefar Hanassi**, near Korazim near the Mahanayim airport east of Rosh Pina, Mobile Post Korazim, tel. 06-6914870. Visitors here can participate in real kibbutz life, taking meals in the large communal dining room.

Kibbutz Kefar Gil'adi Guesthouse, 1 kilometer north of Tel Hay on the road to Metulla, Upper Galilee 12210, tel. 06-6900000, nice views of the Hula Valley, the kibbutz has a museum documenting the history of settlement in the region and the history of Jewish volunteer troops in the British Army in World War I.

BUDGET: **Nature Friends Youth Hostel**, in the old section of Rosh Pina, tel. 06-6937086.

Youth Hostel Tel Hay, Tel Hay, on Route 90 from Qiryat Shemona north to Metulla, tel. 06-6940043.

Restaurants

Baron's Stables, Ha'elyon Street, Rosh Pina, tel. 06-6930666, located in the former stables of Baron Rothschild, bar with adjacent restaurant and German beer on tap.

Achuzat Shulamit, in the old part of Rosh Pina, tel. 06-6931495, serves special cuisine in a nostalgic atmosphere.

Rafa's, in the heart of the old city of Rosh Pina, tel. 06-6936192, gourmet cooking.

Cowboy's Restaurant, Kibbutz Merom Golan, tel. 06-6960206, on the Golan Heights, west of the Syrian city of Quneitra; good steaks in a cowboy atmosphere.

Dag al Hadan, on Route 99, near Qiryat Shemona, opposite the kibbutz Hagoshrim, specializes in trout.

Ein Camonim, on Route 85, 4 km west of the Kadarim Junction, south of Zefat, tel. 06-6989894, good, no-frills food with excellent goats cheese, fresh-baked bread, a wide range of vegetables and local wine; you can buy the cheese in the adjacent shop.

Farmyard Restaurant, Dubrovim Farm, Yesod Hama'ala, near the entrance to Hula Nature Reserve, tel. 06-6934495, one of the best restaurants in Israel, and thus not exactly cheap.

Hagome, on the west side of Route 90 near Rosh Pina, opposite a police station, tel. 06-936250, very good Oriental food.

Hospital

Rivka Ziv General Hospital, Zefat, Harambam Road, tel. 06-6978811.

Tourist Information

All of the kibbutz accommodations listed here are as well provided with information for visitors as any of the official tourist offices, and can also perform the same services, such as reservations or guided tours.

Sights and Museums

TEL HAY: Museum, open Sun-Thu 8 am-4 pm, Fri 8 am-1 pm, Sat 8 am-2 pm.

TEL HAZOR: Excavation site, open daily 8 am-4 pm.

QUALA'AT NIMROD: Nimrod's Castle, April to September Sat-Thu 8 am-5 pm, Fri 8 am-4 pm, March Sat-Thu 8 am-4 pm, Fri 8 am-3 pm.

QAZRIN: Golan Archaeological Museum, open Sun-Thu 8 am-4 pm, Fri 8 am-1 pm, Sat 10 am-4 pm.

AROUND THE SEA OF GALILEE

CAPERNAUM / TIBERIAS
BELVOIR / BET SHEAN
MEGIDDO / BET SHE'ARIM
NAZARETH / CANAAN
MOUNT TABOR

THE SEA OF GALILEE

The Sea of Galilee is 21 kilometers long and 13 kilometers wide at its widest point. Its Hebrew name, Yam Kinneret, Lake Kinneret, comes from a Canaanite town of the same name which was once located on its northern shore. The Arabs call it Ein Allah, the "eye" (or "the source") of God.

Yam Kinneret, at 209 meters below sea level, is the lowest-lying lake in the world after the Dead Sea.

A subtropical climate characterizes the region; winters are very mild and summers are very hot, with temperatures normally reaching and rising above 35° C. While pilgrims in the last century were still complaining that the land around the lake was an absolute desert and that the surrounding mountains looked bare and hostile, this image has changed radically today. Since there is no lack of water, the land around the lake is extremely fertile, and the hillsides are no longer mere patches of mountainous desert, but, thanks to irrigation, have become green and produce a wealth of agricultural products.

Preceding pages: Sunset over the Sea of Galilee. Left: Patient mules are an invaluable help to the region's small farmers and landowners.

Some crops can even be harvested several times a year. But this is not the first time this land has been so productive: Flavius Josephus reported on the various produce and crops that thrived here 2,000 years ago.

CAPERNAUM

The biblical town of Capernaum stands at the northern end of the lake; today it is again called Kefar Nahum, the village of Nahum, as it was at the time of Jesus. The settlement was probably founded around 200 B.C. By the time of the New Testament, it had already grown to a considerable size, extending along the whole northern shore of the lake; its inhabitants lived by fishing.

Since Jesus was unable to attract a group of followers in his home town, he traveled to Capernaum. Here he performed a series of miracles: he cured Peter's mother-in-law of a fever, brought the dead child of the synagogue leader Jairus back to life, cured a leper and a man sick with palsy, exorcised an unclean spirit from a man in the synagogue, and restored the withered hand of another man until it was as healthy and whole as the other one.

Jesus gave one of his most famous sermons in the synagogue of Capernaum,

167

figs. **St. Peter's Church** is an octagonal chapel with a semicircular apse. It dominates a group of humble houses, some dating from as far back as the 1st century B.C. One of the houses, where the names Jesus and Peter can be seen many times in the crumbling plaster, is supposed to have been the dwelling of Peter. The church was built over this house in about 450 A.D. In it, there is a magnificent floor mosaic of a peacock displaying its colorful tail.

You can also visit the ruins of the most beautiful synagogue in the Holy Land, which was constructed of white, cut limestones. A narthex leads to the main hall in which the nave is flanked by two aisles with columns crowned by beautifully ornamented capitals. Stonework embellishments include grapes and Jewish symbols such as the seven-armed menorah and the star of David.

On the Western Shore of the Sea of Galilee

From Kefar Nahum, continue along the lakeside towards the south and to the summit of the **Mount of the Beatitudes**. At its peak, a church built in the 1930s by an Italian missionary group towers high above the Sea of Galilee. The harmonious, octagonal house of worship crowned with a high dome is built of local basalt. It is ringed by a colonnade of white Nazareth stone and Roman volcanic limestone. Inscribed on the walls of the octagon is the Latin text of the famous Sermon on the Mount, which Jesus is said to have given here: "Blessed are the poor in spirit: for theirs is the kingdom of heaven. Blessed are they that mourn: for they shall be comforted. Blessed are the meek: for they shall inherit the earth. Blessed are they which do hunger and thirst for righteousness: for they shall be filled. Blessed are the merciful: for they shall obtain mercy. Blessed are the pure in heart: for they shall see

but here, too, he failed to achieve really large-scale success – the town's inhabitants were not to be inspired to a life of faith.

After the two rebellions against Rome, Capernaum continued to grow, and many Jews from Jerusalem fled and settled here. A new synagogue was built in the town in the 4th century. When the Arabs conquered the town in the 7th century, though, Capernaum quickly lost its importance and became little more than a sleepy fishing village.

Archaeologists have excavated remains of the synagogue and the chapel over Peter's house, as well as houses from Jesus' time. The excavation site is surrounded by an attractive park. The fragments of columns and building stones that lie around are decorated with delicate stonework patterns: leaves, grape vines and palm branches. Reliefs show eagles, stars of David, grapes and

Above: In the ruins of the Holy Land's oldest synagogue at Capernaum.

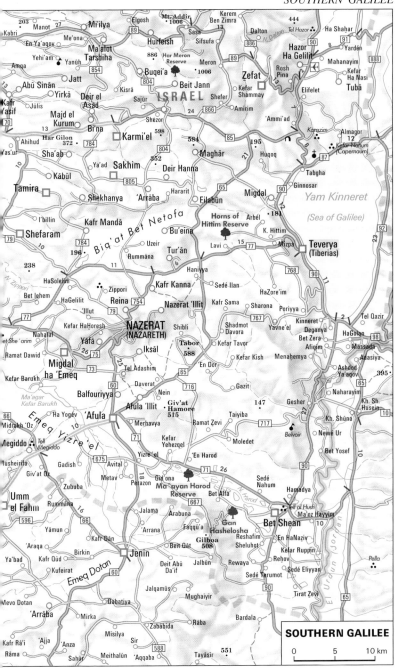

SOUTHERN GALILEE

0   5   10 km

169

God. Blessed are the peacemakers: for they shall be called the children of God. Blessed are they which are persecuted for righteousness' sake: for theirs is the kingdom of Heaven."

In the dome you can read the last Beatitude: "Blessed are ye, when men shall revile you, and persecute you, and shall say all manner of evil against you falsely, for my sake. Rejoice, and be exceeding glad: for great is your reward in heaven: for so persecuted they the prophets which were before you" (Matthew 5, 3-12).

The church is surrounded by a delightful garden with palms and exotic, sweet-smelling plants. Here you are sure to find a shady spot from where you can peacefully enjoy one of the most beautiful views of the Sea of Galilee, especially in the late afternoon, when the water takes

Above: Jesus is said to have given the Sermon on the Mount here, atop the Mount of Beatitudes. Right: Fishermen on the Sea of Galilee.

on a deep blue tone, the lakeside plantations are intensely green, and the Golan Heights on the eastern shore are veiled in a shimmering wave of heat.

After a short drive along the shore of Yam Kinneret, you will see a small outcropping of rock in the water bearing the Church of the Appearance of the Resurrected, more commonly known as the **Church of the Primacy of St. Peter** Here Jesus, resurrected from the tomb appeared to his disciples who had in vain tried to catch fish all night in the Sea of Galilee, and urged them to try one more time. When they succeeded, they realized that they were indeed in the presence of their resurrected Lord.

As they then sat down together for a meal, Jesus then said three times to Peter "Feed my sheep" (John 21:1-17). In those days, a statement repeated three times before witnesses meant the formal conveying of a legal title; Jesus had therefore, formally charged Peter with the leadership of his church. Over the centuries, a total of six churches would

be erected at this spot, each one centered around the *Mensa Domini*, the table at which Jesus and his disciples were said to have sat. The present church is a severe, single-aisled structure made of black basalt, which the Franciscans constructed in the 1930s.

A short distance away is the town of Tabgha. Tabgha is a derivative of the Greek word Heptapegon, which means "Seven Springs," the Crusaders named the place Septem Fontes, and in Hebrew it is called En Sheva, both names also with the same meaning as the Greek. Here the **Church of the Multiplication of the Loaves and Fishes** recalls another of Jesus' miracles: when he transformed five barley loaves and two fish into enough food to satisfy 5,000 hungry people who had come to hear him preach.

The actual town where the miracle of the loaves and fishes was supposed to have happened was on the eastern shore of the Sea of Galilee; at some point, however, the journey to this town seemed to be too far for the pilgrims and the solitary location too dangerous, and so the site of the miracle was simply changed to the settled western shore – so much for the authenticity of Bible story settings in the Holy Land.

The first church was constructed here in the middle of the fourth century, but it soon fell victim to an earthquake. A new house of worship was quickly built but met the same fate.

The basilica you see today is of fairly recent vintage: built in Byzantine style based on designs by an architect from Cologne, it was consecrated in 1981. It stands over the Egyptian-inspired floor mosaics of the structure which had stood there before, mosaics which are justly praised as the most beautiful in the entire country; particularly impressive is the mosaic depicting water birds, with storks, herons, geese, ducks, and swans fluttering around a marsh landscape. The mosaic in front of the altar shows the bread basket with two fish.

Going south from Tabgha, you will soon reach the kibbutz of Ginosar. Here,

171

you should make sure to visit the **Bet Allon Museum**. It honors the memory of Yigal Allon (1918-1980), who fought in the Haganah in the 1940s and served in the 1970s as foreign secretary to Golda Meir and Yitzhak Rabin.

The star attraction in the exhibition building is a 2,000 year old fishing boat that was discovered in the silt of the Sea of Galilee in 1986. To keep it from falling to pieces, the boat was preserved in a chemical solution for over 10 years. It is presently waiting in a tub while an exhibition room is being constructed for it. An interesting film shows how archaeologists dug up the boat. Further exhibitions in Bet Allon familiarize the visitor with the natural history of the area as well as with the story of its settlement; in the top floor exhibit, photos tell about the life of Yigal Allon, the pride of the kibbutz.

Above: 5th-century floor mosaic in the new Church of the Multiplication of Loaves and Fishes. Right: "Salome with the Head of John the Baptist," Titian, 1515.

TIBERIAS

In around the year 18, Herodes Antipas, the son of Herod the Great, named his newly-founded town Tiberias, thereby honoring his Roman overlord, the Roman emperor Tiberias. The choice of location, however, was unfortunate. To construct the town, Antipas had had a cemetery levelled and houses built over it; for Jews, this meant that the place was impure, and when Herodes moved his residence to the new town of Tiberias, he had a hard time finding people to populate it.

Flavius Josephus reports: "Tiberias was, moreover, inhabited by a mixture of peoples, including many Galileans as well as new arrivals who were forced to settle there even though many of them were members of the upper class. But beggars, too, were gathered from around the country, as well as many individuals who may not even have been free men; and all of these people were given housing here and received certain privileges.

To keep them bound to the city, Herod had houses built for them and lands awarded to them, as he was well aware that, according to Jewish law, they should not even have been living there" *Jewish Antiquities* XVIII, 2, 3).

In around the year 32, Antipas separated from his wife, the daughter of a Nabatean ruler from Petra (today in Jordan), in order to marry his sister-in-law, Herodias. Indignation was voiced throughout the country, and John the Baptist publicly denounced him; in response, Antipas had him arrested. Herodias demanded that he be put to death, but her husband did not dare to execute John, who was well-known throughout the country. One day Salome, Herodias' daughter, danced at the court, and Antipas was so infatuated with her that he swore to fulfill her every wish. The girl asked her mother for advice. Herodias saw the chance for revenge and told her daughter that she should demand that Antipas give her the head of John the Baptist upon a silver platter. According to his own overly hasty oath, Antipas had no choice, and so John was beheaded.

But the Nabatean king Aretas – the father of the first, rejected wife of Herod - was not prepared to tolerate such an affront and marched his army to Tiberias. Antipas had the Romans to thank for the fact that his former father-in-law did not bring his life to an untimely end. Several years later, Caligula banished disrespectful Herod Antipas and his wife to Gaul. Tiberias was granted first to his brother-in-law Agrippa I, and then to his son, Agrippa II.

In the 2nd century, Rabbi Simion Bar Zochi came to the hot springs to find relief from his rheumatism. When he indeed started to feel better after lengthy treatment, he declared the town "pure" and from then on, even Jews faithful to their laws of purity could settle there. A short time later the Sanhedrin, the high council of Jews, came to Tiberias, and

soon a yeshiva, a school of Jewish civil and religious law, opened its doors. It was in this period that the Mishnah, a collection of laws, was compiled, as well as the Gemara – a commentary on the Mishnah – a century later; the two together comprise the Talmud. The first churches started to appear around the fourth century, and Tiberias became the seat of a bishopric. In 636, the Arab army came and conquered the spiritual-religious Jewish center without a fight. In 749 and 1033, severe earthquakes almost completely destroyed the town; each time reconstruction work was begun immediately. During the time of the First Crusade, Tiberias changed hands several times between the Franks and the Arabs. In the 16th century, Jews from Portugal settled there; two hundred years later, a large group of Jewish immigrants from Eastern Europe arrived. Ibrahim Pasha, the Egyptian viceroy during the last century, took a liking to the hot springs and developed Tiberias into a luxurious bathing resort.

Today the town, with a population of 35,000, is still a resort, but it can hardly be called luxurious any more, since mass tourism has meanwhile taken over. Tiberias is for the most part a modern, lively, and very populated vacation spot which offers a wide variety of leisure activities and diversions. Cafés and restaurants on the lovely lakeside promenade are inviting places to unwind and take in the view out over the water. The specialty of the local restaurants is a kind of perch known locally as "Peter's Fish." Along the promenade there are also piers for excursion steamboats and a yacht marina. You can rent boats, go water-skiing, or simply swim and sunbathe in the time-honored vacation tradition.

On the shore, built on the location of an old Crusaders' church, you will find the Franciscan church and monastery of **St. Peter** with its harmonious cloisters.

Above: St. Peter's fish, the regional delicacy. Right: A vacationer's paradise – the Sea of Galilee.

The apse, parts of which still stem from the original Crusader edifice, is shaped like a fishing boat.

South of the monastery is the **Town Museum**, housed in a mosque built in around 1880. After a recent course of renovation, objects excavated in and around Tiberias are once again on display here. At the northern edge of the Old City stand the remains of a Crusader castle into which an art center and a restaurant have been skillfully integrated.

Several times daily in the large cement buildings at the marina, *The Galilee Experience*, a half-hour audiovisual show introduces visitors to the history of the southern Galilee region. Parts of the medieval town wall are still standing on Habanim Street, and behind the Scottish Centre in Dona Gracia Street and Gedud Barak Street you can see defensive structures from the time of the Crusades. Also of great cultural significance is the **Tomb of Moses Maimonides** (Moishe Ben Maimon, 1135-1204) in Ben Zakka Street. This famous philosopher and doctor was born in Cordoba, Spain. In 114 his parents fled with him and his siblings to Fez, Morocco, escaping from the Spanish pogroms against the Jews. At the age of 30 he traveled to Cairo where, thanks to his erudition, he soon became the leader of the Egyptian Jews. Maimonides tried to systematize Jewish religious traditions according to Aristotelian philosophy; at the same time, he studied the human body and its illnesses and was eventually appointed the personal physician of the sultan Saladin. Maimonides often recommended the mineral-rich waters of Tiberias for their healing powers; in fact, he was so enthusiastic about the hot springs that he asked to be buried near them – a wish which was accordingly, granted.

High on the mountainside in the Derech Hagevura, you can find the **Tomb of Rabbi Akiva**, the spiritual leader of the Bar Kochba rebellion

gainst the Romans which broke out in
ne year 137; after his capture, Akiva was
xecuted by Roman legionnaires.

Hammat Tiberias

Located just at the southern edge of
iberias are the hot springs of **Hammat
'iberias**, where highly concentrated
mineral water bubbles out of the ground
at a temperature of 60° C. Through cracks
in the earth's crust at the so-called Pales-
nian Fault, water heats as it passes
through fiery magma and rises to the sur-
ace. But there is also a somewhat less
rosaic explanation of how these springs
ame to be. One day, so the story goes,
Solomon wanted to take a hot bath at this
pot; discovering that the region under-
round here was inhabited by devils, he
forced them, with his power, to heat the
pring water. The restful soak so pleased
he great king that he continued to de-
and the services of the little devils, and
even made provisions for baths in his
fterlife: he simply made the hot water

spirits deaf. To this day, they have not
heard of his passing on and, ever in fear,
they are still hard at work, as we can see.

The healing power of the water, which
is particularly effective against rheumatic
diseases, was already well-known in Biblical times. Today, two different spots for
bathing are available: to the right of the
road, the spa "Tiberias Hot Springs" specializes in the treatment of skin disorders;
on the lake to the left is the modern complex of the "Young Tiberias Hot
Springs," which is open to the general
public. You really should not pass up the
pleasure of this unique bathing experience: a large indoor pool and an outdoor
pool with a terrace for sunbathing and a
spectacular view are soothing for both
body and soul.

In Hammat Tiberias, archaeologists
have unearthed the remains of a **synagogue** that was probably destroyed by an
earthquake in the 5th century A.D. A
large, tripartite floor mosaic in the central
nave shows the sun god Helios surrounded by the twelve signs of the zo-

175

diac. The floors of the two aisles flanking the nave are decorated with simple mosaic patterns.

Also located here is the domed **Tomb of Rabbi Meir**, named "Giver of Light" because of his scholarship. In the 2nd century, this important scribe contributed to the compilation of the Mishna, the Jewish book of religious laws.

The Horns of Hittim

About 10 km west of Tiberias, not far from the road to Nazareth, the Horns of Hittim (*Qarne Hittim* means horns, or heads, of wheat) rise abruptly from the plain. You can climb to the top of these twin peaks, parts of the rim of an ancient volcanic crater, in about half an hour. The exertion will be repaid with a marvelous view out over the Sea of Galilee and the countryside of eastern Galilee.

Above: Tiberias' hot springs have been renowned since Antiquity (remains of the Roman baths). Right: On the River Jordan.

The destiny of the Crusaders was decided here. The spark that set off the decisive battle was kindled by Reynald of Chatillon; in 1186, he and his men attacked and looted a richly loaded Arabian caravan. Saladin was understandably indignant, since a cease-fire had calmed relations between Christians and Saracens. He demanded the return of the goods and the immediate release of the prisoners, but the arrogant Reynald refused, and even ignored King Guido's intervention on Saladin's behalf. Accordingly, the sultan assembled an immense army that crossed the Jordan south of the Sea of Galilee in July, 1187, and advanced towards Tiberias. The Crusaders approached from the west under a blazing summer sun through the hills of southern Galilee and fell upon the Arab camp between the Horns of Hittim on the evening of July 3. The entire army suffered unbearable thirst and was already completely exhausted by the rapid march as well as by constant skirmishes with attacking Saracens along the way. Saladin and his men completely surrounded the Franks and closed in the next morning.

The Crusader army tried to escape to the lake, but Saladin managed to keep the Franks from the water. Since the wind was blowing in a favorable direction, he had the dry grasses set on fire so that the flames and smoke caused even more confusion and chaos, until the first infantry troops began to flee and deserted their knights – at which point the battle was effectively decided.

The battle at the Horns of Hittim was a case of unprecedented carnage. The Frankish army was said to have numbered some 63,000 men: half of these were killed, while the other half caused a rapid price fall in local slave markets. Only a few hundred fighters managed to get away; but Saladin netted all of the Christian leaders, including Reynald of Chatillon, who was responsible for the massacre. Saladin himself chopped of

is head, for the Crusader had never kept his word with the sultan. A similar fate was met by the knights of the Orders of Knights Templar and Knights Hospitaler, who had become the most fanatic storm troops in the Holy Land and caused death and destruction wherever they went.

The Crusaders would never recover from the catastrophe at the Horns of Hittim. Over the next few months, Saladin conquered all of the Franks' important bases; finally, on October 2, 1187, he marched triumphantly into Jerusalem.

Kinneret and Yardenit

Several kilometers further to the south, the **Cemetery of Kibbutz Kinneret** appears on the left; a shady path leads to a scenic lookout. From here you get a terrific view of the lake and of the Golan Heights, hazy in the distance. Many Jewish settlers as well as several spiritual leaders of the Zionist movement are buried here, amongst them the poetess Rachel Hameshoreret, who is highly ho-

nored in Israel. Rachel lived in Degania before World War I, then studied in France and, during the war years, took care of refugee children in Russia, where she contracted tuberculosis. Back in Israel, she wrote passionate poems in Hebrew about the beauty of the region. Many of her verses have been set to music and belong to the newer folklore tradition of the country. She died in 1931.

Near to the entrance of Kibbutz Kinneret – which, founded in 1911, is one of the oldest kibbutzim in Israel – is **Yardenit**, a delightful little spot on the River Jordan shaded by high eucalyptus trees. Here, you can often encounter Bible tourists, who hold baptism ceremonies with religious songs and prayers at the river. If, however, the shores should happen to be free, you can jump into the water as a respite from the hot weather. Showers and changing rooms are provided.

A short bit further you will reach the kibbutz **Degania Aleph** (*aleph* means the letter "A" – there is also a Degania Bet, or "B"). This oldest kibbutz in Israel,

177

founded in 1909 by Eastern European Jews, is still famed today as "Mother of the Kibbutzim." A small **museum** informs visitors about the philosophy and history of the kibbutzim.

In the year 636, the Arabs defeated the Byzantine troops, and so cleared the Near East for Muslim conquest. It was also here that the sultan Saladin led his troops over the Jordan in 1187 on the way to the battle of Hittim which brought the end of the Crusader era. A third military event of more recent vintage took place in 1948: after the proclamation of Israel's independence, invading armies from five neighboring Arab states closed in on the new country. Syrian tanks rolled in from the east, overran two kibbutzim and could only be stopped near Degania; the first tank was supposedly put out of action by a Molotov cocktail thrown by a 15-year old.

Above: Baptismal ceremony at Yardenit, on the River Jordan. Right: Daily life in a village.

178

BELVOIR

Once the most powerful Crusade castle in the Holy Land, this edifice wa given a befitting name by the Franks Belvoir, or beautiful view. The pan oramic view from the 550 meter-hig cliff plateau extends far over the country side and, on clear days, all the way to th Sea of Galilee. Both Jews and Arab were inspired by its unique location whe they named it in their own tongues; th former called the fort *Kochav Hayarder* or Star of Jordan; the latter called it *Kau kab al Hauwa*, or Star of the Airs.

The mountaintop was already settled i Biblical times, and a first fortificatio was built there during the Jewish rebel lion against the Romans in the year 66. I 1138, the Crusaders built a small fortres on the strategically important hill; the called their acquisition La Coquette, "th coquettish one." Thirty years later, th Knights of St. John of Jerusalem recog nized the military importance of the pla teau, bought the fortification complex

nd, within a few years, had developed it
nto an invincible and defiant fortress.

The battle of Hittim in 1187 rang in the
nd of the Crusader era in Palestine; sul-
an Saladin then conquered one Frankish
ortress after the other until only Belvoir
emained. He besieged the stronghold for
8 months and had his sappers collapse
ne northeastern tower by digging under
: – but that in no way changed the situ-
tion; Belvoir was still invulnerable. The
Crusaders only surrendered when all
heir other bases had been taken, which
topped their supply of reserves and rein-
orcements. Saladin guaranteed them an
nimpeded retreat, and so the knights
noved to Tyros to the north.

The sultan had the fortress repaired,
ut when the troops of the Fifth Crusade
urged into the Holy Land 20 years later
1219, the Arabs destroyed the fort. In
241 the Franks again ruled the plateau,
ut could not raise the amount of money
ecessary to rebuild Belvoir.

In the 1960s, archaeologists carried out
omprehensive excavation work here,
and today the ruins of Belvoir are an impressive sight. In places where no steep
cliff-drop offered natural protection for
the fortress, the Crusaders carved a
trench up to 25 meters wide and 12
meters deep into the hard ground. The
high walls were more than 3 meters thick
and were further guarded by seven
towers. The main gate was built according to the most advanced military technology of the day; it had a series of
angles and corners that made it easy to
defend, as well as a number of machico-
lations, or high gutters, from which one
could pour hot pitch or boiling oil down
on the heads of attackers. Additional
safety features included escape doors and
extra underground passageways leading
to exits far from the fortress. Furthermore, the castle had a gigantic water cistern and extensive storage areas for food
supplies – all of which explain why Saladin's 18-month siege was inneffective.

The mighty keep, which probably
functioned as a fortress within a fortress,
rises at the center of the walled complex;

it was so fortified that the knights could have held out there for months after the fall of the outer ring of defense walls. But Belvoir was never taken. Several storage rooms and a large water tank were on the lower floor; while the knights dwelled in tracts above them.

Belvoir was one of the many castles which young T. E. Lawrence, the future Lawrence of Arabia, studied in 1909 during work on his master's thesis about crusader castles in Syria and Palestine.

BET SHEAN

Indubitably one of the most important excavation sites in the Holy Land is the comlex at Bet Shean or – to speak in the jargon of archaeology – *Tel al Husn*, the Hill of Strength. The name is fitting, since archaeologists had to dig through an impressive 28 layers of different set-

Above: The ruins of the Crusader castle Belvoir. Right: The prickly pear (opuntia), a thorny beauty.

tlements. On this spot, Egyptians, Canaanites, Philistines, Jews, Hellenes, Scythians, Romans, Arabs, and Frankis Crusaders settled over thousands of year – and small wonder, given that the ruler of this site could dominate the fertil plains of the Jezreel to the northwest a well as its offshoots in the Jordan Valley where there was also a caravan route.

Traces of human habitation here dat back as much as 5,500 years ago, to th late Copper Age, but things only reall started happening in the region when th Egyptians arrived on the scene and real ized the site's strategic importance. Thut mose III conquered Canaan in aroun 1500, and built Bet Shean's first strong hold. Almost all the pharaohs after hir immortalized themselves in Bet Shea either by building temples or by renovat ing and expanding the fortress.

After the Israelites had migrated int "the land of milk and honey," they als began to settle in the Jordan Valley an the fertile Jezreel plain, and divided th land among their tribes. Bet Shean re

nained in Canaanite hands, since in those days the Jews were still a long way from conquering the city-states in Canaan – the Philistines, however, did just that in round 1100, dealing the Israelites a disastrous defeat at Mount Gilboa. Saul and his three sons were killed in the battle. David, however, managed finally to drive out the Philistines for good. Bet Shean lost its importance, and did not gain it back until the Scythians, a much-feared tribe of Asiatic horsemen from southern Russia, penetrated into Palestine and prepared to threaten Egypt. Pharaoh Psammetich went to meet the strangers on their way and presented them with such fabulous gifts that they changed their plans and turned back. A small troop, however, stayed in Palestine and settled in Bet Shean, which was renamed Skythopolis.

With the arrival of the Romans in the 2nd century B.C., the town gained importance as the capital of a ten-state federation. In Byzantine times it was honored as the residence of a bishop. Finally the Arabs came, took over the place by surprise attack, and named it Beisan. Over the following centuries of Arab rule, the place lapsed into a twilight slumber; not even the upheavals of the Crusader era made for much excitement, and so it has remained until today.

In Bet Shean, the **Town Museum** displays interesting local excavation finds and a mosaic with a scene from the *Odyssey*. There's also a small outdoor museum, while the ruins of an amphitheater are at the eastern edge of town. The **seraglio**, a Turkish government building, was built in 1905; the building materials include ancient columns and stones.

The main attraction of the ruins is the **theater**, the largest the Romans built in Palestine. It is still in an excellent state of preservation. At the time of the Roman Empire, it was equipped with every imaginable staging mechanism. Water pipes even bore in precious fluid to enable the staging of Naumachias, gladiator combats fought as mock sea battles, their arena either a gigantic pool or the flooded surface of the entire theater floor. The

181

stage was flanked by two round towers containing flights of steps; from these, actors could be lowered onto the stage or made to "disappear" by being pulled up into the wings, creating, for the 8,000 spectators in the theater's tiered seats, the illusion that gods were appearing from heaven or vanishing again into the clouds.

Between the theater and Tel al Husn runs a **colonnaded street** which is also of Roman vintage and was once lined with shops. Some of these columns have been set back up; these, together with the theater, give the archaeological site a touch of the original atmosphere it must have had in ancient times. A mosaic from the 6th century A.D. was found in a building nearby here, depicting the goddess Tyche with a horn of plenty. At the northern end of the street, steps lead to

Above: Roman-era theater and colonnade at Bet Shean. Right: In spring, the countryside is transformed into a bright carpet of flowers.

the remains of a Roman **Temple of Dionysus**.

A short but steep climb leads to the peak of **Tel al Husn**, the town's fortress mountain, where a Philistine town with an Astarte temple once stood. From this height one can enjoy a fantastic view of the ancient city center. Gigantic Byzantine **thermal baths** rise on the western side, their atrium ringed with columns and decorated with mosaics. A further large thermal bath is presently being excavated in the east. Between them, one sees the streets, monuments and squares of a rich Roman Byzantine city, whose splendor fell victim to an earthquake in the year 749 A.D. At the entrance to this area, one can receive upon request an informative, but not too up-to-date, English-language handbill about the site.

North of the Tel, beyond the river Harod, is the **Monastery of the Virgin**, built in 567 A.D., which has wonderful mosaics: the sun god Helios, the moon goddess Selene, peacocks, and many other birds and beasts.

Mount Gilboa and
the Synagogue of Bet Alpha

Southwest of Bet Shean, **Mount Gilboa** rises from the plain to a height of 508 meters above sea level. A tortuous road leads steeply upwards. It was here that Saul and his three sons died in battle against the Philistines. To intimidate other foes, the victors hung Saul's corpse from the town walls of Bet Shean.

The mountain is known for its wildflowers (including the Gilboa iris), which create a magnificent carpet of blossoms. Ascending the easy panoramic footpath up to the peak, walkers are dazzled with the wealth of natural beauty – which has had considerable help from the environmental organization *Society for the Protection of Nature in Israel* (SPNI). Flower picking is, of course, not allowed!

Just a few minutes' drive further is **Gan Hashelosha**, the Garden of the Three, at the foot of Mount Gilboa. The small national park got its name from three Jewish settlers who were killed during a fight with Arab neighbors. Here, you can enjoy a swim even in winter, since warm springs at 28° C gurgle between the grassy lawns.

A bit further along to the west, at the kibbutz Heftzi Bah, visit the **Synagogue of Bet Alpha**. Built in the 6th century, the synagogue was destroyed by an earthquake only a few years later. Its splendid, perfectly preserved floor mosaic is among Israel's most beautiful. The first section of this large mosaic illustrates the sacrifice of Isaac; the center section depicts the signs of the zodiac; and the last section shows the Ark of the Covenant guarded by lions with a Torah shrine, and two seven-branched menorahs.

Ma'ayan Harod National Park
and Tel Jezre'el

The small **Ma'ayan Harod National Park** is located just a few kilometers fur-

ther to the west, shortly before you reach kibbutz En Harod, about 3 kilometers off Route 71. With its spacious lawns under shade-giving eucalyptus trees, this place is ideal for taking a rest and a picnic; the main attraction – especially on hot days – is a large, natural, spring-fed pool of water which is well-suited for swimming.

More than 3,000 years ago, Gideon's fighters refreshed themselves at this spot – and then proceeded to fall upon their enemies, the Midianites. With only 300 men, the Israelites surrounded the enemy camp at night. Gideon ordered his warriors to blow their horns loudly and light bright torches. The Midianites, drunk with sleep, were disoriented by the noise and the torchlight. In their confusion, they turned their swords upon each other and massacred themselves.

It was not the only battle fought here. In 1260, a Mameluke army halted the advance of the thereto undefeated Mongols. In the 1930s, the English officer Orde Wingate trained Haganah units here; among the men who received Wingate's

rather unorthodox, but undeniably effective lessons in strategy were Moshe Dayan and Yigal Allon, two great Israeli generals who later also became successful politicians.

Proceeding a bit further to the west, one comes to the Kibbutz Yisre'el. Located here is **Tel Jezre'el**, a site where archaeologists from the University of Tel Aviv are working to uncover the remains of a town from Biblical times. The place is mentioned in the Old Testament as the scene of the story of Ahab, the King of Samaria, who wanted to have a vineyard that belonged to Naboth of Jezreel; Naboth, however, did not want to sell. The king's wife, Jezebel, had the unyielding Naboth falsely accused of cursing God and the king, and saw to it that he would be stoned to death for this alleged crime. God punished Ahab and his wife with a terrible death for their outrageous actions (1 Kings 21:1-29, 2 Kings 9:1-15).

Above: The floor mosaic in the synagogue of Bet Alpha is eminently worth a visit.

184

MEGIDDO

Megiddo was once one of the most important metropolises in the region, and guarded the busy trade and military road that led through Palestine from Egypt to Mesopotamia. The city was populated from the 4th century B.C. up to the 4th century A.D., and the Tel of Megiddo shows no fewer than 21 different layers of settlement, the first dating from the late Neolithic period.

1,000 years later, during the Bronze Age in around 3,000 B.C., the first fortified town was constructed, from which archaeologists have been able to locate a small temple.

The Canaanites developed the town further, and the Hyksos secured it with new fortifications. In the year 1468 B.C. the Egyptian pharaoh Thutmose III and his troops conquered Megiddo, then traveled further towards the Euphrates; the capture of the fortified town was recorded as a great heroic feat in Egyptian history. During the time of the "heretic

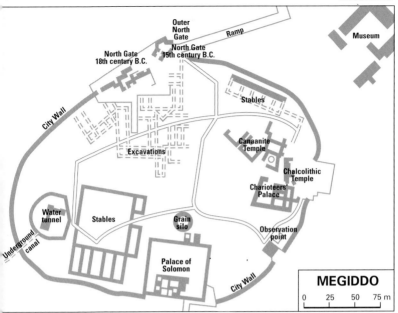

MEGIDDO

0   25   50   75 m

pharaoh" Akhnaten, many of the so-called Amarna Letters record attacks by the Habiru – these incidents probably represent the first tentative attempts at settlement by the Israelite tribes.

The Jewish appropriation of land began in a big way as of 1230 B.C., after the Chosen People had defeated the Canaanites. King David took Megiddo in round the year 1004. David's successor, Solomon, secured the town with strong defensive walls, but this didn't prove to be of much help; the pharaoh Sheshonq I passed through on one of his raiding expeditions from the Nile, descended upon Megiddo, looting everything that was not nailed down. The kings Omri and Ahab but did even Solomon in their efforts to make the town unconquerable; the elaborate and extensive system of water pipes was installed in Ahab's time.

The next arrivals were the Assyrians, who stormed in from Syria; the Israelites submitted to them and regularly paid taxes to their powerful neighbors. In 732 B.C., when King Pekach refused the pay-

ments, the Assyrian ruler Tiglath-Pileser destroyed Megiddo down to the ground. The town was rebuilt immediately thereafter, only to be destroyed by the Assyrians for the second time in 723.

When this pwerful kingdom finally fell, Josiah, king of Judea, seized the Assyrian provinces of Samaria and Megiddo and annexed them to his own dominion. In 609, Egyptians under the pharaoh Necho arrived to conquer Palestine and Syria; and from that point on, the town that had been so proud and wealthy for so many millennia slowly transformed into the sleepy and insignificant place it was to remain ever after. Following the Bar Kochba rebellion of the Jews against the Romans in 135 B.C., the occupying forces built an extensive military complex here. The town's last moment in the sun came in the 4th century when it was given the new name of Maximinopolis after Emperor Maximinus.

A small **museum** is located at the entrance to the ruins. In it you can examine a model of the excavation site, as well as

185

viewing a short film about the history of Megiddo.

Once on the site itself, you can see the remains of a town gate with three chambers, as well as the high city walls, which date from the days of the Canaanites, and a Canaanite **shrine** with a large round altar and an adjacent **double temple**. Farther south is a large, round grain silo from the 8th century B.C.; behind this are the famous **stables** which were once thought to date from the days of Solomon, but which, it has now been established, were actually built by Ahab. These extensive stalls housed the horses for Ahab's chariots of war, said to number 2,000.

Another real highlight of a visit to Megiddo, even for non-engineers, is the water supply system. Southwest of the town, outside the town walls, a spring

bubbled up in a cave; the Canaanites had already built a small flight of stairs leading to it. If the town was under siege however, its inhabitants were not able to reach this vital spot, so Solomon had the so-called "gallery" built: this was a narrow, well-hidden artificial tunnel completely lined with stonework, which led down to the water. Still, the military experts of pharaoh Sheshonq must have discovered it, making Solomon's extensive camouflage useless. To prevent something similar from happening again, King Ahab's engineers dug a shaft more than 50 meters deep through solid rock inside the city walls. From the foot of this immense passage they chiseled out a 70 meter-long tunnel reaching as far as the spring; the cave's interior entrance was then sealed. A first-rate feat of engineering from ancient times!

BET SHE'ARIM

North of Megiddo, where the foothills of the Carmel Mountains begin, and in

Above: Visitors examine a grain silo at the excavation site at Megiddo. Right: Shepherds and their flocks seek shade from the baking noonday sun.

the middle of a lovely national park, is the catacomb complex of **Bet She'arim**. After the Bar Kochba rebellion in the year 135 A.D. and the downfall of Jerusalem, many inhabitants of the plundered town moved to Bet Shary, as it was called in those days. The rabbis of the Sanhedrin, the Jewish high council, moved here as well, and the town quickly developed as a religious center. In around the year 170, Rabbi Yehuda Hanassi compiled the Mishnah here, a collection of religious texts which had, until then, only been passed down orally from generation to generation.

Bet Shary developed into the secret capital of the Jews and a center of religious scholarship. Each time that one of the learned men died, he found his final resting place in the catacombs beneath the town. As the years passed, many Jews from throughout the country wanted to be buried in Bet Shary near the great rabbis, and the necropolis became larger and larger. Since every catacomb was closed with a great stone gate, the town got a

new name: Bet She'arim, the House of the Gates.

In the year 352, the Romans destroyed the town to punish an uprising. In 1936, Alexander Zayd, a Jewish immigrant from Russia, discovered the entrance to a catacomb, and archaeologists began excavation work, which continues to this day. At the highest point in Bet She'arim stands the equestrian statue of Alexander Zayd, who was killed in fighting with Arabs in 1938.

A bit before the entrance to Bet She'arim National Park you can see the ruins of a synagogue with three aisles from the 2nd or 3rd century A.D., and an oil press.

At the catacombs, you can only visit the grave complex number 20 which, with its 26 labyrinthine chambers, is the largest of the catacombs excavated to date. The more than 100 sarcophagi here, all made of local limestone, bear inscriptions in Greek, Aramean, and Hebrew; many of them are decorated with simple Jewish symbols.

NAZARETH

With 60,000 inhabitants of Arab descent – of which about half are Christian – **Nazareth** is the largest Arab town in Israel. Sprawled over a hill nearby is *Nazerat Illit*, Upper Nazareth, which has grown since the 1950s; its 30,000 in habitants are, without exception, Jewish. Visitors here walk in the footsteps of early Christians, but the whole look of the town, with its lively bazaar streets and the old, colorful marketplace, has a decidedly Arab flair and hardly corresponds to the expectations of Christian pilgrims.

Although probably already settled in the 3rd millenium B.C., this town was never important enough to warrant mention. In the era of Herod the Great, a young woman named Mary lived in Na-

Above: Since the 2nd century A.D., Jewish scholars have been buried in the catacombs of Bet She'arim. Right: In the bazaar of Nazareth.

zareth and was betrothed to a carpenter, Joseph. One day, the angel Gabriel appeared to her and told her that she would bear a son whom she should name Jesus. Mary, astonished, asked the divine messenger how that should come to pass, since she was still a virgin. "The Holy Ghost shall come upon thee, and the power of the Highest shall overshadow thee," was Gabriel's response (Luke 1:26-35). In the following years, the boy Jesus grew up in Nazareth.

After the destruction of Jerusalem in the year 70, many Jews settled in Nazareth. The first church was not built here until after the 5th century, a Byzantine edifice called the Church of the Annunciation. This, however, was destroyed by Persian troops in 614. In 1099, the Crusaders erected a new and magnificently decorated house of worship on the same Byzantine foundations.

In 1187, sultan Saladin conquered the town. By the standards of his contemporaries, he showed extraordinary religious tolerance and did not disturb the Chris-

ian sanctuaries. Their destruction was left to the Mameluke sultan Baybars more than 100 years later.

At the beginning of the 17th century, Christians began to settle in Nazareth again, and in 1730 the Turks even permitted the construction of a church. There was a catch, however, to their generous offer: the church had to be built in less than half a year! Thus there was only time to build a small church over a grotto which was hastily converted into a crypt. This provisional church fell victim to the pickaxe in 1954. Finally, in 1969, the present **Church of the Annunciation** was consecrated; today its high dome is visible from a great distance, towering imposingly over the roofs of Nazareth. The church is a favorite with young couples looking for a wedding chapel.

According to Christian belief, Mary's humble house stood at the spot where today this mighty **Basilica** stands. On the western façade, a relief illustrates the scene of the Annunciation, with the angel Gabriel and Mary above, and below, the four Evangelists with their symbols: the eagle (John), the ox (Matthew), the lion (Mark), and the man (Luke). The three portals, depicting scenes from the New Testament, are the work of German sculptor Roland Friedrichsen. On entering, you first come into the lower church with the Grotto of the Annunciation. In this cave, which was formerly used for storing provisions, the angel Gabriel is said to have appeared to Mary.

Two spiral staircases lead to the upper church; you can look down into the grotto through a large, octagonal opening in the floor. Over it rises the dome, measuring 40 meters high and 18 meters wide, shaped like a lily blossom. Through the northern portal in the upper church, you can reach a terrace which looks out over the ruins of the old settlement.

A few steps further is **St. Joseph's Church**, consecrated in 1914. According to belief, Joseph the carpenter had his house and workshop there. While excavating, archaeologists unearthed a baptis-

189

mal font decorated with mosaics. Steps lead to a long grotto, formerly a storage chamber, which was already considered a holy place early on, as the mosaic floor and the wall inscriptions suggest.

If you walk down Casa Nova Street from the Church of the Annunciation, you will soon come to its intersection with Paul VI Street. From here, the loud and lively main street of the town goes off to the left. After about 1 kilometer you will see a modern, white fountain on the left: the Virgin Mary is said to have come here for water.

But the only true spring in all of Nazareth can be found at the end of the street in the Greek Orthodox **St. Gabriel's Church**. Greek Orthodox believers consider this spring a holy place,

Above: Jesus in Joseph's carpenter's workshop; a wall painting in St. Joseph's Church in Nazareth. Right: The soil of the Holy Land is sewed into sacks and sold as souvenirs to tourists.

believing that Mary was visited by the angel Gabriel not in her house, but here while she was fetching water. For a small donation (for which you will receive a small, blessed cross), a Greek Orthodox patriarch will lead you to the spring.

ZIPPORI

The ruins of the city of Zippori lie six kilometers north of Nazareth, on a 289-meter-high hill surrounded by the fertile valleys of lower Galilee. The city rose to importance in the 1st century B.C., when the Roman governor of the province of Syria named Zippori the capital of Galilee. In the 3rd century A.D., the Sanhedrin moved here from Bet She'arim. At that time, Zippori was a wealthy trading town with about 30,000 primarily Jewish citizens. The city became a bishopric in the 4th century A.D., resulting in the building of Zippori's first churches. The city first declined in importance after being conquered by the Arabs in the 7th century A.D. In 1187, the Crusaders set

ut from here for the fatal battle against ultan Saladin at the Horns of Hittim.

Since the start of excavations in 1993, he wealth and beauty of this ancient city re becoming apparent. A theater has een unearthed; another of the dis-overies is a Roman villa with a floor mosaic depicting scenes from the life of he wine god Dionysus, as well as the ountenance of a beautiful woman who as ever since been known as the "Mona Lisa of Galilee." Besides these, the re-mains of the pillar-bordered Roman main treet and of a public facility with its "Nile Mosaic" have been uncovered. Also to be viewed is a gigantic water eservoir which was hewn out of the ock. The **citadel**, which is the only uilding that has been restored and tilized over and over again, today ouses a small museum showing multi-media programs on the history of the city nd providing information about the vater system and the Nile Mosaic. One an get a detailed English-language andbill about Zippori upon request.

CANA

Ten kilometers north of Nazareth, the small Arab village **Kafr Kanna** lies among olive groves. In Biblical times, the place was called Cana. Here, Jesus performed his first miracle, changing water into wine at a wedding (John 2:7).

This miracle is commemorated by not one, but two churches in this friendly Arab village, where Christians and Arabs dwell peaceably side by side; one for Roman Catholic believers and one for those of the Greek Orthodox faith. Each denomination claims that its place of worship was built over the site of the wedding house where the miracle oc-curred. The obligatory souvenir for tipp-ling travelers tracking down Bible sites are bottles labeled "Wine of Cana," avail-able throughout the village.

ON MOUNT TABOR

Twenty kilometers east of Nazareth, **Mount Tabor** rises into the sky from the

plain of southern Galilee. At 600 meters the "mountain of the transfiguration" is the highest point in the region.

According to the Old Testament, an important event occurred at Mount Tabor and the adjoining Jezreel plain: it was here that the Israelites gathered and, following the instructions of the woman judge Deborah and commanded by the military leader Barak, ended their days of oppression under the Canaanites once and for all.

This was one of the first large battles during the Israelite takeover of the land, and was exceptionally well prepared for since the Jews, and not their foes, were able to determine the place and time of the fight. From the mountain, the Israelites were able to observe the movements of the Canaanites under Sisera. Since Sisera's 900 war chariots were unable to attack uphill, the Jews were able

Above: View over Galilee from Mount Tabor.
Right: Years of working in the fields have left their mark on peoples' faces.

to delay the battle until the rainy season They then placed themselves in the narrow Tabor valley for the fight so that th Canaanite chariot units would hav trouble advancing in the muddy terrair Sisera's wagon got completely stuck i the quagmire, forcing him to flee, humil iatingly, on foot. His entire army wa wiped out.

The mountain was already settled i the 2nd century B.C., and Ramses II con quered the town there in the 12th centur during one of his many looting raids. Fla vius Josephus reported that he himself, a commander-in-chief in Galilee, had mighty wall erected within 40 days her during the Jewish rebellion against th Romans in the year 66. But this didn' help very much, since there was no wate up on top of the mountain, and apparentl no cisterns either: the inhabitants there fore had to yield to the hated occupyin, forces.

In the days of the Crusades, Benedic tine monks founded a heavily fortifie monastery on Mount Tabor. Despite re eated efforts, Saladin never managed to onquer the abbey.

After the disastrous defeat in the battle f Hittim, which brought the age of the Crusades to an end, the monks were also orced to leave Tabor. Several years later, he sultan of Damascus had a mighty tronghold built upon the plateau. Yet the mountain once again came into Christian ands (not through war, but through reaty negotiations), until 1263, when Baybars and his troops laid waste to the igh plateau, transforming it into a stony esert. At the beginning of the 17th century, Franciscans came and founded a ew monastery there.

A winding road leads up to the 588 meter mountain plateau, which is shaped ke an ellipse. You can get there by car r with a taxi shuttle service; to have a more authentic experience, however, you hould really go on foot.

Enter the ruins site through the Arab rch, "Gate of the Winds." Canaanites ad set up a shrine here as early as the nd century B.C., and the first churches t this spot were built around the year 00. Fortification walls from Antiquity ircled the outer rim of the plateau. The Crusaders erected a second wall at aproximately the center of Tabor; this enlosed a castle and a church.

Today, you can see remains of various uildings scattered all over the plateau. Greek-Orthodox monks constructed the Church of St. Elijah on the foundations f a building from the Crusader era; it as consecrated in 1911. In 1921-23, the Franciscans commissioned the architect Antonio Barluzzi to build the **Basilica of he Transfiguration** (the Tabor Church). It stands inside a walled cloister with lovely gardens and the ruins of an lder church. Built of light-colored limestone, this monumental basilica features wo massive towers linked by an arch.

Inside, wide arches separate the nave om the side aisles. A mosaic in the ome of the apse shows the scene of the

transfiguration of Christ. Jesus climbed Mount Tabor with Peter, James, and James' brother John. There, he was transformed. His face shone like the sun and his clothing became white as snow. Suddenly Moses and Elijah appeared and spoke to Jesus. A bright cloud threw its shadow on them and from it the voice of God told them that this was his beloved son, and that they should listen to him (Matthew 17, 1-6).

In the eastern end of the church, the Grotto of Christ, with a modern altar room, is set into the old walls of a Crusader church. Two other chapels, the **Elijah Chapel** and the **Moses Chapel**, are located in the towers. The mosaic floor of the Moses Chapel, with its pattern of crosses, dates from around 400 A.D.

From the mountaintop plateau, you have an extraordinary view in all directions – of fertile Galilee to the north, of the Jordan lowlands to the east, over the mountains of Samaria to the south, and to the Jezreel plain and the mountains around Nazareth to the west.

TIBERIAS

Getting There

Buses run regularly to and from Tel Aviv, Jerusalem and Haifa.

Accommodation

LUXURY: **Galei Kinneret**, 1 Kaplan Street, tel. 06-6728888, Tiberias' first big luxury hotel, built in 1943 directly on the lake, recently renovated, excellent French cuisine is served in the Art-Deco restaurant *Au Bord du Lac*, waterskiing and kayak trips are also available.

The Caesar, The Promenade, tel. 06-6727272, newest hotel in Tiberias, all rooms with lake view, with weekly Israeli Folk Evenings organized by the tourist board, indoor and outdoor pools, waterskiing and windsurfing.

Gai Beach, Route 90, Box 274, tel. 06-6700700, at the southern end of the city with a private beach on the lake as well as a pool with wave machine.

Sheraton Moriah, on Habanim Street, tel. 06-6792233, recently completely renovated, rooms with lake view, but not located directly on the water; pool, sauna and fitness center.

Holiday Inn, Route 90, Box 22, tel. 06-6728555, at the southern end of Tiberias on Route 90 right next to the hot springs, lovely shady palm garden, tennis courts, and private beach.

Ron Beach, Gedud Barak Street, tel. 06-6791350, on Route 90 at the northern end of Tiberias, right on the lake, with a private beach and good fish restaurant.

MODERATE: **Astoria**, 13 Ohel Yaakov Street, tel. 06-6722351, family-run establishment, high prices during the Israeli holidays in July and August.

Church of Scotland Centre, Gedud Barak/corner Hayarden Street, tel. 06-6723769, in the city center, built in 1893 as the hospital of the Free Church of Scotland, later transformed into a hospice for pilgrims, today a mid-priced hotel open to everyone, with a lovely garden and its own beach.

Aviv Holiday Flats, Hanoter St., tel. 06-6712272, new, has its own restaurant.

Tzameret, Plus 200 Street, tel. 06-6794951, Tzameret means "peak" in Hebrew, and the hotel is situated 430 meters above the Sea of Galilee; the view is fantastic, and on hot summer days the temperatures are as much as 6° C lower than they are in the hot Jordan valley.

Bet Berger, 27 Neiberg Street, tel. 06-6720850, Berger House is run by a family of the same name, and is located a good way up the hillside, with nice rooms and balconies.

Kolton Inn, 2 Ohel Ya'akov Street, tel. 06-6791641, nice lake views from the rooms' balconies.

Continental Hotel, Alhadif Street, tel. 06-6720018, small, older establishment, with a cozy feel.

Ron Hotel, 12 Ahad Ha'am Street, tel. 06-6720259, modern, simple furnishings and good service.

Prime Tiberias Hotel, Elhadel Street, tel. 06-6791166, quiet family hotel.

Panorama Hotel, Galil Street, next to the Emek Hotel, tel. 06-6720963, simple rooms.

Eden Hotel, Obel Ya'akov Street, tel. 06-6790070, next to the Kolton Inn, simple and good.

BUDGET: **Adina Hostel**, 15 Shiloah Street, tel. 06-6722507.

Hostel Aviv, Galil Street, tel. 06-6720007, comfortable hostel.

Meyuhas Hostel, Hayarden Street, tel. 06-6721775, in the city center.

Nahum Hostel, Travor Street, tel. 06-6721505.

Casa Nova Hospice, Casa Nova Street, tel. 06-6456660, a low-priced Christian pilgrims' hospice.

Restaurants

Au Bord du Lac, im Galei Kinneret Hotel, finest French cuisine, the best restaurant in Tiberias.

Karamba, on the beach promenade, tel. 06-6791546, fish specialties and vegetarian meals; in summer, you can sit outside; open until midnight.

Pagoda and **The House**, both on Gedud Barak Street, on Lido Beach, Chinese and Thai cuisine. Pagoda also has a sushi bar, tel. 06-6721538.

Dex, on Lido Beach, tel. 06-6721538, Argentinian grill restaurant.

Arabeska, excellent Oriental food in the Sheraton Moriah Hotel.

Sights

The Galilee Experience, lakeside promenade at the Lake of Tiberias, presentations in English Sun-Thu 10 am-10 pm, Fri 8 am-5 pm, Sat 5-10 pm.

Tomb of Moses Maimonides, Sun-Thu from sunrise to sunset, Fri until 2 pm.

Hammat Tiberias (hot springs of Tiberias), Sat-Thu 8 am-4 pm, Fri 8 am-3 pm.

Hospitals and Pharmacies

Poriya Hospital, tel. 06-6738211. **Schwartz Pharmacy**, Galil Street. **Center Pharmacy**, Bibass/corner Galil Street.

Tourist Information

Habanim Street, tel. 06-6725666.

SEA OF GALILEE

Getting There

Buses run from Tiberias north and south along the edge of the Sea of Galilee; there are also *Sherut* services from Tiberias.

Accommodation

LUXURY: **Nof Ginosar Guest House**, on Route 90, 10 km north of Tiberias, Mobile Post Jordan Valley 14980, tel. 06-6700300, well-run, comfortable kibbutz guest house with its own beach on the Sea of Galilee,

Ideal for a few quiet days, all kinds of water sports available.

Ramot Resort Hotel, east of Route 92, Mobile Post Sea of Galilee 12490, tel. 06-6732636, on the eastern bank of the Sea of Galilee in the hills, marvelous view, 10-minute drive to the beach.

MODERATE: **En Gev Holiday Village**, on Route 92, 10 km from Tzemach Junction, Mobile Post En Gev 14940, tel. 06-6659800, also on the eastern bank of the lake, but right on the water; boats run to En Gev from Tiberias.

Maagan, on Route 92; 1 km from Tzemach Junction, Mobile Post Jordan Valley, tel. 06-6654400, at the southern end of the Sea of Galilee, sand beach and all kinds of water sports.

Ha'on, on Route 92, 5 km northeast of Tzemach Junction, Mobile Post Jordan Valley 15170, with private beach, tel. 06-6656555.

Restaurants

En Gev Fish Restaurant, in the kibbutz En Gev on the east side of the Sea of Galilee, on Route 92; 10 km from Tzemach Junction, Mobile Post En Gev 14940, tel. 06-6658036, good, moderately-priced restaurant featuring tasty fish specialties and other dishes.

Sights and Museums

Excavation Site of Capernaum, open daily 8:30 am-4 pm.

Bet Allon Museum, kibbutz Ginosar, on the northern shore of the Sea of Galilee, open Sun-Thu 8:30 am-5 pm, Fri 8:30 am-1 pm, Sat 9 am-5 pm.

Church on the Mount of the Beatitudes, open daily 8 am-noon and 2:30-5 pm.

Church of the Primacy of St. Peter, open daily 8:30 am-noon and 2-5 pm.

Tabgha with **Multiplication of the Loaves and Fishes Church**, open daily 8:30 am-5 pm.

SOUTHERN GALILEE

Getting There

Buses and *Sheruts* run regulary to and from Tiberias, Afula, Akko, Haifa and Nazareth.

Accommodation

MODERATE: **Lavi Kibbutz Hotel**, Kibbutz Lavi, on Route 77, Mobile Post Lower Galilee 15267, tel. 06-6799450, 12 km east of Tiberias, run by orthodox Jews, thus no check-in or check-out is possible on Saturdays; offers tennis courts, a pool, and kibbutz tours.

BUDGET: **Ma'ayan Harod Youth Hostel**, in Ma'ayan Harod National Park, on Route 71, on Mount Gilboa, Mobile Post Gilboa 19120, tel. 06-6531660, set in a lovely landscape.

Restaurant

Younes, on Route 77 next to a gas station, 1.5 km west of Golani Junction, no-frills, solid meals.

Sights and Museums

BELVOIR: Crusader Castle ruins, 20 kilometers south of the Sea of Galilee, open Sat-Thu 8 am-4 pm, Fri 8 am-3 pm.

BET ALPHA: Synagogue Bet Alpha with splendid floor mosaic; in the kibbutz Hefzi Bah, open Sat-Thu 8 am-4 pm, Fri 8 am-3 pm.

BET SHEAN: Excavation site, open Sat-Thu 8 am-4 pm, Fri 8 am-3 pm.

BET SHE'ARIM: Excavation site, open Sat-Thu 8 am-4 pm, Fri 8 am-3 pm.

GAN HASHELOSHA NATIONAL PARK: open Sat-Thu 8 am-4 pm, Fri 8 am-3 pm.

KAFR KANNA (Canaan): **Wedding Church of the Franciscans**, open daily 8:30 am-noon and 2:30-6 pm.

MA'AYAN HAROD NATIONAL PARK: open Sat-Thu 8 am-4 pm, Fri 8 am-3 pm.

MEGIDDO: Excavation site, open Sat-Thu 8 am-4 pm, Fri 8 am-3 pm.

MOUNT TABOR: Basilica of the Transfiguration, daily 8 am-noon and 2-6 pm.

YARDENIT: open Sat-Thu 8 am-4 pm, as well as Fri 8 am-3 pm.

NAZARETH

Accommodation

LUXURY: **Marriott**, 2 Hermon St., Nazareth Illit, tel. 06-6028200.

MODERATE: **Galilee Hotel**, Paul VI Street, tel. 06-6571311, small hotel near the town center.

Grand New Hotel, St. Joseph Street, tel. 06-6573020, a bit out of town on the way to Haifa.

Restaurants / Bakeries

Astoria Restaurant, located at the intersection of Casa Nova Street/Paul VI Street, tel. 06-6573497, a small and low-priced restaurant which serves Oriental cuisine.

Riviera, at the intersection going toward Afula, tel. 06-6554963, good Oriental food.

Hospitals and Pharmacies

Nazareth Hospital, tel. 06-6571501.

Holy Family Hospital, tel. 06-6574537.

Farah Pharmacy, Paul VI Street, next to the Egged Bus information office.

Sights

Greek Orthodox Church of Gabriel, open daily 8:30 am-noon and 2-6 pm.

St. Joseph's church, open Mon-Sat 8:30 am-noon and 2-6 pm, Sun 8:30 am-noon.

Church of the Annunciation, open Mon-Sat 8:30 am-noon and 2-6 pm, Sun 8:30 am-noon.

Tourist Information

Goverment Tourist Information Office on Casa Nova Street, tel. 06-6573003.

THROUGH THE NEGEV TO ELAT

BE'ER SHEVA / TEL ARAD

DEAD SEA / MASADA

EN GEDI / HAI BAR

TIMNA PARK / ELAT

THE HEART OF THE NEGEV

IN AND AROUND BE'ER SHEVA

In its extensive areas of new buildings, **Be'er Sheva**, the fifth-largest city in Israel with a population of 120,000, is without a doubt a modern metropolis, with large, airy residential complexes and wide streets. And yet these regions of the Negev capital are somehow lacking in atmosphere. Only in the **Old City** do you get a sense of history and charm, and even this quarter itself is not so very old; the Turks, with the help of a German architect, laid it out in 1900 on a rectangular ground plan.

Every Thursday, the **Bedouin Market** is held at the edge of the Old City, drawing nomads from near and far to offer such wares as leather products, copper goods, and silver jewelry. Passionate haggling is not only accepted but expected. Near the market is **Abraham's Fountain**, beautifully restored, dating not from the days of the Old Testament, but from those of the Turks. You can recover from a visit to the market with refreshments in the restaurant in the airy fountain courtyard. Also in the Old City

Preceding pages: Camels tank up near Be'er Sheva. Left: Sheik in Be'er Sheva – a Muslim patriarch committed to preserving the tradition of his tribe.

is the **City Museum**, housed in a Turkish mosque and displaying early finds from the surrounding area. From the minaret, you have a great view out over the city and the desert around it.

Impressive too, are the mighty buildings of Ben Gurion University; the Arid Zone Research Center here is dedicated to research on the region and the possibilities offered by irrigation.

A fifteen-minute drive away westward along Route 233 is the interesting **Israel Air Force Museum**. Just under one hundred planes are shown here, and the special features of each are explained by women in the army on the guided tours. One exhibit, for example, is one of the four Messerschmidts which comprised the first Israeli Air Force at its founding in 1948, and which stopped the Egyptian advances during the War of Independence. In addition, you can see the Kfir, Israel's first independently manufactured warplane, or a Spitfire flown by the future Minister of Defense, Ezer Weizmann. In the Boeing 707 which flew in a contingent of special troops for the liberation of Israeli hostages at the Ugandan airport of Entebbe in 1977, an informational film gives an overview of Israel's air force.

Some 20 kilometers northeast of Be'er Sheva and near the town of Lahav, the

Museum of Bedouin Culture is housed in the Alon Regional and Folklore Center. This cultural center is named after the pilot Joe Alon, who demonstrated an active interest in the life of the Bedouin and, on his own initiative, helped get the museum off the ground. One central focus are the changes in Bedouin life throughout the latter part of the 20th century, documented with a number of exhibits and displays.

TEL ARAD AND ARAD

Some 40 kilometers further east along Route 31, you can see **Tel Arad** to the north of the road; a Canaanite royal city once stood upon this hill. The region was first settled during the Copper Age, around 4000 B.C.; Arad itself was probably founded in the early Bronze Age,

Above: A teapot changes hands (Bedouin market at Be'er Sheva). Right: Nomad shepherds have dwelt in tents since time immemorial.

after 2900 or so. Over the next millenium, Arad developed into a trade center on the caravan route from Egypt to the north, and its inhabitants prospered. So powerful was the city, in fact, that immigrating Israelites were forced to make a large detour around it to avoid it. Several years later, the Israelis took their revenge for this inhospitable reception by destroying Arad.

Solomon rebuilt the city, only to have it laid to waste once again a century later by the armies of the Egyptian pharaoh Sheshonq. This pattern of settlement and destruction was repeated many times; the Babylonians finally delivered the coup de grâce in 587 A.D.

Archaeologists have unearthed two large complexes: the Canaanite city from the pre-Israelite Canaanite period, and the Acropolis, with buildings dating from the days of the Israelites to the Roman period. Further excavations include remains of the walls of the Israelite fortress, the Yahweh temple, the Royal Palace, and a reservoir.

A few kilometers east of Tel Arad is the modern city of **Arad**, which was founded in 1961 and is today inhabited by 25,000 people. If you make it to this city, take a deep breath. Located 600 meters above sea level, Arad is famous for its dry air, free of dust and pollen; many asthma sufferers come here to find respite from their illnesses.

On Ben Yair Street is the **Arad Museum and Visitor Center**, exhibiting finds from the excavations at Tel Arad. Also interesting here is a film about the desert, which is sometimes inundated with torrential rainfall, and its flora and fauna, which have adapted to this inhospitable climate.

THE DEAD SEA

From Arad, the road wends its steep and winding way downhill for 24 kilometers to the Dead Sea, in the world's lowest declivity, lying 400 meters below sea level; you traverse more than 1,000 meters in altitude along this stretch of road. There are two laybys along the way, where you can park and take in the impressive views of gorges and canyons of the Negev, as well as of the Dead Sea iself.

At **Newe Zohar**, a lakeside spa with sulfur baths, you come to the shore of the lowest-lying lake in the world.

Road signs in this area keep indicating a place called **Sodom** (or Sedom). For Christians, the town's Biblical past is common knowledge: the Lord wanted to find 50 just men in Sodom and Gomorrah. Abraham managed to bargain him down to ten, but was not even able to locate that many. This sealed the fate of everyone else. Two angels quickly evacuated Lot and his family, who were the only virtuous people in the area, hurrying them out to the mountains and enjoining them against looking back; when the sun rose, and Lot and his wife and family were in safety, the Lord sent a rain of sulfur and fire down upon Sodom and Gomorrah, utterly wiping out not only the two offending cities, but also the

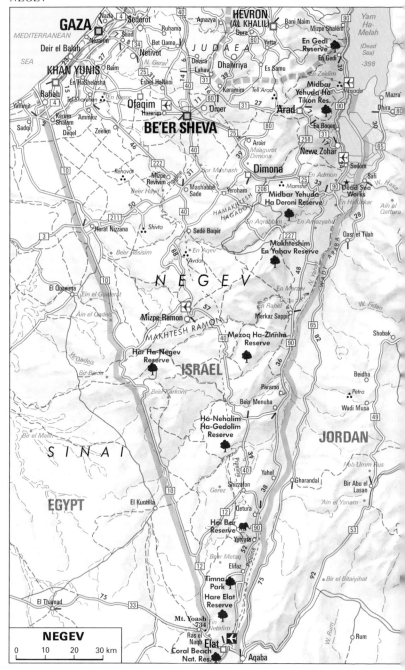

NEGEV

0   10   20   30 km

entire surrounding region. Not a single resident survived this divine punishment. When Lot's wife, despite the warning, looked back after all, she solidifed into a pillar of salt (Genesis 19, 23-26).

According to the Bible, this event took place in the period when Abraham moved into the Negev, around 1800 B.C. Geologists have established that in the middle Bronze Age this region was struck by a tremendous earthquake at the point where the Syrian and African plates collide. When the earth split open in the quake, sulfurous gases and asphalt poured out into the air and ignited. These must have been responsible for a terrible catastrophe.

In the mid-1930s, a settlement of workers was established here under the name Sedom; but it was given up some 20 years later.

At the southern end of the Dead Sea are the **Dead Sea Works**. Here, in large evaporation tanks, bromine, salt, magnesium and potash are extracted from the lake's waters. A visitor here is enveloped in the Dead Sea's heavy, sulfurous air, which tickles the nose with its unpleasant smell.

The Dead Sea is 80 kilometers long and up to 18 kilometers wide, covers a surface area of 1,010 square kilometers, and is as much as 399 meters deep. Because of its unusually high salt content, 30% on the surface and 33% in the depths (the North Sea, by contrast, has 3.5%), there is no plant or animal life whatsoever. The high level of salt is a result of water evaporation from this lake, which, fed by the river Jordan, has no outlets. Because of the salt, you cannot sink, and visitors are fond of photographing one another in the classic pose, reading the paper.

In summer, when temperatures rise to over 45° C, seeking respite from the heat in the oily water is a vain endeavor: the Dead Sea's average temperature in July and August is 30° C, in February, still a respectable 19° C. Running into the water with exuberant splashing is not recommended, as any water that gets into your eyes burns terribly; should this happen, immediately flush out the eye with plenty of fresh water.

At **Newe Zohar**, you will see several white "dams" in the water. The Dead Sea Works is conducting dredging work here; the sea bed rises 20 cm every year due to the deposition of salt sediments as a result of evaporation, which causes rising water levels possibly endangering local hotels. Therefore, there are no more salt formations to be seen, but the atmosphere remains surreal: it is absolutely silent, no sound; not even a bird cries or flies here.

In En Boqeq, Newe Zohar and En Gedi, there are a number of thermal baths, with adjoining hotels, that specialize in the treatment of eczema and other skin diseases, and generally have great success in this area.

MASADA

Driving north along the shore of the Dead Sea from Newe Zohar, you will pass **En Boqeq**, a resort town with hotels and a shore promenade lined with palm trees, on your way to the plateau of **Masada**, 20 kilometers away.

Rising up vertically from the plain, 440 meters on each side, this mighty tableland was, because of its secure and easily defensible location, settled in the earliest days of prehistory; later, a mountain fortress was erected atop it. Herod the Great, who had so many bitter enemies, was in dire need of a stout fortress that could not be taken; he therefore built a mighty castle on the plateau between 36 and 30 B.C., hewed cisterns for water directly out of the rock, constructed two splendid palaces for good measure, and also built storehouses for grain and provisions.

In 66 A.D., when the first uprising against Rome got underway, a group of

Zealots – a radical political minority with strong Jewish nationalist tendencies – overran the Roman garrison at Masada and brought the fortress under their control. Flavius Josephus reports that the Zealots started cultivating grain on the extensive plateau to provide themselves with more supplies; archaeologists, however, have consistently disputed this claim on the grounds that the region around Masada receives a maximum of 40 millimeters of rainfall a year. Recently, however, meteorologists have established that at the time of the uprising, there were completely different weather conditions in Masada, with considerable rainfall; the last 2,000 years have seen quite significant climatic change in the northern Negev.

After the Romans conquered Jerusalem, Masada was the only remaining center of Jewish resistance, and therefore a

thorn in the Roman side. At the beginning of winter in the year 72 A.D., Flavius Silva and his legionnaires marched to the foot of the plateau and put it under siege. Because of the fortress' huge stores of supplies and full cisterns of water, it would have taken years to starve out the inhabitants; therefore, this impregnable fortress would have to be forced by military measures.

Until a few years ago, archaeologists – including the leader of the Masada excavations, Yigael Yadin – were unanimous in their belief that the huge ramp up to the plateau was set up early on by Roman engineers in order to bring troops and a siege tower up to the top. Thus, at least ran the report of Flavius Josephus, whose descriptions had thereto consistently been supported by the evidence of archaeological excavations. But in August 1993, the geologist Dan Gill of the Geological Survey of Israel demonstrated that this sloping surface was of natural origin and, in all probability, only slightly enhanced by the hand of man. In

Above: Finally able to read the paper in peace – the Dead Sea's high salt content keeps your head above water.

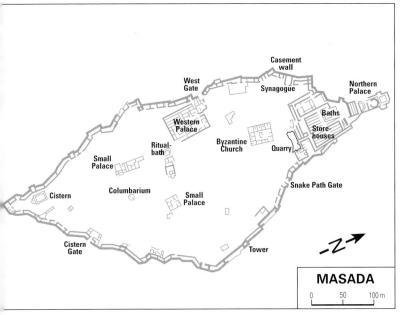

MASADA

0   50   100 m

he few months of the siege, the Romans could not possibly have managed to move the 250,000 cubic meters of earth which Josephus' report described as necessary to the task.

At the beginning of the year 73, the Romans had managed to put a hole in the defensive wall and set fire to the provisional barrier which the Zealots had hurriedly erected behind it. When they stormed the plateau the next morning, everything was dead silent. After a fiery oration from the Zealot leader Eleazar (doubtless a largely fictitious invention of Flavius Josephus), all of the residents of Masada had committed mass suicide – according to Flavius Josephus, a total of 960 men, women and children. Despite the inspirational nature of this story, it has been called into question in recent years whether or not this dramatic event actually took place, and Israel is starting to de-mythify the history of this powerful mountain fortress. Excavations have uncovered only 24 skeletons, and no sign anywhere of a tomb complex, or cemetery. Collective suicide, furthermore, would have gone against the spirit of the Jewish religion; the Jewish tradition emphasizes survival at any cost. There is not a single shred of concrete evidence beyond the say-so of Flavius Josephus – and he was not even there himself.

Until 1967, recruits to the Israeli Army were sworn in on this plateau, taking the famous oath, "Masada shall not fall again."

A cable car carries visitors up to the plateau, although it is classier to ascend on foot along the so-called Snake Path (about 45 minutes). Once you reach the top, you will find a roofed, shady rest area with water taps.

Both the Snake Path and the cable car arrive at the Snake Path Gate, which marks the start of the defensive walls, some 1,400 meters long, which once enclosed the entire area and stood around 8 meters high and 6 meters across. As you go toward the plateau's northern tip, you come upon the bathhouse, Herod's luxurious swimming facility. The walls of

205

the tepidarium (cooling room) and the frigidarium (cold-water bath) are adorned with mosaics, as are those of the caldarium (hot-water bath), which was heated by means of a hypocaust, or hot-air pipe system.

Clinging to the northernmost tip of the plateau is the **Northern Palace**. Herod's private residence. From the upper terrace, the ruler had a spectacular view; a flight of steps descends to the middle terrace, 20 meters lower down, with a round colonnaded courtyard, and continues a further 15 meters down to the lower terrace, with a square courtyard.

Slightly to the west are the remains of the oldest **synagogue** in the world, which the Zealots renovated and fitted out with stone benches. Farther south is a Byzantine-era **church** with a mosaic floor depicting plant and fruit motifs.

Above: The Romans broke Jewish resistance in 72 A.D. – exploring the mountain fortress of Masada. Right: In the cistern of Masada.

The **Western Palace**, halfway between the northern and southern ends of the plateau, directly on the city wall served as the ruler's official residence and was accordingly ornamented in such a way as to impress visitors as much as possible. The former reception room contains the oldest mosaic discovered in Israel. In the throne room, four post holes were possibly used to support a baldachin over the ruler's head. A citadel guarded Masada's southern tip, as the cliffs here were not quite as steep as in other areas; nearby, steps lead down to one of the many gigantic **cisterns** on the plateau, filled in by the rare, but torrential, rainfalls by means of an intelligent system of water pipes. From the plateau, you can clearly make out the remains of the **Roman Camp** at the foot of the mesa.

EN GEDI

Fifteen kilometers north of Masada is En Gedi, the largest oasis in the region, where recreational pursuits range from wimming in the Dead Sea to roaming in he attractive landscape of the nature ark. It was in this region that David ought refuge from Saul, who suspected im of insurrectionary plans, and "dwelt n strong holds...in the wilderness of En-edi" (1 Samuel 23:29-24:1).

A signposted path leads along Nahal David (David's River) through green woodland, past little splashing waterfalls nd natural pools shaded with ferns and igantic rushes, to a **waterfall** cascading nto a pool from a considerable height. You will not find a more refreshing place or a swim anywhere else in the area.

The countryside around the oasis is a paradise for birds, and with a little luck, you may also be able to spot ibex, foxes, nd rock hyraxes. A steep path leads rom here up to the Dodim Cave (Lovers' Cave) and the David Spring; south of this s the Shulamite Spring, named after the erotic figure in the Song of Songs who ings to Solomon, "My beloved is unto me as a cluster of camphire in the vin-yards of En-gedi" (Song of Solomon :14). Camphire, or henna, used to grow ere in days gone by.

From the spring, a path leads south to he Chalcolithic Temple. From here, you can continue on northwest to the "Dry Canyon" or west to the Roman Castle nd the round Israelite Fortress. To take n all of the nature park's sights, allow for a walk of at least five hours.

Overnight accommodations are avail-ble at the En Gedi kibbutz. North of the kibbutz are the ruins of a synagogue with floor mosaic depicting pairs of birds nd a star of David.

On the shore of the Dead Sea, near En Gedi, there is a campground with a res-aurant and youth hostel. Here, you can swim and sunbathe, or coat your body with thick black mud that can be scooped up at the seashore. Let it dry for a while before rinsing off! Rich in minerals, this mud is supposed to be excellent for your skin and for your overall state of health.

HAI-BAR ARAVA – A BIBLICAL WILDLIFE RESERVE

From En Gedi, you pass Masada and Newe Zohar once again as you go south along Route 90, parallel to the nearby Jordan border. The long, solitary drive through the desert is probably of interest only to real desert fans: the shimmering heat blurs colors and shapes, and gives rise to one mirage after another. Red peaks of rock alternate with chains of yel-low or purple hills. Bedouins drive their camels and sheep through the broad emp-tiness, and if it was not for the occasional airplane droning overhead, you could be-lieve that you had been transported lock, stock and barrel back into the days of the Bible.

Near Kibbutz Yotvata, 60 kilometers north of Elat, in the Biblical Wildlife Reserve **Hai-Bar Arava** (*Hai-Bar* means "wildlife"), biologists have settled every breed of animal that is mentioned in the Bible (guided tours at 9 and 10:30 am,

207

noon, and 1:30 pm). Herds of Somalian wild asses gallop across the dry savanna, raising clouds of dust; oryx antelope forage for the sparse grazing here; ibex leap across wide gorges; ostriches bury their heads in the sand. On one side, you may spot a cute little fennec, or desert fox, with its huge pointed ears; on the other, you might see a dangerous-looking lynx, recognizable by the long tufts on its ears. Branded with the stamp of ugliness is the hyena, which nonetheless demonstrates a sense of social solidarity; while one hyena is eating, the others wait their turn until he is done, and females in heat get to go first. Even the last desert leopard in the Negev, 18 years old, receives her food here; and she is no longer the least bit ruffled by tourists. In her younger years, she did honor to her race by taking on the residents of the kibbutz En Gedi, by the Dead Sea; but they, gradually tir-

Above: Mud-pack treatments by the Dead Sea. Right: Oryx antelope at the Hai Bar Reserve.

ing of watching their population of domestic animals being regularly reduced every second day, hired a hunter, who fired on her and critically injured her. Veterinarians saved the animal in an operation which took hours, and she was transferred for the rest of her days to the wildlife reserve. Biologists fear that in the Negev Desert and the neighboring Egyptian Sinai there are no more desert leopards left at all.

Many of the animals on the reservation are threatened with extinction. Among these is the Asian wild ass, which has never been domesticated. The white antelope was once common throughout the Middle East and on the Arabian peninsula; in his *Seven Pillars of Wisdom*, T. E. Lawrence ("of Arabia") mentions that antelope meat was the main nourishment of his Bedouin warriors. Today, the small herds in the reserve may be the only living specimens outside of Africa, where the white oryx population has also been drastically reduced. The future of the desert lynx, which appears to have

urvived only in Israel, also seems uncertain. Many of the animals bred and raised on the reserve are released into the wild when their population has built up sufficiently, in an effort to re-establish them in their natural habitats.

Near this nature park is the lush palm forest of the kibbutz Yotvata, a feast for the eye in the monochrome desert landscape. The numerous springs here quenched the thirst of Moses and his Israelite followers; these days, more prosaically, a pipeline carries their precious waters to Elat.

TIMNA PARK

Not far away is the Negev's next attraction. Half of Timna Park, which extends over 60 square kilometers, is surrounded by a rugged range of mountains 00 meters high. (The park is open daily, 7:30 am until sundown). Sunlight brings out the many rich hues of the rocks and cliffs; the lower part of the mountains consist of sandstone, shimmering in purplish tones, while above this layers of ocean sediment, solidified to chalk, which reflects back the strong glittering light.

In Timna, archaeologists have discovered the oldest mine in the world. Some 6,000 years ago, people began to mine copper ore here and learned how to form it into metal. The region is honeycombed with more than 1,000 mines, and dotted with the remains of kilns, in which simple but effective technology was used to extract the copper from the ore.

Into the stone ovens, which were lined with clay, went charcoal, copper ore, and iron or manganese oxide; the purpose of the latter was to bind the by-products of the ore, such as sulfur, and reduce the fluidity of the molten metal. Two foot-operated bellows were used to pump oxygen into the oven, where the heat reached levels of as high as $1,350°$ C. After five to seven hours, the copper – of which the melting point is $1,083°$ C – had become liquid and had separated from its by-products. The heavy metal sank to the

floor of the kiln, while the lighter waste ash floated on its surface. Now, all that was left to do was to make an opening in the kiln through which the slag and waste products could flow out, leaving behind them an ingot of pure copper.

From the 14th to the 12th centuries B.C., the Egyptian pharaohs exploited Timna's copper mines, mainly through the Midianites, unpopular throughout the region, who lived in the area between Egypt and Palestine as shepherds and traders, but who were also expert in the art of plunder and theft.

Near many of the kilns, archaeologists have found small Midianite temples with altars, sacrificial altars, fonts, and priests' cells. Expeditions of up to 1,000 men came from Egypt to bring the copper into the land of the pharaohs; royal cartridges with the names of the Egyptian rulers are still found along the route through Sinai

Above: King Solomon's Pillars in Timna Park. Right: The beach at Elat on the Red Sea.

and the Negev, and in Timna you can see a number of **cave paintings** from the Egyptian-Midianite period. Clearly recognizable are an ibex and an ostrich, both native to and common in the region; other depictions include a cart pulled by oxen and guarded by Eyptian soldiers with axes and shields as well as a group of hunters armed with knives, bows, and arrows.

At the center of Timna Park tower mighty, purplish rock formations around 60 meters high: **King Solomon's Pillars.** Erosion in the sandstone over millions of years has created these bizarre formations. A flight of stairs which the ancient Egyptians hewed into the rock leads up to a relief, showing Ramses III (who reigned from 1184-1153 B.C.) bringing an offering to the goddess Hathor. In fact Hathor was not only the patron of dancers, musicians and lovers, but also served as the godly benefactor of miners. At the foot of the pillars, the Egyptians built a central shrine which was also dedicated to Hathor.

Once you have taken in all of the shafts, kilns and cliff paintings, you can unwind at the small blue Timna Lake, with its good shady picnic spots. (However, swimming in the artificial lake is not allowed). From here it is only a half-hour drive on to Elat, Israel's tourist center on the Red Sea.

IN AND AROUND ELAT

Elat is at the southern tip of Israel, on the Gulf of Aqaba. Adjacent to the west is the Sinai Peninsula, while to the east, on clear nights, you can see the sparkling lights of the nearby Jordanian harbor city of Aqaba. At this point, Israel is only 15 kilometers wide.

Anyone wanting to venture into one of the neighboring countries, to see, perhaps, the convent of St. Catherine in the Sinai, or the impressive ruins of the former Nabatean capital of Petra in Jordan, will today encounter little difficulty. From Elat, it is no problem to travel into both of these countries, formerly enemies of Israel; large travel agencies are even setting up three-country tours which take in all the main tourist sights of Israel, Jordan and Egypt.

Elat is a modern tourist capital with luxurious hotels and shopping centers, a yacht marina, and a youth hostel. The city is popular with package tourists, with international travelers prepared to sleep on the beach, and with pickpockets. Particularly inviting is the long beach at the city center, where you can find yourself on the fine sand or swim in the warm waters of the Red Sea. It is so warm here all year round that you will hardly want to get out of the water, or crawl out of your beach chair.

One attraction of Elat is the **underwater observatory**, which was built into a coral reef. From a depth of 6 meters, visitors can watch the brighly-colored reef fish through thick panes of glass. Those who would like to make a more detailed investigation into the silent underwater world should take the **Yellow Submarine** on a 45-minute tour through

211

the coral reef; there are, furthermore, legion diving schools in the area, while glass-bottomed boats run regularly out of the small marina.

At the **Coral Beach Nature Reserve**, a bit out of the town center toward the Egyptian border, you can rent flippers, mask and snorkel and snorkel out along the reef to examine the bright fish at first hand.

Do not, however, go into the water without bathing shoes; the ocean floor is covered with bits of dead, razor-sharp coral, and there is also the risk of stepping on a starfish (whose spines can inject you with deadly poison).

But Elat's main attraction is the nearby **Dolphin Reef**; here, a big net screens off the mouth of a bay and prevents dolphins and sea lions from swimming away. With a snorkel (or, if you have a license, with oxygen tanks), you can swim with the

dolphins, touch them, and even let them pull you through the water, a truly unforgettable experience (advance reservations necessary).

A few kilometers northwest of Elat on Route 40, you can drive along a steep dirt road almost to the peak of **Mount Yoash**. From up here, you have a fantastic (and photogenic) view. To the east and south you can see out over Elat to the Jordanian harbor city of Aqaba, a vista of the jagged mountains of Edom, and the Saudi Arabian coast of the Red Sea, while to the west extends the panorama of Moon Valley in Egypt, which is framed by high mountains which glow red in the warm sun.

Nor should you pass up the chance to visit the **Red Canyon**, located a few kilometers farther north on Route 40. Walking from the road, you follow a *wadi*, or dry river bed, for a short distance; this brings you directly into the narrow rock gorge. You can clearly see how, over the millennia, water has eaten out gorges – sometimes no more than 1.5 meters wide

Above: From Elat, you can see the city of Aqaba in Jordan. Right: In Elat's underwater observatory.

- into the red sandstone. With help, when necessary, of handrails, or grips cut into the rock, you can follow the path further and further down, until the gorge opens out again into a broad *wadi*. From here, you can return to the surface by means of a narrow path, with ladders, and walk back along the top of the canyon.

IN THE HEART OF THE NEGEV

On the way from Elat to the north, through the heart of the Negev along Route 40, you will pass some other landscape highlights of the region. After some 100 kilometers of uneventful driving, the road – here called *Ma'ale Ha'atzmaut*, "Pass of Independence" – suddenly becomes steep and starts twisting in hairpin curves.

At the top, you have got a view of the gigantic "crater" of **Makhtesh Ramon**, 40 kilometers long, 10 kilometers wide, and surrounded by vertical rock faces 430 meters high. However, the crater is not of volcanic origin, but came into

being around 70 million years ago, when the region, which was honeycombed with extensive networks of caves, simply collapsed. Paleontologists have found fossils of animals that lived in the area some 200 million years ago, including traces of dinosaurs.

A **visitor's center**, built in the shape of a giant ammonite fossil, provides further information on the geological history of the region. At the northwest rim of the valley is the miners' city **Mitzpe Ramon**, which does credit to its name: *Mitzpe* which means lookout point.

After the flight from Egypt, the Israelites set up camp for a time in this desert crater, which appears inimical to any form of life. It is easy to understand how the Chosen People, on their way to a land supposedly "flowing with milk and honey," balked at their immediate surroundings and could not find anything good to say about Moses or his God: far from flowing with milk and honey, this crater cannot boast even a trickle of running water.

The well-to-do merchant people of the Nabateans, however, set up a flourishing city in the center of the desert, only a few kilometers to the north, in the 3rd century B.C. **Avdat** was an important stop for caravans along the trade route leading from the Nabatean capital of Petra (in present-day Jordan) through Elat to Gaza on the Mediterranean.

In the dry climate of the Negev, the Nabateans made use of an extensive system of cisterns and sophisticated irrigation techniques for agricultural purposes, and were eminently successful.

In the 3rd century, the Romans had a military camp here and built a Temple of Jupiter; in the Byzantine era, the inhabitants were Christianized. After the Persians and Islamic Arabs overran the area in the 7th century, the city was finally abandoned.

Above: Without a hump, you will have to be satisfied with a canteen – hiking in the Negev. Right: Border patrol in the Negev Desert.

Israeli botanists and archaeologists have reconstructed a Nabatean farm, got the irrigation system working again, and have cultivated, very successfully, plants which the Nabateans themselves used centuries before.

The fabulous excavation site contains a wealth of interesting sights: near the upper parking lot is a Roman residential district with a Nabatean wine press and a pottery; through the south gate, you come to the partly-restored **Byzantine Fortress**, with the ruins of a chapel and monastic rooms; two three-aisle basilicas, the **Theodoros Church** and the **North Church**, are also integrated into the castle complex. South of this, at the lower parking lot, are several burial chambers, remains of a Byzantine-era residence, and a Byzantine bath.

Not far from this site is a natural attraction: **En Avdat**. En means spring, and here you can enjoy cool water in the desert heat. The view into the gorge of En Avdat, some 50 meters across, a few kilometers long and several hundreds of meters deep, is truly spectacular. Today a dry bed, the river Zin flowed here for millions of years and etched out a deep track for itself in the soft chalky stone. If you are subject to vertigo, do not even bother to essay the narrow, stepped path and the ladders that lead down into the gorge. At the narrowest points, handholds in the stone provide a measure of extra security.

When you arrive at the bottom, you will find you have left the desert behind altogether. Tamarisk trees cast shade over three small lakes; still further down, there is a fourth pool, fed by a splashing waterfall.

Bordering on the northeastern end of En Avdat are the lands of the kibbutz **Sede Boqer** with the Negev branch of Ben Gurion University in Be'er Sheva; this campus is dedicated to the natural sciences, sociology, archaeology and history. In addition, there is a Natural Solar

Energy Center, where a visitor's center has plenty of information about the latest developments in solar technology.

In front of the library of this desert university is the last resting place of David Ben Gurion (1886-1973), Israel's first Prime Minister, and his wife, Paula. The Gurions were members of the community project of Sede Boqer; after the end of his first term in office, in 1953, David and Paula moved into the newly-founded kibbutz.

You can visit their tiny house, which can hardly hold the 5,000 books (and remember, there are 20,000 more in his house in Tel Aviv); for all the house's small size, Ben Gurion had no qualms about receiving prominent politicians from around the world in it (thereby constantly reaffirming Israel's possession of the Negev).

Mizpe Rivivim, halfway to Be'er Sheva, was the first Israeli kibbutz in the desert. The impetus to settle the Negev came from Ben Gurion himself. The old man knew that when the U.N. drew up its plans for the partition of Palestine, the huge Negev region would only be awarded to the Israelis if they had demonstrated visible efforts to make it arable. In 1947, a U.N. delegation inspected Mitzpe Rivivim and was impressed by the evident success of the kibbutzniks.

A year later, after the State of Israel had been officially proclaimed and the armies of the five neighboring Arabian countries had crossed Israel's borders, the settlers here had to hold at bay Egyptian forces many times stronger than their own. For weeks, the Egyptians shelled the kibbutz with heavy artillery fire, but they were never able to take it. After the war, the inhabitants of the kibbutz preserved their central defense position as a monument.

In this kibbutz, you can examine the accommodations of the earliest kibbutzniks, with original furniture and the defensive trenches, and get a realistic taste of what life was like in the period just after the declaration of Israeli independence.

BE'ER SHEVA

Getting There
From Tel Aviv (central bus station in the south of the city, or from Arlozoroff Station at the train station) and Jerusalem (bus station Jaffa Road), buses run several times a day to Be'er Sheva. There is also a *Sherut* service from Tel Aviv and Jerusalem.

Accommodation
LUXURY: **Hilton Hotel**, 1 Henrietta Szold St., tel. 07-6405444.
MODERATE: **The Desert Inn**, Sderot Tuviyahu, tel. 07-6424922, renovated in 1998, has center for alternative medicine.
BUDGET: **Bet Yatsiv Guest House**, 79 Haatzmaut Street, tel. 07-6277444, the guest house has an adjacent youth hostel. **Hotel Aviv**, Hagetaot Street, tel. 07-6278059, in the Old City. **Hotel Hanegev**, 26 Haatzmaut Street, tel. 07-6277026.

Restaurants
Bulgarit, 112 Keren Kayemet Le Yisrael Street, itel. 07-6289511, in the pedestrian zone of the Old City, with plenty of tradition and low-priced Eastern European and Oriental dishes. **Pitput**, 122 Herzl Street, tel. 07-6237708, light meals of every description, from pizza and sandwiches through pasta and vegetable casseroles to omelettes, soups, and so on.
There are a number of other cafés and small restaurants in the huge concrete shopping center at the bus station. The two American fast food chains Pizza Hut and Burger King have branches here, but you can also find the thoroughly acceptable Chinese restaurant **China Town** and the **Café George**, which offers light snacks, with air conditioning.

Museums
Israel Air Force Museum, 15 kilometers west of Be'er Sheva on Route 233, Sun-Thu 8 am-5 pm, Fri 8 am-noon.
Museum of Bedouin Culture in the Alon Regional and Folklore Centre, 20 kilometers northeast of Be'er Sheva in the village of Lahav, Sun-Thu 9 am-4 pm, Fri 9 am-2 pm, Sat 9 am-4 pm.

Hospitals and Pharmacies
Soroka Hospital, Hanassaim Boulevard, tel. 07-6400111.
Yerushalayim Pharmacy, 34 Herzl Street as well as **Super Pharm** in the huge concrete shopping mall at the bus station.

Tourist Information
Tourist Information Office, Hebron Street, corner of Keren Kayemet, tel. 07-6234613.

EN BOQEQ

Accommodation
LUXURY: **Hyatt**, tel. 07-6591234. **Nirvana**, tel. 07-6584626. **Sheraton Moriah**, tel. 07-6591591.
MODERATE: **Carlton-Galei Zohar**, tel. 07-6584311. **Hod**, tel. 07-6584644. **Lot**, tel. 07-6584321-4. **Tsell Harim**, tel. 07-6584121-2.

ARAD

Getting There
Buses run several times a day from Be'er Sheva; there is also a *Sherut* service from Be'er Sheva.

Accommodation
LUXURY: **Margoa**, Moab Street, tel. 07-9951222, known for a quarter of a century for its asthma clinic, best hotel in Arad. **Nof Arad**, Moab Street, tel. 07-9957056, opposite the Margoa, and almost as good, yet somewhat cheaper. *BUDGET:* **Blau-Weiss Youth Hostel**, Arad Street, tel. 07-9957150, named after a Zionist German youth group.

Restaurants
Steiner's, at the entrance to the city on Route 31, near a Delek gas station. This is Arad's oldest restaurant with a wide range of delicious but reasonably-priced meals.

Museum and Sights
Arad Museum and Visitor Centre, Ben Yair Street, Sun-Thu/Sat 9 am-5 pm, Fri 9 am-2 pm.
Tel Arad, Sun-Thu 8 am-5 pm, Fri 8 am-4 pm.

Hospitals and Pharmacies
First Aid Station, Yehuda Street, tel. 07-9959333.
Pharmacy in the Commercial Centre near the tourist information office.

Tourist Information
Tourist Information in the Arad Visitor Centre, 28 Ben Yair Street, tel. 07-9954409.

ELAT

Getting There
Arkia Airline has flights several times a day from Sde Dov Airport in the north of Tel Aviv, as well as several flights a day from the Atarot Airport 10 kilometers north of Jerusalem and 3 times a day from Haifa Airport to Elat. The airport is located in the middle of the city.
Buses run several times a day from the Central Bus Stations in Tel Aviv and Jerusalem. It is definitely worth your while to reserve a seat, especially in high season.

Accommodation

LUXURY: **The Neptune**, The Promenade, North Beach, tel. 07-6369369, good views over the marina, the beach and the ocean. **The Sport Hotel**, North Beach, tel. 07-6303333, fitted out with every imaginable manner of sports equipment. **King Solomon Palace**, The Promenade, North Beach, tel. 07-6363444, the name indicates the level of luxury of the hotel itself. **Ambassador Red Sea Sports Club Hotel**, on Route 90, toward the Egyptian border, special diving hotel, tel. 07-6382222. **Princess Hotel**, near the Egyptian border, tel. 07-6365555.

MODERATE: **The Edomite**, New Tourist Centre, tel. 07-6379511, in the center of Elat. **Etzion Hotel**, opposite the bus station, tel. 07-6374131, **Adi Hotel**, New Tourist Centre, on Yotam Boulevard, tel. 07-6376151. **Dalia**, tel. 07-6334004 and **Americana**, tel. 07-6333777, both reasonably-priced establishments, although located within the expensive hotel district on the lagoon.

BUDGET: **Sunset Hostel**, 130 Retamin Street, tel. 07-6373817. **Elat Youth Hostel**, Arava Road, tel. 07-6372358. **Spring Hostel**, Ofarim Street, tel. 07-6374660. **Nathan's White House Hostel**, 131 Retamin Street, tel. 07-6376572. **Taba Youth Hostel**, Hativat Hanegev Street, tel. 07-6375982. **Bet Arava**, 106 Almogim Street, tel. 07-6371052. **Elat Field School**, Harava Road, tel. 07-6371127, opposite Coral Beach; if the hostel is full, you can set up your tent in the hostel's campground. **Sinai Hostel**, Hativat Hanegev Street, tel. 07-6372826, simple lodging. **Shalom Hostel**, Hativat Henegev Street, tel. 07-6376544, simple lodging.

YOUTH HOSTEL: **IYHA Youth Hostel**, Arava Road, tel. 07-6372358, member of the International Youth Hostel Association.

CAMPING: **Almogim Camping** is the city campground, on Harava Street opposite Coral Beach, tel. 07-6371911.

For additional campsites, see **Elat Field School**.

Restaurants

El Morocco, New Tourist Center, tel. 07-6371296, Moroccan specialties and grilled dishes.

Red Sea Star, Hadromint Sq., tel. 07-6340250, near the Meridian Hotel, the first underwater restaurant in the world, exclusive fish specialties, bar.

Eddie's Hideway, Almogim Street, tel. 07-6371137, American-inspired cuisine, all manner and size of steaks.

Fisherman's House, on Coral Beach, tel. 07-6379830, self-service fish restaurant.

Hard Luck Café, 15 Almogim Street, tel. 07-6232788, budget café-restaurant with fish & chips and a range of pasta.

Last Refuge, on Route 90 on Coral Beach, tel. 07-6372437, this is the best seafood restaurant in Elat.

Mai Tai, Yotam Street, tel. 07-6372517, Thai cuisine.

Mandy's Chinese Restaurant, on Coral Beach, tel. 07-6333879, good Chinese food.

Tandoori, King's Wharf, on the lagoon, tel. 07-6333879, very good Indian food with corresponding prices, often accompanied by Indian music and dance performances in the evening.

Sights

Dolphin Reef, Elat, tel. 07-6371846, daily 9 am-5 pm, advance reservation required.

Underwater observatory at **Coral Reef**, tel. 07-6364200, Sat-Thu 8:30 am-4:30 pm, Fri 8:30 am-3 pm.

Hospitals and Pharmacies

Yoseftal Hospital, Yotam Street, tel. 07-6350011. **Michlin Pharmacy**, opposite the bus station.

Diving

Aqua Sport International Red Sea Diving Centre, Coral Beach, tel. 07-6334404.

Manta Diving Club, on Coral Beach, in the Ambassador Hotel, tel. 07-6333666.

Lucky Divers, Marina and Coral Beach, tel. 07-6335990.

Tourist Information

Municipal Tourist Office, Arava Road, corner of Yotam, tel. 07-6372111.

NEGEV

Sights and Museums

EN AVDAT: Nabatean Farm Avdat, open daily 8 am-4 pm. **En Avdat**, open Sun-Thu 8 am-5 pm, Fri 8 am-4 pm.

EN GEDI: En Gedi National Park, open Sat-Thu 8 am-4 pm, Fri 8 am-3 pm.

HAI BAR RESERVE: daily 8 am-3 pm, buses for round-trip tours depart from the Hai Bar Visitor Centre at 9 am, 10:30 am, noon, and 1:30 pm.

MASADA: open Sat-Thu 8 am-3:30 pm, Fri 8 am-1:30 pm.

MIZPE RAMON: Makhtesh Ramon Visitor Centre, open Sun-Thu and Sat 9 am-4:30 pm, Fri 9 am-2:30 pm.

MIZPE RIVIVIM: former war bunkers in the kibbutz Mizpe Rivivim, 30 km south of Be'er Sheva, open Sun-Thu 9 am-3 pm, Fri 9 am-noon, Sat 10 am-4 pm.

SEDE BOQER: House of Ben Gurion, in the kibbutz Sede Boqer, open Sun-Thu 8:30 am-3:30 pm, Fri 8:30 am-1 pm, Sat 8:30 am-2:30 pm.

TIMNA PARK: open daily 7:30 am to sunset.

EXCURSIONS TO JORDAN

JERASH / AMMAN
DESERT PALACES
MADABA
MOUNT NEBO
KERAK / PETRA
WADI RUM / AQABA

JERASH

About 50 kilometers north of Amman is the ancient city **Gerasa** (today called **Jerash**). Gerasa was founded by the Greeks in the 2nd century B.C., but settlements from the Neolithic Age and the Bronze Age have also been identified. The town saw its first great flowering, however, in the days of the Romans, when the population grew to 25,000. From 63 B.C. until 106 A.D., Gerasa belonged to the Decapolis, the federation of ten free cities in the Roman province of Syria. After 106 A.D., the Decapolis was combined with the former Nabatean kingdom to the south to comprise the Roman *Provincia Arabia*. Specializing in trade and commerce, but also surrounded by fertile countryside, Gerasa benefitted from its central position within the province, as well as from the new network of Roman roads and the fact that the Romans protected its borders; the ruins that you see today are from building projects from this period, partly financed by Rome, but also underwritten by wealthy merchant families from Gerasa itself.

Preceding pages: Temples in the landscape – a fantastic combination in Petra (here, Ed-Deir). Left: Bedouin woman from Siq al-Barid.

Towards the end of the 3rd century A.D., this phase of prosperity came to a temporary end, precipitated by the late Roman Empire's political problems both at home and abroad. All building projects were stopped; Gerasa's population had to content itself with maintaining the buildings that already existed. In the early Byzantine period (5th/6th centuries) the town, which had in the meantime become Christian, flourished a second time, something to which the many churches built in this period attest. Temples were converted into churches; in addition, stones and columns from temples were used in the construction of new churches.

In the early 7th century, Gerasa was conquered, first by Sassanids, then by Muslims. A terrible earthquake in 747 razed Gerasa to the ground, and the town remained uninhabited for more than 1,000 years. Not until 1878 did Cherkassian immigrants settle in the eastern part of town, and they used the ancient ruins as a source of building materials.

While the eastern section is full of modern buildings, the well-preserved western area still gives some indication of its former importance as a Roman province town – which is why Gerasa today is famous, second only to Petra, as one of the most important sights in Jordan. From the south, you reach the ruins

221

through a Visitors Center, where there is also a detailed model of the city.

Gerasa is entered through its **south gate**, which sports Corinthian pilasters and barrel-vaulted passageways. The gate is set into the city walls, which formed a ring about 3.5 kilometers long and an average of 2.5 meters wide; constructed in the 1st century, the walls are best preserved around the south gate. Only a few meters further on, you will reach the **Oval Forum**, the most unusual town square from Antiquity that is known today. Edged with a colonnade, the square was built on 7-meter high foundations to compensate for the unevenness of the terrain. The reason for its curious shape was that a transitional element was needed between the northwest-southeast orientation of the adjacent **Temple of Zeus** and the north-south layout of the Roman road network. The original Zeus temple dated from the Hellenic period; later Roman additions from the 1st and 2nd centuries A.D. are temporarily closed for renovation work.

From the Oval Forum, a steep path leads to the **South Theater** (end of the 1st century A.D.), which has been painstakingly restored, but is not true to the original. It once accommodated as many as 5,000 spectators. From the top row you have a fantastic view over the ruins.

Approximately 700 meters in length, the **colonnaded main street** (Cardo Maximus), which was expanded in the 2nd century, runs from the northern end of the Oval Forum (Corinthian columns, paving stones laid diagonally, and a raised sidewalk). After about 150 meters this street is crossed by another road, Southern Decumanus; the circular intersection is marked by a **tetrapylon** (a gate with a dome supported on four columns). A few meters further, a path to the left leads to the **cathedral**. This edifice is ac-

tually two churches joined together; the lower eastern end of the building was built on the foundations of an ancient temple of Dionysus. Above the cathedral and set perpendicular to it, is **St. Theodore's Church** (4th/5th centuries).

If you continue to follow the colonnade, you will see, on your left, the semicircular **nympheum** (a splendid fountain from the 2nd century); we can now only imagine the extravagance of its original ornamentation. Shortly after this, wide steps to the left lead to the Artemis Temple; but first turn right and go into the **propylaeum court** (2nd century A.D.), since this was a terminus for processions from the eastern residential areas. At the narrow end of the courtyard, niches were built into the walls, holding basins of water in which the faithful could wash. After crossing the Cardo, you climb directly up wide steps to the altar-terrace. Here, hundreds of believers could participate in or observe the ceremonies of cult sacrifice; today, all that remains of the altar are its foundations.

It takes a bit of time for the vast dimensions of the **Temple of Artemis**, once a magnificent place of worship, to sink in: a flight of steps 120 meters wide leads up to the broad temenos, or temple courtyard, which was once surrounded by a hall with columns. More steps lead to the cella or shrine of Artemis, originally faced in marble. Artemis was the town's patron goddess, and a statue of her, painted in bright colors, stood in the niche at the back of the temple.

From here, continue westward over the hill to a complex of three Byzantine churches, built in 529-533 A.D. The newest, the **Church of Ss. Cosmas and Damian**, had already been destroyed by the time that 8th-century Islamic iconoclasm was disposing of many other edifices; you can admire its beautiful mosaic floors from a wall built around the ruins. The oldest of the churches is the **Church of St. George**, a three-aisled basilica.

Right: The ruins of the Temple of Artemis at Jerash.

Before you leave Gerasa to travel south towards Amman, take a look at Emperor Hadrian's **triumphal arch** (129 A.D.). The hippodrome (horse racetrack) used to be to the north of it.

AMMAN

A century ago, it was a mere Cherkassian village; today, Amman is the country's modern capital, with 1.5 million (mainly Palestinian) inhabitants.

Today, Amman betrays little of its past as the **Philadelphia** of antiquity, a city which, like Gerasa, belonged to the Decapolis. The **theater** from the 2nd century A.D., one of the largest Roman theaters in Jordan, could accommodate 6,000 spectators. It lay in ruins for centuries and was not restored until 1970. The **Folklore Museum** and the **Museum of Popular Traditions**, housed in the two wings of the stage building, are worth a visit. To the right in front of the amphitheater stands the **Odeon** (2nd century A.D.), a small, roofed theater with

500 seats. Today, the plaza in front of the theater only represents a fraction of the size of the ancient forum, which is estimated to have covered 7,500 square meters; if this figure is accurate, it would have been the largest forum in the whole eastern portion of the Roman Empire.

An absolute must in Amman is a trip up the hill of the **citadel**. From the ruins of the **Temple of Hercules**, which dominated the acropolis, there is a fabulous view of the town and the amphitheater opposite. Important finds from throughout Jordan – the Dead Sea Scrolls, Nabatean ceramics from Petra, a hand from the 9-meter-tall statue of Hercules, examples of Islamic calligraphy – are displayed in the **Archaeological Museum**. To the north of the citadel you can see the foundations of an Umayyad palace from the early 8th century (a house with an inner courtyard, in Iranian architectural tradition), as well as a Byzantine basilica from the 4th-5th centuries.

Also worthwhile is a detour to the **suqs**, located behind the **King Hussein**

Mosque (built in 1924) with its variously-formed minarets. The largest mosque in Amman was not comleted until 1989: in the **King Abdallah Mosque**, you can get an impression of modern Jordanian architecture. The **Abu Darwish Mosque** in the south, with its black-and-white façade, is also well worth a visit.

25 kilometers southwest of Amman is the **Qasr al-Abd** (Palace of the Slaves) in Wadi es-Sir. This palace building from the 2nd century B.C. is impressive for its huge blocks of stone and its well-preserved reliefs of lions.

THE DESERT PALACES

In Syria, Lebanon, Israel, and Jordan, there are a total of over 20 so-called Umayyad "Desert Palaces." Three of these which are particularly worth seeing are east of Amman. Today, the exact building date or the function of these edi-

fices are still open to question, since Umayyad builders (7th-8th centuries) had no characteristic style of their own, but rather were known for borrowing elements from other architectural epochs. Many theories have attempted to explain the significance these desert palaces may have had for the caliphs of Damascus. Did the caliphs come here to feel at one with their Bedouin ancestors? Were they better able to live as they pleased in these spots distant from their cities? Traces of irrigation sytems have been found; were the palaces simply large farmhouses? Or were they used for holding court from time to time, to show the nomads the strength of the new Islamic empire, and thus win their loyalty?

A good main road runs southeast from Amman to Azraq. On the right, after 55 kilometers, you will see **Qasr al-Kharane**, a square two-story building measuring 35 meters on a side, with round corner towers and semicircular towers halfway along each side. The openings in the walls are not slits for fir-

Above: Evening bustle in the Jordanian capital, Amman.

g at enemies, but rather served to venti-
te the rooms inside. The entrance hall is
n the south side; to the left and right of it
re two large stables or storage rooms.
eading off from the rectangular inner
ourtyard are three separate residential
partments. A low staircase leads to the
pper story, where the living quarters are
iterconnected, forming a virtual laby-
nth; they are also decorated much more
vishly than the rooms on the lower
oor. Much about the architecture hints
at the building could have been used as
Persian caravanserai, but the palace is
robably an original Umayyad structure.

After another 5 kilometers you will
ach **Qasr Amra**, which was discovered
1 1898 by the noted Bedouin expert,
lois Musil. From a three-aisled audi-
nce room, with a niche for the throne in
e central aisle, there is access to a bath-
ouse with a changing room, a tepida-
um (with a hypocaust system for floor
eating), and a steam bath. The heating
om, storage room and pump room are
lso accessible from outside. There is
othing odd about this juxtaposition of an
udience room and bathhouse since, in
e true Oriental tradition, Umayyads
ften held conferences in the bath. Qasr
mra is famous for its figurative frescoes
on the left wall of the audience room are
e "Great Bathers," six major leaders
rom world history and youths engaged
1 sports; on the right wall are scenes of
unting and craftsmen at work). The fre-
coes in the bathhouse, which reflect a
horough knowledge of Greek mytho-
gy, might well be the work of a master
f the "Madaba School." From an art his-
orical point of view, these wall paintings
re downright sensational, given the fact
hat such images are strictly forbidden by
slamic law.

From Qasr Amra, it is another 50 ki-
ometers to the oasis Azraq, which was
ettled as early as the Neolithic period. In
he northern part of town is a fortress of
lack basalt: **Qasr Azraq**. Its history has

been eventful. In the 3rd/4th centuries A.D., Qasr served as a Roman border fortress. In the 8th century, the caliph Walid II converted the building into a base for hunting expeditions (with a mosque in the courtyard). Later Qasr served as military headquarters for the Ayyubids in battles with the Crusaders (13th century). In the winter of 1917/18, T. E. Lawrence took shelter here before his attack on Damascus, and described the heavy basalt slab of the back gate.

If you want to avoid going back the way you came, leave Azraq on the main road to Zarqa, and visit **Qasr Hallabat**, a fortress which, almost completely in ruins, dates back to the Roman era.

MADABA AND MOUNT NEBO

From Amman, a road southwest leads about 30 kilometers to **Madaba**. This is the starting point of the Kings' Highway,

Above and right: Qasr Amra is famous for its figurative frescoes.

an old caravan road which leads through breathtaking landscape.

Madaba was already famous in Biblical times: it was here that David's army defeated the Ammonites and Moabites. In the 6th century A.D., the town gained new importance as a bishop's residence; its mosaic workshop was also renowned. In the 8th century an earthquake destroyed the town, burying the church's mosaics under rubble; they were not uncovered until the end of the 19th century.

Famous, too, is the **Map of Palestine** in **St. George's Church**. It represents the Holy Land the way Moses must have seen it from Mount Nebo, and helped to orient worshippers en route to the Middle Eastern pilgrimage towns. The area shown extends from northern Egypt to southern Lebanon; in the center of the map is Jerusalem (complete with town walls and gates), the Jordan river valley and the Dead Sea. The composition is enlivened with place names in Greek (with a few spelling mistakes!) and images of plants and animals.

Another famous mosaic is in the ruins of the **Church of the Apostles** (on the road to Kerak): the **Thalassa Mosaic**. This round image depicts a sea goddess surrounded by all manner of animals and plants. Characteristic of the Madaba school are the plastically-rendered images of people and animals, which reflect Greek influence.

About 10 kilometers north of Madaba is **Mount Nebo**, from which Moses is said to have looked out over the Promised Land (a monument marks the spot), and where he is supposed to have died and been buried. Not only do you have an extraordinary view of the Jordan Valley and the Dead Sea from here, but you can also survey 4,000 years of history. Nebo came to dubious fame when King Mesha had all 7,000 inhabitants of the town massacred in the middle of the 9th century B.C. In the 4th century A.D., Egyptian monks settled here and founded a monastery. The churches with their wonderful Madaba school mosaics, of which the original foundations still exist, date from the 6th century. Like Madaba, this place also declined in the 8th century. Not until 1901 did Alois Musil rediscover the Byzantine churches on both peaks of Mount Nebo. These spectacular findings inspired the Franciscan order to purchase the whole mountain.

The mosaics in the **Monastery Basilica of Siyagha** depict a number of different wild animals, hunters, a scene of a grape harvest and the process of making wine, and a personification of the earth. Not far from Siyagha, in the **Church of Ss. Lot and Procopius** on the hill of Khirbet al-Mukhayyet, you can admire other mosaics with wine-making motifs and hunting and music scenes.

KERAK ON THE KING'S HIGHWAY

From Madaba, it is another 90 kilometers south to Kerak. The drive leads through majestic countryside along the famous trade route of the King's Highway. It is not known where this caravan road got its name, but it is certain that for thousands of years, the most diverse kingdoms struggled to control this important route. As early as the Neolithic period, people were settling and farming these valleys, thanks to their favorable climate. As a trade route, the safe King's Highway was always preferable to the desert road further east, which was constantly threatened by thieving nomads.

So **Kerak**, too, can look back on a long history: Moabites, Assyrians, Jews, Greeks, Romans, Byzantines, and the Arab Umiyyads followed closely on each other's heels, until the town started to decline in importance around the 8th century. This situation did not change again until the time of the Crusades, when Kerak, at a key strategic position, became indispensable for anyone who wanted control of the southern Dead Sea and the eastern desert road. In 1142, Payen le Bouteiller had the invincible fortress expanded; in case of siege, the occupants could call for reinforcements with signal fires visible from as far away as Jerusalem. In 1170, Reynald de Chatillon, the new, cruel master of the fortress, and Saladin, the founder of the Ayyubid dynasty, began to fight over control of the fortress. The Crusader had threatened Muslim caravans and even Mecca. Saladin was not able to conquer the fortress until he had defeated the Christian army at Hattin in 1187. His brother Adil had the stronghold further developed with a bailey and a palace. In the 13th century the Mamelukes succeeded the Ayyubids and built more castles, including Baybar's bastion in northern Kerak.

When you visit the fortress, you can distinguish, from the different building materials used, which parts of the building were built by the Franks (reddish-black volcanic stone) and which by the Ayyubid-Mamelukes (yellowish limestone). Behind the main gate, steps lead down to the lower fortress with its museum and underground hall. If you follow the steps upwards, you can see the Ayyubid-Mameluke keep, the fortified tower of the stronghold, opposite. In front of it, you can make out the remains of the palace. Directly to the right by the entrance gate is a long, dark vaulted hall which served the Crusaders as stables.

From Kerak, the King's Highway continues further to the south, through Tafila and **Shobak** (about 120 kilometers) to Petra (another 50 kilometers). After Kerak, Shobak is the most important Crusader castle in Jordan. The location is memorable, but the fortress lies in ruins.

PETRA

Petra, the old capital of the Nabatean empire, is unquestionably the highlight

Right: Tombs of kings hewn out of the living rock in Petra, the unique city of the Nabateans.

of any trip to Jordan. Plan to spend at least one whole day visiting the ruins.

From the Desert Highway, the road branches off at Ma'an (about 200 kilometers south of Amman) towards Wadi Mousa, a village near Petra. Day tickets are sold at the **Visitors Center**; you can also buy a pass valid for several days for a reasonable price. If you are not comfortable walking, you can rent a carriage here (since 1995, you are only allowed to ride horses along the short stretch up to the mouth of the gorge).

History and Culture

The Nabateans were a nomadic tribe from southern Arabia who settled in the region in the 4th century B.C. At first they lived as livestock breeders and traders, transporting asphalt from the Dead Sea to Egypt, or aromatics such as incense and myrrh from southern Arabia to the Mediterranean. They had neither houses nor established forms of agriculture. In the course of the 2nd century B.C., they developed a monarchy, taking the Greeks as their model, and expanded the limits of their dominion; in the 1st century B.C., it reached as far as Damascus. They never viewed their borders as rigid, however, and other peoples who lived on their territory were accorded respect and their own cultural identity.

In the year 63 B.C., Petra was conquered by the Romans, but was able to buy back its independence by paying tribute. After the beginning of the Christian Era, the Nabateans developed into a prosperous people who lived in permanent houses, engaged in thriving trade and agriculture, and raised livestock; in this period, Petra had 30,000 inhabitants. As traders, however, the Nabateans struggled with increasing competition from the Ptolemies who, with their ships, now dominated the transport of goods between southern Arabia and the Mediterranean. In the year 106 A.D., Petra be-

came part of the Roman province Arabia and the Nabateans became increasingly Romanized.

To date, not much is known about Nabatean culture; one characteristic, however, is their mingling of ancient Arab and Hellenic influences. Famous, for example, are their fine red ceramics, painted with a wide range of different designs in a darker red. Their cleverly devised system to supply the population with water is also notable. Nabatean writing is reminiscent of Aramaic, and is considered a precursor of Kufic Arabic. The large necropolises with their ornate tomb architecture raise many questions about the Nabatean cult of the dead. The Nabateans worshiped their gods in special cult areas, as well as with faceless, non-figurative stone sculptures which they placed in niches in the cliffs (Betyl). The gods were not given recognizable forms until the advent of the Romans. Their main god, Dhushara (Lord of the Crests of Petra), was himself made of stone and was comparable with Dionysus or Zeus.

The Arabian goddesses Allat and al-Uzza correspond to Aphrodite and Venus; Shai al Qaum was the protector of caravans, and Qaus was the god of weather.

Following the earthquake of the year 363, the town was almost completely deserted. The eastern Roman church had a cathedral consecrated in Petra in 446. Another serious earthquake shook the city in 747. After that, it was uninhabited and forgotten until 1812, when Johann Ludwig Burckhardt, a young Swiss traveler and adventurer, rediscovered Petra while searching for the tomb of Aaron. The news of this sensational find triggered a wave of European travelers to Petra in the middle of the 19th century.

Sightseeing

The path down to the ruins leads through the **Siq**, a narrow gorge with walls towering more than 70 meters. It was not erosion which formed this natural wonder, but plate tectonics. The red sandstone is streaked with veins of green,

yellow, and blue-gray. Beyond the embankment left of the path, you can see the remains of an ancient water transport system which was fed by the Moses Spring. Above, you can still see the beginnings of an arch which once spanned the gorge. The path was originally paved with stone slabs. On the way, you can make out reliefs shaped like pointed arches in the canyon walls, the so-called Nefesh (souls) which were meant as reminders of the dead, and votive niches (Betyl), which held images of gods.

Suddenly, the narrow gorge widens out and reveals the **Khazne al-Firaun** (treasure house of the pharaoh, probably from the 1st century A.D.), the most impressive structure in Petra (25 meters wide and 40 meters tall); although it is still open to question whether it served as a temple or a grave. Its richly articulated façade was carved directly into the ca-

Above: An urn tops the temple of Ed-Deir. Right: Landscape of bleak beauty – the Wadi Rum.

230

nyon wall. The six tall columns with floral capitals support a massive attica. The upper story is dominated by a tholos or round structure; the columns to the left and right bear a so-called "broken pediment," an architectural peculiarity of Petra. On the tholos stands an urn which is 3.5 meters tall, and is commonly said to have contained the legendary "treasure of the Pharaoh." Shot-holes in its front are evidence of thieves' numerous attempts to break into it over the years. The steps lead through the columned entrance hall into the inner room, which measures 12 x 12 meters.

To the right, the path leads further through the **Outer Siq**, the row of tombs belonging to the theater necropolis. Especially on the right wall of the gorge, you can see a great variety of tomb façades (1st century B.C.); only their upper parts are visible, since the valley floor has risen several meters over the course of time. From here, a steep path leads left to the large sacrificial area; sacrifices were made to the gods on a high altar. The way up is strenuous, but the view is worth the effort. The path leads on past a relief of a lion and a stone altar to a garden temple, a statue tomb, and the **Colored Hall** where feasts were held in honor of the dead. With its red, blue and white sandstone, the room is aptly named.

One end of the Outer Siq is formed by the **Roman Theater** (1st century B.C.) which could accommodate 8,000 spectators. The semicircular form is typically Roman; the location on the side of a hill was more typical of Greek theaters.

From here, a path branches off to the right to the **King's Wall**. The southernmost façade is that of the **Urn Tomb**; its interior, measuring 17 x 18 meters, displays the entire color palette of the local sandstone. In 447, this tomb was consecrated as the cathedral of Petra. Adjoining to the left are the **Colored Tomb** (or **Silk Tomb**); the badly weathered, two-story **Corinthian Tomb** (without Corin-

thian capitals!); the gigantic **Palace Tomb**, with classical echoes; and finally the **Tomb of Sextius Florentinus**, the Roman governor. All the tombs are from the 1st and 2nd centuries A.D.

Now follow the Roman **colonnaded street** past the **marketplace** (on the left) and the **nympheum** (a richly decorated fountain on the right). On your right is the area which is said to have once been the former residential area of Petra; but there are no surviving remains of the houses, which were probably of clay brick – unless, of course, they were tents.

After passing the ruins of a large gate, bear left to reach the **Qasr al-Bint Fa-raun**, the "palace of the pharaoh's daughter," which was in fact the temple of the Nabateans' main god, Dhushara. The six columns in the entrance hall and the massive walls of the cella, as well as the altar in front of the temple, lie in ruins. Directly opposite is the **Lion-Grif-fin Temple**; next to this, Petra's **museum** exhibits finds from the Nabatean, Roman, and Byzantine periods.

To the right, there is a difficult but rewarding path (you can rent donkeys!) up to **Ed-Deir**. Measuring 47 meters across and 43 meters in height, the façade of this "monastery" is truly gigantic. The Nabatean temple and the open area in front of it were used for rituals and festivities. Another few meters further and you can see over to the white dome of Aaron's Tomb and into the Wadi Araba from the Dead Sea to Aqaba.

WADI RUM

40 kilometers north of Aqaba, a fork off the Desert Highway leads to **Wadi Rum**. Here a landscape of indescribable beauty awaits you: huge, weathered rock formations in a vast desert steppe. Before you get to the desert police station at the foot of the Jebel Rum (particularly popular with rock climbers), you will see the rocks of the Seven Pillars of Wisdom on the left, where Lawrence of Arabia once pitched camp. In the village of Rum there is a small rest house, and you can rent a

Land Rover or a camel to continue your journey. In the valley, there are more traces of Nabatean civilization: the ruins of a temple to the goddess Allat (1st century A.D.). The rock formations on the other side of the village are famous for their prehistoric drawings. In late afternoon, to the delight of photographers, the sun brings out the yellow and red of the rocks even more intensely.

AQABA

When you arrive in **Aqaba** (335 kilometers from Amman, 120 kilometers from Petra), you just might believe you have landed on another planet. Highlights here are the bizarre corals in the waters of the gulf and the many colorful species of sea fauna. Water sports, especially snorkeling and scuba-diving, are first priority here. One reason for this are the reef perch, parrotfish, lionfish, angelfish, and many other varieties teeming along the coast, where the sea floor falls steeply into the depths. But you can also keep your feet dry and marvel at the rainbow beauties of the underwater world at the **aquarium**.

Nabateans, Ptolemies, and Romans recognized the trade advantages which the harbor here could offer. Aqaba became very important to the Arabs, and not only as a stop for pilgrims on the way to Mecca. The **old city** still offers genuine Oriental charm. The 12th-century **Crusader castle**, conquered in 1170 by Saladin and later by the Mamelukes and Turks, is worth seeing. In 1917, the fort was conquered by Prince Faisal, who drove the Turks out of the city and the country, and established the dynasty of the Hashemites, which still rules today. Behind the fortress is the **visitor's center** and **museum** (in the house of King Hussein's great-great-grandfather).

Right: Waiting for tourists before the colorful sandstone backdrop of Petra.

JORDAN
Accommodation

AMMAN: *LUXURY:* **Marriott**, Shmeisani, tel. 06-5607607, near airport. **Intercontinental**, 3rd Circle, Jebel Amman, tel. 06-4641361. **Regency Palace**, Queen Alia St., tel. 06-5607000.
MODERATE: **Amra Forum**, tel. 06-5510005, quiet, a bit out of the city in the diplomats' neighborhood. **Ocean**, Um-Utheina, tel. 06-5517280, new, attractive, quiet. **Rhum Hotel**, Basman St., tel. 06-4623162, city center, with restaurant and bar.
BUDGET: **Al-Monzer Hotel**, tel. 06-4639469, by the Abdali Bus Station. **Lords Hotel**, King Hussein St., tel. 06-4622167. There are many cheap hotels along King Faisal Street.
AQABA: *LUXURY:* **Alcazar Hotel**, Corniche, tel. 03-2014131. **Holiday Inn**, Corniche, tel. 03-2012426. *MODERATE:* **Aquaba Beach**, tel. 03-2012491. **Aquaba Tourist House Hotel**, tel. 03-2015165. **Miramar**, Corniche, tel. 03-2014341.
KERAK: **Rest House**, tel. 03-2131148.
PETRA: *LUXURY:* **Petra Forum Hotel**, tel. 03-2156266, right at the entrance to the ancient sites. **King's Way Inn**, Wadi Mousa, tel. 03-2156799 reservations: 00962-6-4647118; small hotel opened in 1995.
MODERATE: **Rest House**, tel. 03-2131142, right by the entrance to the ancient sites.
DEAD SEA: *MODERATE:* **Dead Sea Spa Hotel**, Sal Land Village, tel. 05-3252002. Amman office: 06-5601544. Has a spa center specializing in skin and respiratory ailments.

Restaurants

Nearly all of the better hotels have good restaurants. Also worth recommending is the state-owned restaurant chain "Rest House," at popular tourist sites (Petra, Kerak, Gerasa, Madaba, Azraq).

Hospitals

AMMAN: **King Hussein Medical Centre**, Wadi es-Sir, Suweilah, tel. 06-5856856. **University Hospital** University St., tel. 06-5353444.
AQABA: **Princess Haya Hospital**, tel. 03-2012122.

Embassies

Embassy of the U.S.A, Jebel Amman, tel. 06-820101. **Embassy of Great Britain**, Abdoun, P.O Box 6062, tel. 06-823100/188. **Australian Embassy** Jebel Amman, 4th Circle, tel. 06-673246.

Emergency

AMMAN: Police, tel. 06-4651048. Emergency, tel 192, 193. Medical emergency, tel. 199.

Tourist Information / Airline

Ministry of Tourism and Antiquities, P.O. Box 224 Jebel Amman, tel. 06-4630359. **Flight information** at the Queen Alia International Airport, tel. 06-4453200. **Royal Jordanian Airlines** (Alia), reservations and tickets, tel. 06-5678321.

KIBBUTZ AND MOSHAV

In 1909, the first kibbutz was founded in Palestine – in Degania, south of the Sea of Galilee. It was Eastern European Jews who first conceived of a community of equal members in which all people owned exactly the same amount. No one should stand out in the community through his or her material possessions. This held true even for children; rather then receiving preferential treatment from their parents, they should all grow up under the same conditions, which meant living in separate children's houses. A cornerstone of the kibbutz concept is the idea of determining oneself how much and when one works, and equal compensation for all; important decisions regarding the community are decided by a plenary meeting of all members. Unfortunately, in practice, kibbutz life today is increasingly moving away from these lofty ideals.

The new Zionist society was supposed to orient itself on the model of the kibbutz; the ideal was the chalutz, a farming pioneer. The microcosm of the kibbutz was supposed to reflect on the level of the macrocosm of society, and thereby give rise to a new Jewish identity based, unlike in the diaspora, not on traders, merchants, and people in the service sector, but rather on agriculture, people who till the soil and actively make the land their own.

In Israel today, there are about 250 kibbutzim in which approximately 110,000 people live and work. The kibbutzniks lead the world in agricultural productivity as well as in industrial production, and they are among the best-educated people in Israel. On average, around 400 people work in each of these communal projects; only very few kibbutzim have a population of more than 1,000 members. The kibbutzim account for almost half of all agricultural produce in Israel, and their output in the industrial fields of metal, plastic, and wood is comparably high. 10% of all kibbutz products are exported abroad. Nonetheless, many kibbutzim today are deeply in debt.

With their special sense of community, kibbutz members keep the national morale high; in the Israeli army, 85% of the kibbutzniks in military service join combat divisions, a disproportionately high number become officers, and more than 30% of all kibbutzniks serve in the Israeli Air Force.

Today, the kibbutzim are known as the home of the so-called planter aristocracy and their descendents: those pioneers, that is to say, who at the beginning of this century came to Palestine and made the land arable. These were without exception European Jews; the percentage of Oriental kibbutz members, therefore, has never been more than 8%.

63% of all Israelis are sympathetic to the goals of the communal projects, and the social prestige of the kibbutzniks is as high in Israel as it has ever been. That, of course, has something to do with the country's history since, above all in the 1930s and 40s, the settlements not only paved the way with pioneering work and agriculture, but also played a significant role in the country's defense. The Zionist movement could always rely without question on kibbutz members who were, if necessary, ready and willing to make great sacrifices and who, perhaps more than any other group in Israel, were essential in the process of the founding and preservation of the state of Israel.

But now, in the late 20th century, this mode of living has lost much of its attraction and is in crisis. Young kibbutzniks show hardly a trace of interest in founding new settlements; 45% could imagine living a completely non-kibbutz life; and 60% of all young Israelis have no interest in living in a kibbutz.

Right: Collective agriculture – melon harvest at the kibbutz of Ha On.

If anyone is interested in finding out what life is really like in such a communal settlement, it is easy enough to do so: many kibbutzim have guesthouses where foreign visitors are accommodated and introduced to the rudiments of everyday life on the kibbutz. You can even participate as a worker in a kibbutz, and help out in the orchards or on a chicken farm. You will not get paid, but food, lodging, and medical care are free, and many friendships have developed between kibbutzniks and guests from Europe or America.

In 1921, a group of chalutzim, as the agricultural pioneers in Israel were called, split off from the kibbutz movement and opened the first moshav – at Nahalal in Galilee. Today, there are over 450 similar settlements. In these places, community spirit and the ideal of equality are not as emphatically promoted as they are on a kibbutz; moshav members can also have private possessions and consume as much as their wallets allow. One of the first moshavniks was Schlomo Dajan, the father of the famous general who showed exceptional strategic performance in the Six-Day War. Every member receives an equal-sized parcel of land and can cultivate on it or build on it as he pleases. Distribution of produce and the purchasing of materials are centralized – a moshav is therefore a co-operative.

From the very beginning, however, the moshavim have never enjoyed the same high regard among the general population as the kibbutzim have, although they were equally involved in the development of the country and also made considerable sacrifices; even the left-wing political parties have always treated the moshavim like stepchildren.

After the declaration of independence in 1948, however, more moshavim than kibbutzim were founded – after all, the desire for private property was, and still is, great. These co-operatives also have by far more Oriental Jews among their members than do the collective settlements.

ISRAEL'S CUISINE

Visitors will search in vain for a genuine "Israeli" cuisine. For rather than a single style of cooking, the food here is influenced by Jewish immigrants from Eastern Europe, Asia, Africa, southeastern Europe and the Orient. Each of these groups brought their own individual cooking style with them into their new homeland of Palestine.

Consider the spices: caraway, onion, mint, garlic, coriander, saffron, cardamom, and green and black pepper, together with golden olive oil, confer upon the dishes here an incomparable aroma.

The Middle Eastern influence is certainly apparent in some of the country's ubiquitous specialties. Take *tahini* or *tehina*, a sesame sauce in which you dunk bread; seldom absent from any table, it is

Above: Conjuring with vegetables – a vegetarian snack bar in Tel Aviv. Right: Chicken and rice served in a kosher restaurant.

especially popular when further combined with eggplant. Eggplant itself i present in countless forms, from fried to pickled, each of them magnificent *Mashi*, stuffed eggplant, is just one example.

Hummus is one of the primary food stuffs in the Near East; it consists o boiled, puréed chickpeas spiced with tahini, lemon juice, garlic, and olive oil.

Popular at lunch, dinner, or between meals is *falafel*, which you can buy or every street corner for a few pennies These are small, crispy chickpea "burgers," deep-fried and served in pita bread; at the kiosk salad bar, you fill the fresh bread with the greenery of your choice, add a dollop of hummus if you so desire, and enjoy. At lunchtime, the falafel stands are surrounded by workers Equally cheap, popular and tasty is *shwarma* (known as *doner kebab* in Turkey); slices are shaved off a large piece of meat cooking slowly on a spit, and served in pita bread with various sauces, lettuce and other vegetables.

At the harbors of Akko and Yafo you can sit around the water in traditional surroundings and eat fresh-caught fish, calamari (fried squid) prepared in a variety of ways, and shrimp in a spicy herb-garlic sauce. In Tiberias, on the Sea of Galilee, the local specialty is the so-called St. Peter fish, a kind of perch. Trout are also popular and feature on most menus. *Marimeh* is the name of an Arabian fish dish, hot and spicy thanks to its component of peppers, rounded off with a sauce including garlic, tomato and cumin.

Known in most countries is *shish kebab*, beef or lamb roasted on a skewer and served with lettuce and bread. *Seniya* is a dish of beef or lamb in thini; also popular is stuffed chicken pigeon. Vine leaves stuffed with rice and served with lemon juice are a popular side dish or snack. In Israeli homes, especially on the Sabbath, *Shulent* is often served; this is a Yiddish bean stew which is begun several days before serving.

One frequent dessert choice is the Middle Eastern pastry *baklava*, comprised of flaky pastry with a sweet nut filling, drenched in honey syrup. To aid digestion, mint tea or Turkish coffee may be served after a meal, although here both of these are so sweet that you can stand your spoon up in them. If you prefer something a little less sugary, be specific about it when you are ordering.

Between meals, people snack on *blintzes*, sweet or savory crepes filled with fruit or cheese, or eat *za'atar*, a long thin bread roll filled with a mixture of spices.

A central term in Jewish cooking is "kosher," which means pure and edible, or something prepared in the appropriate manner, and denotes foodstuffs which are permitted by the Jewish religion. Kosher meat is meat from fowl or beasts that have been killed with a knife and allowed to bleed to death – for blood is seen as bearing the soul of a living being. Not kosher, and therefore impure, is, for

example, pork – as it is for Muslims, as well. Other non-kosher foods include the meat of meat-eating animals and certain fish, including shellfish.

Meat may not be cooked or eaten together with milk products. One may not have milk products until five hours after having eaten meat; and after partaking of a milk product one must wait two hours before eating meat.

The *Allgemeine Jüdische Wochenzeitung* (a Jewish weekly paper) reports the following: "In London, active Jewish believers have come up with a new idea. Ads in the Jewish press announce that anyone with questions on religious customs can call a certain telephone number at given hours. Two young rabbis will be available to answer questions and give advice. One question was: 'Do I need two automatic dishwashers, one for milk and one for meat products?' The rabbi's answer: 'Open the machine after use and look in. If, as is probable, foodstuffs have remained inside, then you will need two – one for milk and one for meat products.'"

JEWISH HOLIDAYS

On September 11, 1999, the year 5760 of the Jewish calendar began with **Rosh Hashanah**, the Jewish New Year. Together, the two holidays of Rosh Hashanah and **Yom Kippur**, the Day of Atonement (celebrated ten days later), are called the High Holy Days. According to Jewish tradition, it was on Rosh Hashanah that God created the world (in the year 3759 B.C., to be precise). On New Year's Day, the *shofar*, the ram's horn that heralded the revelations on Mount Sinai, sounds to move people to prayer and repentance. There follow, until Yom Kippur, ten days of reflection during which the faithful prepare themselves for the holiday of atonement. On Yom Kippur, public life in Israel comes to a standstill; public transportation and private cars stay in the garage; radio, tele-

Above: Succoth, the Feast of the Tabernacles, was ordained by the Lord after he delivered the Children of Israel from Egypt.

vision and telephones fall silent; and nothing interferes with the process of fasting a prayer. "When the eve of Yom Kippur nears, an atmosphere falls over Jerusalem which cannot be put into words. There are hordes of self-avowed atheists who, while they do not enter a synagogue on these days, also do not let a morsel of food pass their lips from dawn to dusk. If you ask them why they do this, they will search, embarrassed, for some kind of answer; the truth is that some vestige of irrationality remains," writes Israeli author Yehoshua Amir.

Also in September/October is **Succoth**, a joyful festival centered around the simple huts which God described after the Flight from Egypt when he told Moses, "Speak unto the children of Israel, saying, The fifteenth day of the seventh month shall be the feast of tabernacles for seven days unto the Lord...And ye shall take you on the first day the boughs of goodly trees, branches of palm trees...and willows of the brook...Ye shall dwell in booths seven days" (Leviticus

24:34, 40, 42). Here, a historic tradition mingles with the seasonal cycle of harvest and wine-making, as well as the beginning of the winter rainy season. These agrarian elements of the Succoth festival are documented in the daily blessing, throughout the festival , of the "Four Species," branches of palm, myrtle, willow, and lemon trees. Anyone who can builds a small hut of branches and boughs in his garden or on the balcony; many hotels and restaurants also build such huts, and then serve meals in them.

The last day of Succoth is marked by the **Simhat Torah**, the festival of joy in the Torah, honoring one of the central sources of the Jewish religion, the revelations of God. The Torah is read throughout the year in services at the synagogue; this day marks the completion of the annual reading, after which it is started again from the beginning.

At about the same time that Christians celebrate Christmas, Jewish believers observe **Hanukkah**, the eight-day Festival of Lights. This holiday commemorates the victory of Judas Maccabeus, who led a people's rebellion to reclaim the Temple from the Hellenic rulers who had taken it over and restored it to members of the Jewish faith. The holiday lasts eight days, in keeping with the tradition that, when the victorious Jewish people reclaimed the temple, they found only a small vial of oil, enough to keep the lamps burning for only a single day. Miraculously, however, the oil lasted for eight days, by which time they were able to procure more of the oil so essential to the practice of their religion. These eight days are symbolized by the menorah, a nine-armed candelabra; on every day of the holiday, a new candle is lit, until finally all the candles are burning.

Tubi Schwat, which falls in January/February, is accounted the beginning of spring. Singing traditional songs, children plant little trees, and fruit is picked and eaten.

In February/March, adults anticipate with childish glee the advent of **Purim** (*Purim* means Fate), which commemorates the story of the Biblical book of Esther. At the insistence of his advisor, Haman, the Persian emperor Ahasuerus issued a decree ordaining the extermination of the Jews, but this plan was thwarted by Esther and her adoptive father, Mordecai. This gave rise, among the Jews, to rejoicing that continues to the present day. Everyone dons costumes and lets his hair down; as one Jewish author notes, "Even the most pious synagogue-goer won't turn down a small shot of brandy at this time." Rabbinic law permits Jewish believers, on Purim, to drink alcohol "until they no longer know the difference between Blessed be Mordecai and Accursed be Haman." A favorite Purim delicacy is the triangular pastry called "Haman's Ears."

March/April sees observance of the holiday **Passover**, in remembrance of the last plague, the Angel of Death's slaying of all firstborn sons until the Pharaoh finally conceded that the Jews might leave Egypt. Passover is traditionally a family holiday, celebrated at home; the ritual festival meal that is eaten every night is punctuated by readings of the historical events from the Haggadah, as well as songs. The social nature of the Passover holiday is sometimes emphasized to the degree that the table is set not only for family members and friends, but also for fellow-men who are in need or have fallen on hard times. During the seven days of the festival, Jewish believers may eat no bread; in its place is the unleavened *matzoth*, the bread of misery.

Shavuot, in May/June, celebrates the receiving of the Ten Commandments; it is also a kind of Thanksgiving, on which Jews eat only milk products and honey.

The **Tish be-Av** in July/August is a day of mourning and fasting to commemorate the destruction of the First and Second Temples.

239

METRIC CONVERSION

Metric Unit	US Equivalent
Meter (m)	39.37 in.
Kilometer (km)	0.6241 mi.
Square Meter (sq m)	10.76 sq. ft.
Hectare (ha)	2.471 acres
Square Kilometer (sq km)	0.386 sq. mi.
Kilogram (kg)	2.2 lbs.
Liter (l)	1.05 qt.

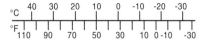

PREPARING FOR YOUR TRIP

Climate / When to Go

Israel's location between desert and sea has a decisive influence on its weather; winters are mild and wet, summers hot and dry. The first rains fall in October, the last in April. Between December and February it can be quite wet.

Israel's wettest area is in northern Galilee, around Zefat and north toward the Lebanese border. It is driest in the Negev desert between Elat and the Dead Sea. Northern Galilee has some 70 days of rain a year, in Jerusalem and the Judaic Mountains there are about 50 days of rain a year, and in the Negev there are about 10 days of rain.

Winter in Israel is generally harmless; temperatures below freezing are indeed rare. The lowest temperature ever recorded in the country was -7° C. Snow does fall in the mountain regions of northern Galilee, as snow lies on the hilltops there. As well as rain, hailstorms are not an infrequent occurrence, often accompanied by strong winds. As a rule, all of the country's precipitation comes from the west and the Mediterranean.

Summers are dry and very hot. The country's hottest areas are the Arava Valley in the Negev Desert, the beaches of the Dead Sea, the Jordan Valley and the Valley of Bet Shean; the highest ever temperature of 54° C was recorded in the Jordan Valley, below sea level. In Jerusalem, the mercury has risen to 44° C.

A normal occurrence are hot winds from the East, called *khamsin* in Arabic and *sharav* in Hebrew; when these are blowing, you have the uncomfortable sensation of sitting in a sauna with a hairdryer held in your face.

The best times to visit the country are the months of April and May.

Average Annual Temperatures

January	21° C
February	23° C
March	26° C
April	31° C
May	35° C
June	38° C
July	39° C
August	39° C
September	36° C
October	33° C
November	27° C
December	22° C

Average Water Temperatures

	Mediterranean Sea °C	Sea of Galilee °C	Dead Sea °C	Red Sea °C
Jan	18	17	21	22
Feb	17.5	15	19	20
Mar	17.5	16.5	21	21
Apr	18.5	21	22	21.5
May	21.5	24.5	25	24
June	25	27	28	25
July	28	28.5	30	26
Aug	29	29.5	30.5	27
Sept	28.5	29.5	31	27
Oct	27	27.5	30	25
Nov	23	24	28	25
Dec	19	21.5	23	24

Clothing / What to Pack

Light cotton clothing, comfortable shoes that are well broken in, and head covering against the strong sun are all essential travel gear. For winter trips to Is-ael or on cool desert nights, you will also need to bring along a thick sweater.

Despite the heat, clothes exposing too much skin should be avoided – not only when visiting synagogues, churches or mosques, but also where the populace tends to be conservative, e.g. in the Old City of Jerusalem. Here, one should not wear shorts, short skirts, and sleeveless T-shirts and blouses, or else bring something along to put on over them.

A small backpack is good to have along for day trips; and a Swiss Army knife or the compact multi-purpose Leatherman tool always comes in handy when traveling. A thermos, a small flashlight and a good pair of sunglasses with UV protection are also worth bringing.

Information

You can get more information about Israel from the Israeli Government Touring offices the world over.

In **North America**:

Northeast U.S.: Uzi Gafni, 800 Second Avenue, New York, NY 10017, tel. (212) 499 5650, fax (212) 499 5645.

Midwest U.S.: Tsion Ben David, 5 S. Wabash Avenue, Chicago, IL, 60603, tel. (312) 782 4306, fax (312) 782 1243.

Western U.S.: Rami Levi, 6380 Wilshire Blvd., #1700, Los Angeles, CA 90048, tel. (213) 658 7462 (ext. 03), fax (213) 658 6543.

South Central U.S.: Rafi Shalev, 5151 Belt Line Road, Suite 1280, Dallas, TX 75240, tel. (214) 991 9097, fax (214) 392 3521.

In **Canada**: Ruth Ben Tzur, 180 Bloor St. West, Toronto, Ontario M5S2V6, tel. (416) 964 3784, fax (416) 964 2420.

Visas

Citizens of Australia, Canada, New Zealand, the United Kingdom and the United States in possession of a valid passport will be issued with visitors' visas upon arrival in Israel, which are valid for up to three months. However,

citizens of a number of other countries, including many African and South American countries, do need to get a visa from their local Israeli consulate before they go. If you are not sure, check with your local Israeli diplomatic mission or tourist office.

If you plan to travel in Arab countries, you can, rather than having your passport stamped, have the entry stamp on a separate piece of paper; but make sure not to lose that piece of paper.

If you are planning to stay in Israel longer than three months, you will need a special permit from the Ministry of the Interior; the same is true if you are planning to work here. Addresses (in Israel): Jerusalem, Generali Building, Rehov Shlomzion Hamalka 1, tel. 02-6290222; Tel Aviv, Shalom Meyer Tower, Visa Department, 9 Rehov Ahad Ha'am, tel. 03-5193333; Haifa Government Building, 11 Hassan Shukri, tel. 04-8616222.

For more information on entry and visa requirements, you can contact the visa department of your local Israeli embassy.

Australia: Consulate General of Israel, 37 York Street, 2000 Sydney, Australia, tel. 2-264 7933.

Canada: Israeli Embassy, 50 O'Connor Street, Suite 1005, Ontario K1P6L2, Canada, tel. (613) 567 6450.

United Kingdom: Israeli Embassy, 2 Palace Green, London W8 4QB, U.K., tel. (020) 937 8050.

U.S.A.: *New York:* 800 Second Avenue, New York, NY 10017, tel. (212) 499 5400.

San Francisco: 456 Montgomery Street, Suite 2100, San Francisco, CA 94104, tel. (415) 398 8885.

Houston: 24 Greenway, Suite 1500, Houston TX 77046, tel. (713) 627 3780, fax (713) 627 0149.

Traveling into Egypt and Jordan

If you plan to travel from Israel into Egypt or Jordan, you will have to get a visa in advance of your trip.

You can travel to the Egyptian-held Sinai Peninsula via the border crossing at Taba, 5 km southwest of Elat's city center. It is open 24 hours a day. (Information: tel. 07-6373110). You can get a Sinai visa right at the border if you only plan to visit the Convent of St. Catherine or to dive in Sharm al Sheikh; but this visa does not allow travel beyond the peninsula. Travelers to Cairo or the Nile Valley need to obtain a visa in advance; these are available at the Egyptian consulate or embassy in your home country.

In **Australia**: Consulate of Egypt, 124 Exhibition Street, 9th floor, Melbourne, Victoria, 3000, tel. 654 88 69.

In **Canada**: Consulate General of Egypt, 3754 Cote des Neiges, Montreal, QCH3H 1V6, tel. (514) 937 7781.

In the **United Kingdom**: Embassy of Egypt, 25 South Street, London W1Y 6DD, U.K., tel. (020) 499 2401.

In the **U.S.A.**: Egyptian Consulate, 1110 Second Avenue, New York, NY 10022, tel. (212) 759 7120.

Once you are in **Israel**, you can still apply to the Embassy of the Arabic Republic of Egypt in **Tel Aviv**, 54 Basel St., tel. 03-5464151, for a visa to visit the neighboring country.

You may not enter Egypt in an Israeli rental car. You can, however, rent cars in the Taba Hilton, just past the border. Without a visa, you cannot stay longer than 7 days in Egypt. One other border crossing between Israel and Egypt is at Rafiah (55 km SW of Ashqelon, information: tel. 07-6734274, open 24 hours).

Now that a peace treaty with **Jordan** has been negotiated, you can cross from Israel into Jordan over the famous Allenby Bridge at the height of Jericho if you have a visa. It is open Sunday to Thursday from 8 am-11 pm, Friday and Saturday from 8 am-2:30 pm (information: tel. 02-9942626). At the other two border crossings, it is possible to acquire a visa on the spot. One is a few kilometers north of Elat, at the Arava

checkpoint. The Egged buses 15 and 1 run about every 20 minutes from th Central Bus Station in Elat to Arava; o the Jordanian side, you can continue you trip by taxi. The border crossing is ope Sunday to Thursday, 6:30 am-10 pm; Fri day and Saturday from 8 am-8 pm. Thes times are subject to change, especially o high Jewish and Islamic holidays. (Infor mation: tel. 07-6336811). A fee is levie for travel across the border in either d rection.

The second crossing is the *Jorda River Crossing*, which leads over th King Hussein Bridge into Jordan. It is lc cated south of the Sea of Galilee at th level of Bet Shean, and is open Sunday t Thursday, 6:30 am-10 pm (informatior tel. 06-6586444). You cannot cross o foot, but a shuttle bus runs back and fort across the border. The larger Israeli ca rental firms can have a car ready for yo on the other side of the border as soon a you have finished the border-crossin formalities.

You can get visas to enter Jordan at th **Jordanian Embassy** in your hom country. **Australia**: 20 Roebuck Stree Red Hill, 2603 ACT Canberra, tel. (0€ 295 9952. **Canada**: 100 Bronson A\ enue, Suite 701, Ottowa, Ontario KI 6G8, tel. (613) 238 8091. **Great Britair** 6 Upper Phillimore Gardens, London W 7HB, tel. (020) 9373685. U.S.A.: 86 United Nations Plaza, Suite 540, Nev York, NY 10017, tel. (212) 355 934: For those already in **Israel**: 14 Abb Hille St., **Tel Aviv**, tel. 03-7517722.

Currency / Money Exchange

The country's official currency is th New Israeli Shekel (NIS). The America dollar serves as a semi-official secon currency, and even the official tourist in formation offices admit that you can pa with German marks virtually throughot the country – a sign of just how highl the shekel is esteemed in its own country Credit cards – Visa, American Expres and Eurocard – are accepted virtually everywhere. Banks exchange Eurochecks and all brands of travelers checks.

Shekels are divided into 100 agorot; there are coins in denominations of one, five, and ten shekels, and bills of 20, 50, 100 and 200 shekels.

There is no limit to the amount of shekels or foreign currency you can bring into the country, but there are restrictions to the amount of shekels you can take out. You can exchange shekels back into another currency only up to a value of 100 US\$, unless you can prove, with receipts, that you exchanged a higher amount of some foreign currency into shekels within Israel. It is more economical to exchange money once you are in Israel than to exchange at home before you go.

Health Precautions

No special inoculations are required for a trip to Israel. Particularly in summer, make sure you take adequate precautions against the heat and sun: suntan oil with a high protection factor, a sun hat, and a good pair of sunglasses are indispensable. Also be sure to drink enough throughout the day to avoid the risk of dehydration. You can now get injections against Hepatitis A and B, and it is not a bad idea to go ahead and get these shots before your trip.

As a rule, you can eat whatever you want without worrying whilst you are in Israel; the most frequent cause of the diarrhea that often plagues travelers are drinks that are served too cold.

Your traveling medical kit should contain diarrhea medicine, pain relievers, insect repellent, bandages and disinfectant, scissors and tweezers, and any medication you take regularly or occasionally. You should also bring some kind of cold medicine with you: as all the better hotels, shops, and tour buses are strongly air-conditioned, you find yourself coming in from the heat, pouring with sweat, into an ice-cold lobby or store several times a day, forming the ideal preconditions for sniffles, coughs, hoarseness, or even a full-blown cold. All doctors and pharmacies in Israel speak English. The **emergency phone number** for Magen David Adom (Red Star of David. the Israeli Red Cross) is 101; for the police it is 100, and for the fire department, 112.

TRAVELING TO ISRAEL

By Plane

Israel's international airport, Ben Gurion Airport, is 15 km east of Tel Aviv and 50 km west of Jerusalem. The national airline, El Al, has regular direct and non-stop service from several international airports to Ben Gurion; other airlines with direct flights to Israel include TWA, British Airways, and United; Lufthansa has daily flights from Frankfurt.

One should definitely get to the airport at least two hours ahead of time, since it sometimes happens that one's entire baggage gets thoroughly searched; these security checks can take over half an hour.

When you leave the country, security personnel will again subject you to a rigorous and stressful "interrogation" and check your baggage again; this can again take a good half hour, but is certainly understandable in light of the possibility of terrorist attack. When leaving Israel, therefore, you will also have to get to the airport 2 to 3 hours before flight time.

AIRLINE OFFICES IN ISRAEL:

Austrian Airlines, 1 Ben Yehuda St., Tel Aviv, tel. 03-5115110. 8 Hayam St., Haifa, tel. 04-8370670.

El Al, 12 Hillel St., Jerusalem, tel. 02-6770200. 32 Ben Yehuda St., Tel Aviv, tel. 03-52161222. 5 Palyam St., Haifa, tel. 04-8612612.

Lufthansa, Tel Aviv airport, tel. 03-9711285.

Swissair, Hilton Hotel, Jerusalem, tel. 02-6240094. 1 Ben Yehuda St., Migdalor Building, Tel Aviv, tel. 03-5116666.

By Boat

Israel's largest passenger harbor is Haifa; car ferries and boats of the Stability Line and the Arkadia Steamship company run between Piraeus (Athens) and Haifa. For additional information on boat service to Israel in North America, contact Atlantic Mediterranean Lines at (415) 989 7434. Mediterranean cruise ships also always stop at the Holy Land.

To bring your own car into Israel, you need only a green insurance card.

By Land

You can travel into Israel by land through Jordan or Egypt. The normal Israeli visa and entrance regulations remain in effect. (For border crossings, see also Visas / Entering the Country.)

TRAVELING IN ISRAEL

By Train

Trains run hourly from Tel Aviv along the northern Mediterranean coast to Nahariyya, by the Lebanon border, and back. Train tickets are cheaper than bus tickets. The train cars are old, but in good condition, and there is always a dining car. There is no train service on the Sabbath or on Jewish holidays. Students (with student ID) get a 10% discount (information: tel. 03-5774000).

By Bus

Buses are the most important transport link between Israel's cities, towns and villages. Prices are low. The *Egged Line* runs the largest network (intercity bus information; tel. 03-6948888). In any Egged Tallim office, you can get discount tickets for 7, 14, or 21 days, and valid for any trip within the country, with one exception of city transportation within Tel Aviv. (In Tel Aviv: 59 Ben Yehuda St., tel. 03-5271222; Jerusalem: 8 Shlomzion St., tel. 02-6221999).

Buses run from 5 am until quite late: the main routes between Jerusalem and

Tel Aviv and Haifa run until 11:30 am. Within the three above-mentioned cities, buses run until midnight. Buses, like trains, do not operate on the Sabbath. Students with student identification get a 10% discount off the ticket price.

By Plane

The two domestic airlines, Arkia Israel Airline and Isra Air, run regular shuttle services between the following cities: Tel Aviv, Jerusalem, Rosh Pina, Elat, Haifa, Be'er Sheva and Mitzpe Ramon.

For information, contact: **Arkia Israel Airline**, Sde Dov Airport, Tel Aviv, tel. 03-9712557; 11 Frishman Street, Tel Aviv, tel. 03-6902222,; 8 Shlomzion St., Jerusalem, tel. 02-6255888; 84 Haatzmaut St., Haifa, tel. 04-8611617.

Isra Air, 23 Ben Yehuda St., Tel Aviv, tel. 03-7955888.

By Taxi or Sherut

Taxi drivers are legally obliged to turn on the meter for all rides and to refer to the meter when asking for payment. For longer trips, you can negotiate a fixed rate, if you like. If you take a taxi into western Jordan, use one of the Arab drivers who are stationed by the Damascus Gate in Jerusalem. To summon a taxi, simply hail one on the street.

Sheruts are shared taxis, Mercedes stretch limousines, which take off as soon as all seven to ten seats are occupied. In general, they follow the bus routes, and you can take a sherut to any major town in Israel. The prices are slightly higher than bus rates, and you have to pay an additional surcharge on the Sabbath.

Car Rental

Israel is easy to drive around, and renting a car is a good way to see the country. The roads are good, and driving rules conform to American and European standards: driving is on the right side of the road. You can reserve a rental car before you go at any of the international firms; you then simply get into your car at Ben Gurion Airport, and take off.

Considerably cheaper, by as much as 50%, are local firms. In Tel Aviv, on the northern end of the Tayelet beach promenade which runs into Hayarkon Street, there are many small car rental companies, all trying to underbid each other.

Before traveling into Palestinian areas, you should find out exactly whether the car insurance will cover all damages along your route; whether the areas in question can safely be driven into with an Israeli rental car; and whether it is generally a safe time to enter these areas.

Starting in April or May, make sure that your car has air conditioning, even in a small car. This only costs a bit extra, and if you do not take this precaution, a drive through the Negev to Elat will be more like a drive through a sauna.

Israel has right-hand driving: if you are coming from the left, you have the right of way, unless otherwise marked (the street signs and road markers correspond to international norms). In towns, the speed limit is 50 kilometers/hour, in the country, it is 90 kilometers/hour. Distances on street signs are given in kilometers. Signposts are in English and Hebrew, and frequently in Arabic, as well. Orange-red signs indicate tourist highlights and sights.

The Automobile and Touring Club of Israel (MEMSI) is linked to the *Federation Internationale de l'Automobile* (FIA) as well as the *Alliance Internationale de Tourisme* (AIT), and thus has international connections with the world's leading automobile clubs.

Members of automobile clubs will find that the Israeli counterpart offers every possible form of help and service. Cars from the club patrol the country's roads from 8 am-5 pm; towing is free of charge up to 25 kilometers, although there's a surcharge after 5 pm.

Addresses: 20 Harakevet St., Tel Aviv, tel. 03-5641122; 31 Ben Yehuda St., Jerusalem, tel. 02-6250661. 1 Nevi'im St., Haifa, tel. 04-8667820. Emergency calls: 03-5641111.

Distances in Kilometers

	Jerusalem	Tel Aviv
Jerusalem		60
Tel Aviv	60	
Arad	104	158
Be'er Sheva	84	113
Elat	312	354
Haifa	159	95
Qiryat Shemona	210	185
Nazareth	157	102
Netanya	93	29
Rosh Ha Niqra	201	137
Tiberias	157	132

PRACTICAL TIPS FROM A-Z

Accommodation

The international star system of hotel classification (* = simple, ***** = luxury) is used in Israel as well. A double room in a five-star hotel in Tel Aviv or Jerusalem will generally cost you around 180 US$, while three-star establishments average at around 80 to 100 US$. If you can forego the comfort and you have nothing against shared sleeping quarters in a hostel, you will be able to find a place to lay your weary head in Tel Aviv or even in Jerusalem for less than 8 US$ a night.

Alcohol

A number of Israeli vintners' co-operatives produce excellent white and red wines, so you do not need to seek out expensive, imported vintages. Among the best Israeli wines are those from the Carmel region south of Haifa and those from the Golan Heights. The locally-brewed beer is equally wonderful, and a popular drink at the end of a long, hot day. Bars and restaurants also serve cognac and other forms of hard liquor, which are often made locally; imported versions can be extremely expensive.

Archaeological Excavations

If, during your holiday, you would like to learn more about the country's history, you can help out on a real archaeological site. For more information, contact: Harnet Menahem, Israel Antiquities Authority, tel. 02-6204622, or via internet: www.mfa.gov.il/mfa/go.asp? MFAH00wk0.

Every year in January, Dr. Yitzav Hirschfeld of the Hebrew University needs volunteers for the excavations at En Gedi by the Dead Sea. Contact Ms. Hani Davis by e-mail: hani@act-com.co.il; tel. 02-5812452, Internet: www.hum.huji.ac.il/archaeology/engedi.

Banks

Even the smallest villages have banks where you can cash traveler's checks or Eurochecks, and where you can use your credit card to get cash, including US$ or Deutschmarks.

Camping

For information about number, location and facilities of Israeli campsites: the Israeli Camping Union, P.O. Box 53, Nahariyya, tel. 04-925392.

Customs

The maximum duty-free allowances are 1/4 liter of perfume, 2 liters of wine and 1 liter of spirits as well as 250 g of tobacco or 250 cigarettes. Gifts may not exceed a value of 125 US$. You may not import fresh meat, fruit, books or newspapers from Arab countries, weapons or knives which could be used as weapons, pornographic materials, or narcotics. Upon leaving the country, you will have to pay an airport tax of about 10 US$.

Diplomatic Representation in Israel

Australian Embassy, Beit Europa, 4th floor, 37 Shaul Hamelech Blvd, Tel Aviv, tel. 03-695 0451, fax 03-696 8404.

Canadian Embassy, 220 Hayarkon St., Tel Aviv, 63405, tel. 03-527 2929.

Consulate General of Great Britain, 192 Hayarkon St., Tel Aviv, 63405, tel. 03-524 9171.

Consulate General of the United States, 71 Hayarkon St., Tel Aviv, 63405, tel. 03-517 4337.

Eating and Drinking

Hygiene is excellent throughout the country. You can drink tap water without any problems; but those who want to play it safe should also avoid lettuce, unpeeled fruit, raw vegetables, mayonnaise, ice cream, and ice cubes.

Electricity

Israel's current is 220-volt; you will need a transformer if traveling from the United States. Plugs have three prongs, so even European hair dryers, electric razors, etc. require an adaptor – whether acquired at home or bought here.

Emergencies

The emergency phone number for Magen David Adom (Red Star of David, Israel's answer to the Red Cross, with ambulances) is 101; the emergency number for the police is 100, and for the fire department 112.

Festivals and Special Events

In June, the annual Israel Festival is held, which is centered in Jerusalem but also includes events in the Roman theaters of Caesarea and Bet Shean. Famous ensembles under renowned conductors give concerts in Tel Aviv and in other cities around Israel. Every year during Passover, the kibbutz En Gev on the Sea of Galilee hosts the famous *En Gev Music Festival*, with classical concerts and presentations of folk traditions and music.

Every third year, harpists from around the world take part in the *International Harp Contest*; also triennial is the *Zimriya*, an international choral festival. April of these years sees the Rubinstein competition in Tel Aviv, visited by young pianists from around the world.

Spring in Jerusalem and *Spring in Tel Aviv* are spring festivals with varied programs of music, theater, dance and folk events. On Independence Day, May 4, there are street fairs, other special events and commemorative celebrations. Every March, the International Book Fair is held in Jerusalem; the largest and most important in the entire Middle East.

Haifa is known for its *International Flower Show* (Floris), when the whole city becomes a floral ocean; for the *International Folklore Festival*, international groups pour into this harbor city.

Film and Photography

Film is expensive here. Photographing military facilities is strictly prohibited. If carrying a video camera, you have to register it and leave a deposit of 1,000 US$; the easiest way is with a credit card. The sum is returned, or taken off your credit card, when you leave the country.

Try to be tactful when photographing or filming; the country's Arab residents, in particular, have considerable reservations about being captured on film.

Hours of Business

Banks: Sun, Tue, Thur 8:30 am-12:30 pm and 4-5:30 pm; Mon and Wed 8:30 am-12:30 pm; Fri and before holidays 8:30 am-noon.

Shops are generally open from 8 am-1 pm and 4-7 pm. On Fridays and before holidays, shops close at 2 pm.

Post Offices: 8 am-12:30 pm and 3:30-6 pm. Main post offices are open all day long. All post offices are closed on the Sabbath.

Working on a Kibbutz or Moshav

If you are burning with desire to work on a kibbutz, you can get more information from: **United Kibbutz Movement** (*Takam*), 18 Frishman Street, Tel Aviv, tel. 03-5278874.

Those who find the kibbutzim too socialist, and want to try a moshav, can get more information from the **Moshav Movement in Israel**, Leonardo da Vinci Street 19, Tel Aviv, tel. 03-6968335.

Language

In Israel, Hebrew and Arabic are the two main *linguae francae*; in addition, nearly every Israeli speaks English. French is also very common, and German not infrequent. Many Israelis also speak Eastern European languages.

Nature Preserves and National Parks

The Israeli conservation association is called the *Society for the Protection of Nature in Israel* (SPNI). The SPNI has a toll-free number in North America: 1-800-411 0966. From them, you can also order the free brochure *Israel Nature Trail*, which suggests tours off the beaten track for individual travelers.

If you would like some hands-on involvement, you can plant a tree on your visit to the country; for information, contact the Jewish National Fund (*Keren Kayemeth Leisrael*). The national office for the United States is at 42 East 69th Street in New York, tel. (212) 879 9300.

In Israel, there are currently 42 national parks encompassing regions of archaeological or scenic interest. These include the excavation site at Megiddo, Caesarea, Bet Shean, Masada, etc. There is a *Green Card* which allows you to visit any and all of the parks you wish within a two-week period. You can save a lot of money by buying one of these cards from the cashier at any of the national parks.

Pharmacies

Even in smaller towns, you can find pharmacies with a complete range of American- or European-standard wares. As international pharmaceutical companies make products specifically for and in Israel, some product names may vary from what you are used to.

If you regularly take any kind of medication, you should have your own pharmacist provide you with a list of its ingredients before you set off on your holiday. All pharmacists in Israel speak English.

Post Offices

You can recognize Israeli post offices from the distinctive logo depicting a leaping deer on a red background. The mailboxes for letters within a city are yellow; those for destinations outside a city, including international mail, are red.

Press

Israel can boast more than 200 different daily papers, some of which appear in English. Of these English-language papers, the one with the best reputation is the Jerusalem Post; its Friday edition is sold with a thick weekend supplement including theater, cinema, and concert schedules, and the television program for the week ahead. This paper is not printed on Saturdays (the Sabbath).

Radio and Television

Kol Israel, the Israeli Radio, broadcast news in English several times a day on its fourth channel. On television, there are educational broadcasts for children and adults in the morning, children's programs in the afternoon, and Arabic and Hebrew broadcasts in the evening.

You can easily pick up Jordanian television in Israel; one channel broadcasts a variety of international shows, mainly in English, and regular news in English.

On both Jordanian and Israeli television stations, foreign films and series are shown in the original language with subtitles, rather than being dubbed.

Safety

Generally speaking, Israel is a very safe country and there is hardly anything which needs to be mentioned by way of warning. Both Israelis and Arabs are usually very interested in meeting foreigners and travelers and are open, friendly and helpful. Still, a couple of precautionary measures cannot hurt. One should beware of pickpockets, especially in the Old City of Jerusalem and on the Mount of Olives; children and itinerant merchants are particularly adept at pickpocketing, but they are never violent. Nightly strolls in Arabic cities are not to be recommended – one is generally more or less alone in the darkened streets.

When traveling to the West Bank with a rental car (entry into the Gaza Strip with a rented car is not permitted), one should avail oneself of an Arabic rental company, since the insurance they offer is also valid in the autonomous and occupied territories (e.g. Petra, tel. 02-5820716, or Good Luck Rent-a-Car, tel. 02-5835786. Both of these are on the main street of Shuafat in the northern part of Jerusalem.). Before visiting one of these areas, it is worth calling the Tourist Information service or the Tourist Police (tel. 02-5931254), in order to find out about possible dangers and/or recommended security measures.

Palestinian-led guide tours (in English) in the West Bank and the Gaza Strip are offered by Mr. Abu Hassan; who is based in the Jerusalem Hotel on Nablus Road in the eastern part of Jerusalem (tel. 02-6277216 or 052-864205). These tours also include an introduction to the culture, history and present situation of the Palestinian people.

In summer, Heartland-Christian Biblical Tours also offers day tours to Judea and Samaria (the West Bank), tel. 02-9400422. Information leaflets are available at the Sheraton Plaza Hotel in Jerusalem.

Shopping

Relatively reasonably priced souvenirs include jewelry and diamonds, antiques and Oriental rugs, silver, copper, and leather goods, sculptures, ceramics, and religious articles (so-called Judaica).

Exporting antiques (any objects dated from before 1700) is prohibited without an export permit from the Cultural Ministry. This means presenting the object in question at the Department of Antiquities of the Rockefeller Museum, Suleyman Street, Jerusalem (at the NW corner of the Old City Walls); you can set up an appointment by calling 02-6204624.

Spas and Thermal Baths
The dry climate around the Dead Sea is ideal for those suffering from all kinds of skin diseases, from psoriasis and allergic eczema to acne, rheumatism, etc. A few addresses: **En Gedi Thermal Springs**, 86910 Dead Sea, tel. 07-6594813; The **Sheraton Moriah Dead Sea Spa**, 86930 Dead Sea, tel. 07-6591391.

Sports
For comprehensive information about schedules and sports activities, contact:

Diving: **Federation for Underwater Activities in Israel**, P.O. Box 6110, Tel Aviv.

Golf: **The Israel National Golf Club**, P.O. Box 26069, Tel Aviv.

Hang-gliding, hot-air ballooning, and *paragliding:* **Aero Club of Israel**, 67 Hayarkon Street, Tel Aviv

Mountain Climbing: **The Israel Alpine Club**, P.O. Box 53, Ramat Hasharon, Tel Aviv.

Riding: **National Assoc. of Horseback Riding**, 8 Haarba Street, Tel Aviv.

Sailing: **Yachting Center**, Solot Yam, M.P. Sharon.

Tennis: **The Israel National Tennis Association**, P.O. Box 20073, Tel Aviv.

Telephones
Nearly all public telephones are card operated phones; but for older telephones located in more remote places you may need to buy a chip or *asimonim.* "Telecards" are available at post offices as well as at many kiosks. Some public phones allow credit card usage. In addition, many stores and small kiosks have coin phones, from which you can easily call anywhere in the world. Israel's country code is 972.

Time
Clocks in the Holy Land are 2 hours ahead of Greenwich Mean Time, 7 hours ahead of New York, 11 ahead of Los Angeles, and 8 hours behind Sydney. Clocks are set forward in the middle of April for the summer period and set back again in the middle of September.

Tipping
In hotels, restaurants, bars and pubs, one tips about 10%. You do not tip sherut drivers, nor is it common to tip taxi drivers, although they will be happy to accept. A small tip, however, is appropriate and recommended for other services.

Weights and Measures
The metric system is used in Israel.

GLOSSARY
Hebrew

Peace (greeting)	*shalom*
Good morning/day	*boker tov*
Good evening	*erev tov*
Good night	*layla tov*
How are you?	*ma nishma*
Very well	*tov m'od*
Is everything all right	*hakol beseder?*
It's OK	*kacha kacha*
yes	*ken*
no	*lo*
Are there ... ?	*yesh?*
Yes, there are ...	*ken, yesh*
No, there aren't	*lo, en*
please	*bevakasha*
thank you	*toda*
I	*ani*
you (m)	*ata*
you (f)	*at*
he	*hu*
she	*hee*
we	*anachu*
you (plural, m)	*atem*

you (plural, f)	*aten*
they (m)	*heym*
they (f)	*heyn*
left	*smol*
right	*yamin*
when	*matay*
how	*ech*
where	*le'an*
doctor	*rafeh*
friend	*chaver/a*
help!	*hasflu!*
hotel	*malon*
house	*bayit*
room	*cheder*
post office	*do-ar*
stamp	*bulim*
toilet	*sherutim*

1	*achat*
2	*shtayim*
3	*shalosh*
4	*arba*
5	*chamesh*
6	*shesh*
7	*sheva*
8	*shmoneh*
9	*tesha*
10	*eser*
11	*achat esre*
12	*shtem esre*
13	*shlosh esre*
14	*arba esre*
20	*esrim*
21	*esrim ve achat*
22	*esrim ve shtayim*
23	*esrim ve shalosh*
30	*shloshim*
40	*arba'im*
50	*chamishim*
60	*shishim*
70	*shivim*
80	*shmonim*
90	*tishim*
100	*mea*
200	*matayim*
300	*shlosh me'ot*
400	*arba meot*
500	*chamesh me'ot*
1000	*elef*

Food and Drink

beer	*bira*
bread	*lechem*
butter	*chem'a*
chicken	*of*
coffee	*kafeh*
food	*ochel*
fish	*dag*
glass	*kos*
ice cream	*glida*
milk	*chalav*
restaurant	*mis'ada*
rice	*ores*
salt	*melach*
soup	*marag*
sugar	*sukar*
tea	*te*
wine	*yayin*

Arabic

Good morning	*sabah al cheir*
Good day/evening	*masa al cheir*
Good night	*tisbah ala cheir*
Hello (greeting)	*marhaba*
How are you?	*izzayak?*
Fine, Allah be praised	*mabsut*
	al hamdullilah
please	*min fadlak*
thank you	*shukran*
Where are you from?	*inta minen*
I am from ...	*ana min ...*
I don't understand	*ana mesh fahim*
I am a tourist	*ana sayih*
Where is ...	*fen ...*
Are there ...	*fi ...*
yes	*naam/aiwa*
yes, there are ...	*aiwa, fi ...*
no	*la*
no, there are not	*la, mafish*
all right / OK	*tamam*
how much does it cost?	*addaish?*
it's too expensive	*hada tamaam ghali*
good	*quassis/tayyib*
help	*musa'ada*
left	*shamal*
right	*yamin*
airport	*matar*

us . . . . *utubes*
ar . . . . *arabiyya*
doctor . . . . *duktur, hakim*
mbassy . . . . *sefarit*
hospital . . . . *mustashfa*
hotel . . . . *funduq*
market . . . . *suq*
police . . . . *shurta*
ea . . . . *bahr*
tation . . . . *mahatta*
icket . . . . *tazkara*
elephone . . . . *tilifon*
rain . . . . *atr*

Food and Drink

beer . . . . *bira*
bill . . . . *hisab*
bread . . . . *aish*
chicken . . . . *farcha*
coffee . . . . *kahwa*
egg . . . . *bedah*
fish . . . . *samak*
food . . . . *akl*
emonade . . . . . . *lemunada/gazoz*
knife . . . . *sikin*
meat . . . . *lahma*
olive . . . . *zeitun*
spoon . . . . *mala'a*
sugar . . . . *sukkar*
ea . . . . *shay*
vegetables . . . . *chadar*
water . . . . *mayya*
wine . . . . *nabid*

AUTHORS

Hans-Günter Semsek, author of the *Nelles Guide Israel*, studied sociology and philosophy. He lived for a period in Egypt while working on two sociological research projects; during this time, he visited Israel on a regular basis. Today, he is based in Cologne, where he works as a freelance journalist and author with a particular focus on the Near East.

Dr. Carmella Pfaffenbach, a geographer with a focus on the Near East,

wrote the chapter on "Jordan." She also conducts study tours to this country.

Ulrike Plochmann is a resident of Jerusalem. She has studied Oriental and Germanic languages and history, as well as Art History, and presently conducts study trips in Israel and Cyprus. Ms. Plochmann is responsible for the updates in the present edition.

PHOTOGRAPHERS

AKG, Berlin 12, 14, 15, 16, 17, 18, 19, 20, 21, 22, 23, 24, 25, 26, 27, 29, 30, 31, 38, 40, 41, 43, 44, 45, 132, 173
Becker, Frank 230
Bondzio, Bodo 37, 61, 67, 70, 73L, 86, 100/101, 108, 128, 129, 134, 136,60, 191
dpa 46, 47
Eifler, Klaus 91, 179
Gottbrath, Till 33
Greune, Jan 35, 56, 73R
Hoyer, Uwe 8/9, 62, 68, 75, 78, 81, 82, 85, 87, 96, 127, 135, 142, 155, 158, 175, 181, 188, 200, 201, 209, 212, 213, 235
Janicek, Ladislav (Mainbild) 72, 204
Janicke, Volkmar, E. 233
Mendrea, Dinu (cover) 74, 152L, 239
Mendrea, Sandu 36, 48, 51 52/53, 54/55, 60, 65, 66, 80, 83, 102, 120, 133, 140, 152R, 153, 156, 157, 161, 164/165, 166, 168 170, 172, 176, 177, 182, 190, 192
Neifend, Harald 88, 123, 130
Rudolph, Walter 10/11
Schindler, Günter (Mainbild) 148
Schmidt, Friedrich 193, 218/219, 223, 224, 226, 227, 229, 231
Scholten, Jo 95, 113, 118, 125, 171 174, 196/197, 198, 208, 236
Semsek, Hans-Günter 139
Stockmann, Reinhard 111, 116/117, 138
Tetzner, Marina 34, 64, 79, 141, 146/147, 180, 183
Thiele, Klaus 71, 76, 89, 90, 94, 104, 105, 110, 126, 159, 178, 184, 186, 187, 189, 206, 207, 210, 211, 214, 215, 220, 237
Wiese, W. (Mainbild) 124.